Constructing Strong
of Early Literacy

This text provides a comprehensive understanding of the foundational literacy knowledge, skills, behaviors, and attitudes necessary to guide emerging readers and writers in early childhood.

Centered on the critical question of why some children learn to read easily, while others do not, this text walks readers through developmentally appropriate goal setting based on the foundational literacy skills that are critical for preschool and kindergarten children to develop. Written in an authoritative yet accessible style, chapters offer instructional strategies, insights, and scenarios from educators, self-reflection, and a variety of methods for implementation. Each chapter also includes differentiation for children with language and learning challenges as well as dual language learners, exploring methods for valuing the home language while building critical literacy skills in the classroom.

Providing critical skills for guiding all emerging readers to an independent reading level, this is an essential resource for both students in early childhood, literacy, and special education courses and educators in early childhood public education, non-profit preschool settings such as Head Start, home and daycare settings, and private and corporate care and education centers.

Malinda E. Jones is an Associate Professor Emeritus of Early Childhood Education at Metropolitan State University of Denver. She began her career teaching preschool through second grade. She taught courses in early childhood education, literacy development (birth through aged 5), and primary (K-1) literacy with field supervision. She earned her B.A. in Early Childhood Education from Towson State University, and her M.A. in Early Childhood Education and Ed.D. in Reading Education from the University of Northern Colorado. She believes that intentional responsive teaching is both a powerful mindset and a pedagogy critical to ensuring all children become those for whom reading and writing comes easily and remains personally meaningful.

Ann E. Christensen has been an educator for more than 40 years. She has been a classroom teacher, a teacher coach and professional development leader, and a district level Early Childhood Specialist and Intervention Coordinator. She earned her B.A. from the University of Northern Colorado, her M.A. from the University of Colorado at Denver, and achieved National Teacher Board Certification in Language Arts. She is currently retired and working as a substitute teacher. Ann believes in the power of planning for responsive teaching and supports teachers in developing that power and expertise. She actively supports inclusion, equity, and non-racist education for children and for the adults who nurture and teach them.

Constructing Strong Foundations of Early Literacy

Malinda E. Jones and
Ann E. Christensen

Routledge
Taylor & Francis Group

NEW YORK AND LONDON

First published 2023
by Routledge
605 Third Avenue, New York, NY 10158

and by Routledge
4 Park Square, Milton Park, Abingdon, Oxon, OX14 4RN

Routledge is an imprint of the Taylor & Francis Group, an informa business

Library of Congress Cataloging-in-Publication Data
A catalog record for this title has been requested

ISBN: 9780367247119 (hbk)
ISBN: 9780367247133 (pbk)
ISBN: 9780429284021 (ebk)

DOI: 10.4324/9780429284021

Typeset in Bembo Std
by KnowledgeWorks Global Ltd.

Contents

Figures

Contributors

We profoundly thank the following colleagues for their expertise and contributions to the book.

Chapter 13: Phonological Awareness

Krista M. Griffin: Associate Professor of Elementary Education and Literacy at Metropolitan State University of Denver, USA.

Dr. Griffin is a former director of a non-profit childcare center and a primary classroom teacher. She teaches undergraduate and graduate literacy courses, focusing on preparing teachers to be confident and competent in teaching literacy, and empowers them to meet their future children with a strong toolbox of strategies to help them become proficient, lifelong readers. Dr. Griffin is the author of *"Listening to the Voices of Boys: Exploring the Motivation of Primary Boys to Engage in Reading"*.

Chapter 17: Delays in Literacy Development

Rebecca L. Dennis-Canges: Associate Professor of Special Education at Metropolitan State University of Denver, USA.

Dr. Dennis-Canges started her career as a Special Education teacher in California where she implemented district-wide awareness programs to promote acceptance of students with disabilities. She teaches undergraduate and graduate special education literacy courses. Dr. Dennis-Canges currently researches methods for improving teacher preparation programs so all teachers can better support students with disabilities in their classrooms.

Content on Multi-Language Learners

Vicki L. Nilles: Associate Professor of Culturally and Linguistically Diverse Education at Metropolitan State University of Denver, USA.

Dr. Nilles had the privilege of being a bilingual classroom teacher for 17 years, working with students ranging in age from early childhood to Grade 6. As a teacher educator, she strongly believes in the professional preparation for all teachers to effectively work with multi-language children. Effective quality literacy instruction is the key as they embark upon the challenging journey of learning multiple languages.

In Gratitude

A most heartfelt thank you to our husbands, Bruce and Pete, and our children, Lee, Taylor, Brennan, and Austin, who encouraged and supported us during the entire process of writing the book. They listened to us read aloud, discuss, and rewrite chapters many times. They willingly took over responsibilities, chores, and dinner prep when we needed to stay focused on the book. We thank our children for teaching us so much about constructing strong foundations of literacy during their early childhood years.

We cannot express sufficient gratitude to our close friend and mentor, Dr. Karen Buie, Professor Emeritus at the University of Northern Colorado, for her wisdom and relentless support with reading and revising, for her many thought-provoking questions that encouraged us to rethink, confer, reread, and rewrite, for her belief in us and our book, and the cheerleading and inspiration she provided all along the way.

A big thank you to a dear friend and colleague, Judy Cardenas, kindergarten teacher in Denver Public Schools, for help with photographs and permissions. Thank you to the families that shared pictures of their children and of their children's work.

Thank you to the many MSU Denver students we have taught, supervised, and with whom we have become colleagues and friends. We will never forget you. Teaching you has enabled us to present the ideas in *Constructing a Strong Foundation of Literacy* with clarity. Thank you to our MSU Denver colleague, Jennifer Stover, who spent hours with us, designing, redesigning, and teaching classes to best prepare future literacy teachers. Thank you to Emily Lambert, who shared her journey from student, to teacher, to principal with us. The time we spent with her at her school deepened our conversations about literacy development and professional development. Thank you to MSU Denver student, Vanessa Sanchez, whose commitment to children, learning, and teaching inspired us to put her picture on the cover of the book. And to the hundreds of school children with whom we have taught and shared classrooms, you shaped our thoughts and taught us to keep striving to be better teachers.

Thank you to the many Colorado classroom teachers who enthusiastically welcomed us into their classrooms, for supporting our students through field experiences and student teaching, and with whom we have become colleagues and friends. We have learned so much from you and look forward to our continued partnerships.

We are also deeply thankful for our loyal, steadfast, and ever-patient K9 writing companions, Scout, Daisy, and Lorelei, who kept our feet warm with their fur and reminded us to take walks when the going was tough.

1 Early Literacy

Essential Understandings

Focus and Big Ideas

- Factors that impact children's ability to learn
- Early literacy experiences
- The critical role of the teacher
- Proficient literacy
- Supporting multi-language learners

Introduction

We, the authors, live in a fast-growing metropolitan area where omnipresent construction cranes slice the horizon. Skyscrapers seem to spring up overnight, competing for space, one higher than the last. Frequent walks around town, however, reveal the significant time it actually takes to dig a hole and prepare a single foundation. Month after month, we watch the crew dig deeper and deeper. The workers pour a sturdy cement base and pound in anchors to hold the foundation steady as the building itself begins to emerge above ground. Building and anchoring a foundation is challenging, complex, and exacting work.

We are struck by how similar this process is to our early childhood teaching. We work incredibly hard to help each child build and anchor a strong foundation for literacy learning. We are exacting. We plan thoughtfully and intentionally, ensuring that each foundational layer is secure and sturdy so that it will support the next layer and the next and the next. The skyscraper we are constructing with young children has no height limits because literacy learning extends over a lifetime. Therefore, the foundation must be especially wide, deep, and strong.

Once a physical skyscraper is complete, no one notices its foundation unless it gives way, leaks, or cracks. The same can be said of the literacy foundation we build with young children. The work of early childhood teachers is sometimes overlooked or undervalued unless the foundation fails to support the next stage of literacy instruction. The purpose of this book is to help teachers ensure such failure does not happen. Effective pedagogy alone, however, is not enough. With it must come a teacher's depth of understanding and the

DOI: 10.4324/9780429284021-1

effective means to explain the value and nuance of their work to others, specifically administrators, colleagues, preservice teachers, paraprofessionals, parents, and the media.

Many Factors Impact Children's Ability to Learn

Variations in children's early literacy foundations are the result of many factors within their unique life and learning circumstances. When children present risk in several areas, it can be particularly challenging for teachers to tease out the specific factors that are creating barriers to learning. Consider how each factor in Figure 1.1 could act as either a potential challenge or a positive contribution to a child's construction of a strong literacy foundation.

Figure 1.2 is an example of how a teacher accommodated her practice when she recognized that a physical acuity factor (a hearing impairment) was significantly impacting a child's potential for literacy learning.

Factors that Impact Children's Literacy Foundations

Physical acuity: The extent to which a child can accurately hear, see, and access text and instruction, clearly articulate speech, and coordinate physical motor activity.

Cognitive factors: The extent to which a child can take in and comprehend information, develop schema, remain focused, regulate attention and emotions, and access information stored in long- and short-term memory.

Psychological factors: The extent to which a child can maintain a positive self-concept, motivation, and confidence to learn, a feeling of trust in adults and others, positive dispositions toward learning and literacy, and coping with trauma.

Language and literacy processing abilities: The extent to which a child can interpret information taken in by sight and sound, perceive and process visual and auditory information, and extend language comprehension and development.

Ecological factors: The extent to which a child's family or caregivers can access community resources and opportunities, maintain financial stability, meet the child's physical and safety needs, and support their language and culture.

Early language and literacy experiences: The extent to which a child has substantive conversations with adults and peers, and frequent positive interactions with more literate others who read aloud, converse, build background knowledge and vocabulary, draw attention to literacy in their environment, provide access to age-appropriate literacy materials, and offer positive affirmations to their emerging literacy behaviors and understandings.

Figure 1.1 Factors that Impact Children's Literacy Foundations

Anchor Under Construction

A Factor of Physical Acuity:

Ms. C, a teacher with many years of experience, had a child born with only one ear who started kindergarten with her. She suddenly felt that she did not have the skill to be a good teacher for this child. Ms. C sought out assistance from the special educator who helped her think about how to create the best opportunities for Samantha to learn. Attention to noise level, the classroom arrangement, the child's line of sight so she could see the teacher's face, frequent checking for understanding using a hand signal, adding visual signals to whole group instruction, and using physical touch on the shoulder to get attention before talking were changes she made in the classroom. Not surprisingly, many children benefited from these more mindful communication routines. Because many young children have temporary hearing loss due to ear, nose, and throat issues, attention to detail in communication is critical. If the child cannot hear, or is not aware of the learning taking place, they cannot participate in the cognitive experience. The early childhood teacher must be aware of signs that a child's limited language and focus may be due to physical acuity such as hearing loss or impaired eyesight, and that with thoughtful consideration and accommodations in the classroom can be made to support the child's success.

Figure 1.2 A Factor of Physical Acuity

Early Literacy Experiences

All modalities of language (reading, writing, speaking, and listening) are interwoven to create "literacy." An individual who can integrate and apply all modalities of oral and written language is considered literate. From infancy, children begin to construct understandings about each of the modalities as they find patterns, organize, store, and retrieve information about the world, the sounds and structure of oral language, and the function and forms of written language.

Early home and care literacy environments are defined as the interactions between parents, caregivers, and young children related to language and literacy development and the availability of literacy materials in the home and care settings. They are more specifically defined as the extent to which a child has substantive conversations with adults and peers, and frequent positive interactions with more literate others who read aloud, converse, build background knowledge and vocabulary, draw attention to literacy in their environment, provide access to age-appropriate literacy materials, and offer positive affirmations to their emerging literacy behaviors and understandings (see Figure 1.3). These experiences have been shown to be a major factor impacting both the development of children's literacy competencies and their dispositions (attitudes, inclinations, and beliefs) toward literacy and literacy learning (Hirsh-Pasek et al., 2015; Niklas, Wirth, Guffler, Drescher, & Emig, 2020).

Anchor Under Construction

A Factor of Limited Early Language and Literacy Experiences (limited experience in the classroom language **and** limited early literacy experiences in all languages):

When Daniel entered kindergarten, he spoke only Spanish, and both he and his mother appeared uncertain about school. Ms. C. had learned a few essential phrases in Spanish and was able to say Hello. I am glad you came to school. (*Hola, Daniel. Yo me gusta a ver a la escuela*). Learning to say a small number of Spanish (or other represented language) phrases is one strategy for including and reassuring children who do not speak English.

In addition to speaking a language that was different from English, Daniel appeared to have had few literacy experiences in any language. He had not learned to read or write his name, he watched and imitated the actions of other students as they participated in a Shared Reading, and he did not attend to text being read aloud from the morning message. As with a hearing-impaired child, Ms. C must consider what she will add to her teaching routines to meet Daniel's needs.

Ms. C talked to Daniel using motions, realia, pictures, and objects, so the talk was contextual. She provided books in Spanish at the listening center and sent home a book each day for his mother to read to him in Spanish. Ms. C valued and expressed the value that he knew more than she did in Spanish, often asking for the name of an object or action and attempting to say the words. She respected his silent period when he was listening to and taking in English but not producing ideas in English. She provided language experience lessons that encouraged Daniel to focus on the print as it was written and then read.

These accommodations supported both his success as a literacy learner and his membership in the classroom community. He was using English for simple social communication by mid-year and would continue to build academic strength in both languages.

Figure 1.3 A Factor of Limited Early Language and Literacy Experiences

Research indicates that early home and care literacy environments that provide frequent positive and supportive language and literacy experiences **reduce the risk** that children will experience difficulty learning to read and become proficient readers and writers (Lonigan & Shanahan, 2008). These are called early **literacy-enriched environments**. In contrast, early home and care literacy environments that provide fewer opportunities for young children to develop and use language and literacy **increase the risk** and are called **limited literacy environments**. The degree and quality of children's early literacy experiences are one of the factors that early childhood teachers have the opportunity to mitigate in the classroom.

Limited Literacy Environments

Research has shown that ecological factors such as a family's reduced access to financial stability, community resources, and educational opportunities are associated with homes that can be considered **limited literacy environments** (Payne, Whitehurst, & Angell, 1994). Limited literacy environments, however, can be found across all socio-economic levels. A limited literacy environment may be the result of insufficient access to resources such as children's books and other print materials, poor quality childcare settings, insufficient healthcare, the effects of trauma, or repeated ear infections. It may also be a result of adults' lack of time and energy to engage in reading aloud, substantive conversations, and *walks around and talks about the world*. While risk factors for learning to read and write exist at all socio-economic levels, literacy success is harder to achieve and more important than ever for children living in poverty (Parrett & Budge, 2016). The foundation of literacy constructed in limited early literacy environments is often tenuous and weak. As a result, these children depend on their teachers in preschool, elementary school, childcare, and community settings to help them develop strong and well anchored foundational literacy that will support future learning.

Advocates of universal preschool and full-day kindergarten make the case that children will have a better chance of long-term school success if they spend more time in the classroom as young learners. This "promise" of results is grounded in the premise that the children who have not had extensive early literacy opportunities and interactions will automatically reset to a successful pathway of proficient literacy. Fulfilling that "promise," however, is not simply about **more time** in the classroom. **It is about what happens in the classroom**. This rests squarely on the teacher.

Defining *Teacher* and *Instruction*

Throughout this text, we will use the term ***teacher*** to refer to ALL individuals who care for and educate children, including parents. Any person in one of these positions plays a vital role in impacting the future and constructing the foundation for children's literacy success or failure. This includes those adults in:

- early childhood public school classroom teachers (preschool, kindergarten, and first grade);
- home daycare settings;
- non-profit preschool settings such as Head Start;
- before and after school care;
- private or corporate care and education centers;
- parents and family.

All of these adults provide ***instruction***. This term means that they reinforce and extend children's applications of the ten Foundational Anchors as they:

- model tasks, procedures, and activities;
- share tasks, procedures, and activities with the child;
- provide encouragement and reinforcement of productive learning behaviors;
- explain, clarify, and label concepts and information;
- engage in substantive conversations that involve lots of child-talk;
- break tasks into parts the child can successfully perform;
- provide support needed for the child to be successful in their attempts;
- provide opportunities for children to apply and practice what they have learned and are learning.

Regardless of experience, language, or culture, the foundational literacy knowledge and skills that children bring with them to any learning situation are valuable. These will become the **"known"** on which teachers help children build and connect with the "unknown" ... new information and learning. For example, a child who does not know many letter names may point to the letter B on a letter chart and say, "That's like Burger King!". Knowing how and where children learned about print helps teachers to use life–literacy connections to scaffold new learning. "Yes, and that letter is a B. It says /b/, Burger King," the teacher responded. For this child, referencing familiar environmental print is a starting point for constructing new understanding about the Foundational Anchors of literacy. Unfortunately, some educators neither recognize nor value the early and diverse literacy understandings children bring to a situation. These previous connections are frequently dismissed as unrelated to learning to read and write or future formal literacy instruction.

Clearly, a whole group **instructional model** does not acknowledge individual children's current foundations of literacy. As a result, instructional inequity in the classroom is created and/or exacerbated. Inequity increases when the children who already know more get more. Consider the impact of implementing a whole group instructional model on those children who have several risk factors from Figure 1.1, Factors that Impact Learning to Read and Write. When children with weak foundations of literacy are always taught the same content at the same time as those with stronger foundations, only some children benefit from the instruction. Can you guess which ones? As a result, a teacher cannot use a strictly whole group curriculum to create a solid literacy foundation for all children. Children from limited literacy environments are **heavily dependent** on instructional early childhood settings to ensure a strong foundation. Teachers help them to build on what they know in order to anchor a foundation that will effectively prepare each child to make sense of future literacy instruction.

Making accommodations for individuals and small groups can be confusing for teachers and parents, but cutting a child's food into bite size pieces so they won't choke and can access nourishment is no different. The child will

---

⛏ Anchor Under Construction

Aaron and DeVon came to kindergarten lacking the experience to recognize their names in print. They watched as other children in the class identified their names and put their name tags in the pocket chart for attendance count. Noticing their confusion, the teacher, Mr. R, put a sticker on each of their name tags. Aaron got an apple and DeVon got a deer, matching the picture alphabet chart on the wall. He showed the boys the stickers and related their names to the letters on the chart. He understood that a lack of experience does not mean a lack of ability. He understood that these boys would not yet benefit from work with isolated sounds and letters as suggested in the curriculum. He would begin with the letters in their names.

Figure 1.4 Children from Limited Literacy Environments Are Heavily Dependent on Early Childhood Settings

---

eventually manage to take on larger chunks or cut their own food because they will learn to use a knife and fork. Making accommodations for a child with less literacy experience, less school experience, linguistic or cultural differences gives them access to the teachers' nourishing lesson (see Figure 1.4).

A teacher less knowledgeable than Mr. R in Figure 1.4 may make incorrect assumptions about these boys, believing that children who arrive at school with a wealth of language and literacy experiences are "smart" or "bright," while inexperienced children are not. The less knowledgeable teacher would begin the year inundating them with letter names and sounds, as suggested by the curriculum. Both teachers are working hard, but the learning outcomes will be vastly different.

The teacher must assist the children to construct the foundation required for them to achieve proficient literacy.

Proficient Literacy

Literacy learning occurs over a lifetime and holds infinite potential. It does not start when children begin formal instruction, nor does it end when they have finished schooling. Just as a proficient musician continues to practice, learn, and enjoy new understandings about music and their instrument, proficient readers and writers continue to use and enjoy literacy, discover new personal interests with and through literacy, and engage in literacy learning throughout their lifetimes. Even as adults, we can challenge ourselves to read complex or difficult texts, follow the assembly directions for building a bookcase, or teach ourselves physics. When a child reads for pleasure or to accomplish a task, when they write a letter, or a supply list, we see them move to extend their own capabilities, their own proficiencies.

But what does the term *proficient* actually mean? *Proficient* is often used on standardized reading tests to refer to readers who have reached a required score on a specific set of tasks. On another reading test, children may be asked to perform a different set of tasks. Thus, *proficient* is a term the teacher must clarify when analyzing assessment information because proficiency may mean a different score or performance on dissimilar tasks and on different tests.

Proficient, according to the Cambridge Dictionary, means "good at doing something because of practice" and provides "skilled" and "competent" as synonyms. Throughout this book, we will use the term ***proficient*** readers to mean **skilled, competent readers who continue to enjoy and improve their reading at or above grade-level expectations.** Ensuring that all young children are traveling a solid path to becoming proficient readers and writers demands that a teacher know a great deal about each child's current and past literacy experiences and understandings, as well as the factors that may have impacted the child's literacy learning. **The teacher is central to the child's** success and continually refers to knowledge about the individual child, knowledge about the foundations of literacy, and knowledge about effective appropriate pedagogy. They look across all Foundational Anchors to provide the wide and deep learning the child needs in order to perceive literacy as a goal they can achieve.

What Does a Strong Foundation of Literacy Look Like?

Researchers have identified key literacy competencies that comprise the knowledge, skills, and dispositions that are the components of a strong foundation of literacy. These have been shown to support children's preparedness for formal reading instruction and later reading success (Cartwright, 2015; Guthrie, Wigfield, & You, 2012; Lepper, Corpus, & Iyengar, 2005; Lonigan & Shanahan, 2008; Snow, Burns, & Griffin, 1998; Sulzby, 1985). By the time children start formal reading instruction in kindergarten or first grade, there are already large individual differences in their foundational literacy competencies. The degree to which children have developed these competencies can impact the ease with which they learn to read and write. These competencies, referred to in this text as the **ten Foundational Anchors of literacy,** should be the focus of curriculum in early childhood classrooms (see Figure 1.5). The relationship of each anchor to the others and how they impact schooling success will be explored and explained throughout this book. A deep understanding of each of these anchors should be used to guide planning of curriculum, pedagogy, and assessment. In this, the teacher is pivotal.

The foundation of any building is constructed to purposefully meet the requirements to support that structure over the long term. The authors make a comparison between that architectural requirement and the foundations of literacy. This foundation of literacy is meant to support a cognitive structure that can grow infinitely (lifelong literacy learning.) So how are foundations for the world's tallest buildings made strong and secure enough to hold these

---

The Ten Foundational Anchors of Literacy

1. Oral language
2. Vocabulary and background knowledge
3. Book awareness
4. Phonological awareness and phonemic awareness
5. Alphabet knowledge and phonics
6. Print concepts
7. Emergent reading
8. Emergent writing
9. Positive dispositions about literacy and literacy learning
10. Executive function

Figure 1.5 The Ten Foundational Anchors of Literacy

buildings steady? The **foundations are anchored** in place with deep pillars called anchors. These anchors work together to increase the strength of the entire foundation. The Foundational Anchors of literacy are like the anchors in the foundation of a skyscraper, strong, deep, and interdependent, holding all the learning that will follow. Of course, a skyscraper does not begin to grow taller without builders but learners take on the task of extending their own literacy knowledge, once they experience the joy, satisfaction, power and purpose of their own literacy. The ten Foundational Anchors are meant to support these life-long learners.

Supporting Multi-Language Learners (MLLs)

As indicated earlier in the chapter, all children accumulate knowledge about literacy before they arrive at school. They develop understandings of the world around them, the role of adults, and their place and value in the world. When children come from homes where a language other than the school language is spoken, **multi-language learners (MLLs)**, our work as teachers is to add a language to their already developing language(s) (Umbel, Pearson, Fernandez, & Oller, 1992). The variety of these situations is reflected in the nuanced terminology used to define them (see figure 1.6).

Being fluent in more than one language is an advantage to be acknowledged and valued. It is important for children who are learning a new language at school to continue to develop their primary language. Background knowledge and literacy development in the primary language accelerate the learning of another language because languages are interdependent (Cummins, 2000; Freeman, Freeman, & Ebe, 2011). Proficiency in the primary language transfers to learning another language because there is **common underlying proficiency**. "This concept of common underlying proficiency helps explain why students who enter school in the United States with grade-level literacy in their first language succeed academically at higher rates than students who

---

Glossary of MLL Language Terms

Heritage language: The language spoken in the culture and community to which the child belongs. The child does not always have strong control of this language.

Home language: The language spoken in the home by the parents or caretakers.

Native language: The home language the child learned in the home and maintained.

Primary language: The language a person uses in most situations. For many children, their primary language is their native language, but for others, their primary language is another language.

Academic school language: Academic school language is the language of instruction and the oral language used by the teacher throughout the school day. In the United States, English is most often the school language.

Social language: Social language reflects children's use of the language of school to informally converse with peers and teachers about their needs, preferences, thoughts, and in play. The child's focus is on communication and meaning. Teachers may falsely assume that children's proficiency of social language spoken in the language of school indicates that the child is equally proficient in academic language. This may not be the case.

Bilingual: The ability to speak fluently in two languages.

Multilingual: The ability to speak fluently in more than two languages.

Multi-language learner: When children come from homes where a language (s) other than English (or the school language) is spoken.

Figure 1.6 Glossary of MLL Language Terms

enter with limited formal schooling and little or no native language literacy" (Freeman et al., 2011).

Teachers must create a strong partnership with families in order for the adults to understand and support the child's important development of complex language skills in their primary language. The goal is for each child to learn to think, communicate, and problem-solve in their native or primary language, while also learning a new language within the school environment. This task takes time and requires the child to receive consistent exposure to **comprehensible input,** the home and school language that a child can understand, despite them not being able to understand all of the words and grammatical structures (Oppenheim, Griffin, Peña, & Bedore, 2020).

Spotlight

It cannot be overstated that all children need a reliably anchored foundation in literacy to support the abstract, complex, and challenging process of learning to read and write. Whether a child has a strong beginning to their foundation, or very little at all, there is still much building and anchoring to be done. Teachers must recognize that they are <u>not</u> filling a gap for children. Rather, they are helping them **construct** their foundation (Hirsh-Pasek, 2018). The historical view of "school readiness" was that the school was a static, standard institution for which the children must be ready. As contemporary early childhood educators, however, we recognize that <u>the school</u> ③ <u>and the teacher must be prepared and ready for the individual children who</u> arrive. Teachers must explore and discover what each knows and build from there. Each child must be taught, supported, and assisted to build and anchor a strong literacy foundation on the understandings they bring with them. This foundation will support all subsequent learning. The stage during which this learning is constructed is called the **Foundation Stage** of literacy development. What the foundation consists of and how to anchor it for strength and durability are essential teacher learnings.

> Much attention has been focused on a persistent achievement gap in literacy between MLLs and their English-speaking peers (National Reading Panel, 2000). Unfortunately, by the time children arrive in kindergarten, differences in foundational language and literacy have often already set the stage for this disparity in future achievement (Garcia & Miller, 2008).

The good news, however, is that recent research has shown that high-quality early childhood education programs can change that trajectory and significantly impact children's later academic achievement. Research-based early childhood programs that provide developmentally relevant opportunities and comprehensive instruction in all of the Foundational Anchors of literacy can ensure that MLLs enter school and begin formal literacy instruction equipped to be successful learners in kindergarten and beyond (Ballantyne et al., 2008).

This book describes foundational knowledge, skills, and dispositions critical to young children progressing and becoming proficient readers and writers. It describes how early childhood teachers <u>must identify and use children's current foundations of literacy</u>:

- to <u>design effective learning</u> contexts, instruction, and interactions that can facilitate the literacy learning process for all young children;
- to <u>analyze</u> behaviors and children's responses to instruction in order to distinguish between a child's lack of literacy experience and other risk factors;
- to <u>mitigate weak foundations</u> that may have resulted from limited literacy learning environments.

Like the foundation of a building, the foundation of experiences that underlie literacy development must be strong, stable, reliable, intentional, and predictable. A building's foundation is well planned and carefully constructed, then anchored into place. The anchors are strong pieces of steel drilled deep into the concrete to give the foundation overall strength and stability. If you are building a garage, a slab of concrete with no anchors at all would be adequate but a skyscraper needs strong deep anchors. Literacy is a complex, infinitely tall structure, and the Foundational Anchors of literacy must be strong and deep to support the learner. The teacher owns the critical role that determines whether the child constructs their foundation of literacy as dependable, stable, and well-anchored, or as a thin slab. **The teacher makes ALL the difference**.

References

Ballantyne, K. G., Sanderman, A. R., & McLaughlin, N. (2008). Dual language learners in the early years: Getting ready to succeed in school. *National Clearinghouse for English Language Acquisition & Language Instruction Educational Programs.*

Cartwright, K. B. (2015). *Executive skills and reading comprehension: A guide for educators.* Guilford Publications.

Cummins, J. (2000). *Language, power and pedagogy: Bilingual children in the crossfire.* Multilingual Matters. https://doi.org/10.21832/9781853596773

Freeman, Y., Freeman, D., & Ebe, A. (2011). Bilingual books: Bridges to literacy for emergent bilinguals. In R. Meyer & K. Whitmore (Eds.), *Reclaiming reading: Teachers, students, and researchers regaining spaces for thinking and action* (pp. 224–235). Routledge.

García, E. E., & Miller, L. S. (2008). Findings and recommendations of the national task force on early childhood education for Hispanics. *Child Development Perspectives, 2*(2), 53–58.

Guthrie, J. T., Wigfield, A., & You, W. (2012). Instructional contexts for engagement and achievement in reading. In Sandra L. Christenson, Amy L. Reschly, & Cathy Wylie (Eds.), *Handbook of research on student engagement* (pp. 601–634). doi:10.1007/978-1-4614-2018-7_29

Hirsh-Pasek, K. (2018, June 1). Retrieved November 27, 2021, from https://www.cpr.org/2018/06/01/lets-stop-talking-about-the-30-million-word-gap/.

Hirsh-Pasek, K., Adamson, L. B., Bakeman, R., Owen, M. T., Golinkoff, R. M., Pace, A., & Suma, K. (2015). The contribution of early communication quality to low-income children's language success. *Psychological Science, 26*(7), 1071–1083.

Lepper, M. R., Corpus, J. H., & Iyengar, S. S. (2005). Intrinsic and extrinsic motivational orientations in the classroom: Age differences and academic correlates. *Journal of Educational Psychology, 97*(2), 184–196. doi:10.1037/0022-0663.97.2.184

Lonigan, C. J., & Shanahan, T. (2009). Developing early literacy: Report of the National Early Literacy Panel. *Executive Summary. A Scientific Synthesis of Early Literacy Development and Implications for Intervention. National Institute for Literacy.*

National Reading Panel (2000). *Teaching children to read: An evidence-based assessment of the scientific research literature on reading and its implications for reading instruction.* U.S. Government Printing Office.

Niklas, F., Wirth, A., Guffler, S., Drescher, N., & Emig, S. C. (2020). The home literacy environment as a mediator between parental attitudes toward shared reading and children's linguistic competencies. *Frontiers in Psychology, 11*(1628), 1–10. https://doi.org/10.3389/fpsyg.2020.01628

Oppenheim, G. M., Griffin, Z., Peña, E. D., & Bedore, L. M. (2020). Longitudinal evidence for simultaneous bilingual language development with shifting language dominance and how to explain it. *Language Learning, 70*(S2), 20–44. doi:10.1111/lang.12398

Parrett, W., & Budge, K. (2016, January 13). *How does poverty influence learning?* Retrieved November 27, 2021, from https://www.edutopia.org/blog/how-d?oes-poverty-influence-learning-william-parrett-kathleen-budge.

Payne, A. C., Whitehurst, G. J., & Angell, A. L. (1994). The role of home literacy environment in the development of language ability in preschool children from low-income families. *Early Childhood Research Quarterly, 9*(3–4), 427–440. doi:10.1016/0885-2006(94)90018-3

Snow, C. E., Burns, M. S., & Griffin, P. (1998). *Preventing reading difficulties in young children.* National Academy Press. doi.org/10.1002/pits.10011

Sulzby, E. (1985). Children's emergent reading of favorite storybooks: A developmental study. *Reading Research Quarterly, 20*(4), 458–481. doi:10.1598/rrq.20.4.4

Umbel, V. M., Pearson, B. Z., Fernandez, M. C., & Oller, D. K. (1992). Measuring bilingual children's receptive vocabularies. *Child Development, 63*(4), 1012–1020. doi:10.1111/j.1467-8624.1992.tb01678.x

-children learn at their own pace, some may have different skill set than others → need to accommod

-10 Foundational Anchors of Literacy

-teaching is like building a skyscraper, strong anchors + foundation

2 The Foundational Anchors of Literacy

Focus and Big Ideas

- The ten Foundational Anchors of literacy
- Emerging literacy
- Supporting and scaffolding children's literacy understandings
- Bridges to literacy for multi-language learners

The Goals of an Effective Early Literacy Curriculum

As introduced in Chapter 1, children's foundation of literacy should include the specific knowledge, skills, and understandings that have been shown to support successful learning to read and write (Cordova & Lepper, 1996; Gambrell, Palmer, Codling, & Mazzoni, 1996; Guthrie, Wigfield, & VonSecker, 2000; Iyengar & Lepper, 1999; National Early Literacy Panel, 2008; Sesma, Mahone, Levine, Eason, & Cutting, 2009; Snow, Burns, & Griffin, 1998; Sulzby & Teale, 1985; Sulzby, 1985; Worthy & McKool, 1996). These key literacy learnings have been organized by the authors into **ten Foundational Anchors of literacy** (listed in Figure 2.1). This chapter will introduce the reader to each of the ten anchors. The remaining chapters will provide a deeper explanation of each of the anchors and **how they are interwoven and how they support one another,** in order for a child to grow a strong literacy foundation. The pivotal role of teachers and the type of effective decision-making they must engage in to ensure all children develop a strong foundation with ten anchors will be a thread throughout.

1. **Oral language**

   Children's oral language (1) comprehending language produced by others **(receptive language)** and (2) constructing and producing language to communicate **(expressive language)** with others. The most concentrated period of speech and language development is during the early years of life when the brain is rapidly growing and developing. As the structures for speech (the jaw, lips, and tongue) and voice mature, an infant learns to make controlled sounds such as cooing, followed later by

DOI: 10.4324/9780429284021-2

The Ten Foundational Anchors of literacy

1. Oral language
2. Vocabulary and background knowledge
3. Book awareness
4. Phonological awareness and phonemic awareness
5. Alphabet knowledge and phonics
6. Print concepts
7. Emergent reading
8. Emergent writing
9. Positive dispositions about literacy and literacy learning
10. Executive function

Figure 2.1 The Ten Foundational Anchors of Literacy

babbling. By the end of year one, most children have mastered the ability to say a few simple words. Children learn the power of those words as others respond to them.

"By eighteen months of age, most children can say eight to ten words. By age two, most are putting words together in crude sentences such as 'more milk.' During this period, children rapidly learn that words symbolize or represent objects, actions, and thoughts." At ages three, four, and five, children's vocabulary rapidly increases, and they begin to master syntax, the rules of their language (A*dapted from: The National Institute on Deafness and Other Communication Disorders. (2000). Speech and Language Developmental Milestones. NIH Publication No. 00-4781).Reading Rockets. (2017, August 24). Retrieved October 26, 2021, from https://www. readingrockets.org/article/speech-and-language-developmental-milestones.*

2. **Vocabulary and background knowledge**

   Vocabulary is the number and range of words a child can either understand or use. The number of words a child can control seems limitless, more than 170,00 words in English. The individual develops a bank of vocabulary with exposure and use. **Background knowledge** includes children's accumulated knowledge of the world, how it works, and the vocabulary to label, think, and talk about it. Background knowledge is also called **prior knowledge** or **schema**. Children's oral language, vocabulary and background knowledgethere are combined to form their **language comprehension. Language comprehension** is at the center of oral language development (Vukelich, Enz, Roskos, & Christies, 2020). We see evidence of language comprehension when a child listens and participates in shared book read-alouds, engages in conversations, responds to open-ended questions, and asks questions seeking clarification or additional information. Children with language comprehension difficulties risk low performance in school and problems with social interaction. Research has shown, however, that it is possible to improve language comprehension in children with language difficulties in an early childhood setting (Hagen, Melby-Lervåg, & Lervåg, 2017).

3. **Book awareness**

    Book awareness is noticing, thinking about, and interacting successfully with books. When a child carries a book to an adult and cuddles up in preparation for a story, we see evidence of book awareness. Opening a book, labeling the pictures, making up a story about each of them, or retelling the story from memory, each episode demonstrates awareness of books. Book awareness also includes recognizing the various purposes for using books, how they are organized, and how each genre is "read."

    Book awareness substantially increases as adults engage children in frequent read-alouds across multiple genres. Children participate differently when listening to narratives, predictable books, rhyming books, fairy tales, informational books, and poetry, for example. A child reading a book about life in the ocean may want to start with the chapter on sharks, rather than at the beginning. Conversely, a storybook is read front to back to follow the plot and learn about the characters. Reading diverse genres with young children also develops their familiarity with various types of **literary language**, the language of authors, which is different from the oral language children typically use in day-to-day conversations. Book awareness prepares children to comprehend the diversity of texts they will read in the future.

4. **Phonological and phonemic awareness**

    Phonological awareness is noticing, thinking about, and working with (manipulating) the sounds of oral language at the sentence, word, and phoneme (individual sound) levels. Children develop or demonstrate phonological awareness when they engage with rhymes in chants and songs, count the number of words in a sentence, and clap the syllables in their names, for example. **Phonemic awareness** is the highest level of phonological awareness. It is noticing, thinking about, and manipulating the *individual sounds* in spoken words.

    Phonemic awareness should be explicitly taught (National Reading Panel, 2000). In addition, engaging activities, songs, and routines that provide opportunities for children to reinforce and practice hearing, playing with, and manipulating sounds in language should also be planned for children throughout the day.

5. **Alphabet knowledge and phonics**

    English is an alphabetic language and letters provide critical visual information requisite for a reader to construct accurate meaning of a text. Children from literacy-rich home and care settings typically solidify their alphabet knowledge between the ages of three and five. Children learn to recognize the shape of letters, identify the names of an increasing number of uppercase and lowercase letters, and increase their speed of letter recognition over time. The first letters that children learn tend to be the letters of their first name. Tasha notices the T in Target and says "That's my name!" Her familiarity with the capital T demonstrates that she is starting to notice print in her environment and searching for letters that she already knows.

The **alphabetic principle** is the concept that letters represent specific sounds. **Phonics,** also referred to as **grapho–phonics**, is the relationship between the letters or groups of letters (graphemes) of written language and the sounds of spoken language (phonemes). As children begin to associate sounds with the correct letter or letters, they are developing a Foundational Anchor that will support later decoding (reading) and encoding (writing) of text. Children begin to learn about letters and sounds through informal interactions with adults and from listening to alphabet books read aloud. However, research has clearly shown that kindergarten children need explicit, systematic instruction to learn and use the alphabetic system effectively (National Reading Panel, 2000).

6. **Print concepts**

Figuring out how readers read and writers write is initially a puzzle, a mystery to young children. Learning that one reads from left to right and proceeds top to bottom requires lots of intentional occasions for children to observe literacy in action. They need focused opportunities to observe readers and writers model and scaffold the processes and then to transfer that understanding by repeatedly trying it themselves.

Children learn **concepts of print** from the more general to the specific. These concepts include how to follow print and write left to right and top to bottom with return sweep, the concept of a word, spacing between words, voice-print match (one spoken word matches one written word), and page orientation. As children have more high-quality experiences with reading and writing, they learn the details of written language called the **conventions of print**. These include understanding what defines a letter, a word, the use of punctuation marks and capital letters, etc. All of these are critical understandings and support learning to read and write with success and confidence (Clay, 2017)

7. **Emerging reading**

Reading-like behaviors begin to *emerge* as children develop the Foundational Anchors. From this point, until the child can independently read unfamiliar, accessible text, the child is an *emerging* **reader**. The reading behaviors children demonstrate before they can read and write conventionally reflect their accumulated literacy experiences, both contextual and targeted, with more literate others.

During **emerging reading**, children use reading-like behaviors and the information they have at hand to reconstruct the narrative and meaning of a text. They demonstrate their immature, emerging knowledge of the purposes of print and the process by which readers read. They begin by reenacting what they can see adults doing, turning pages and referring to pictures. When rereading familiar books, children use their memory

Figure 2.2 Significant Growth Occurs Long before Emergence, Both in a Plant and in Emerging Reading

of the story, the pattern of the genre or the text, repeated predictable phrases, and reference to the pictures. They draw on all their previous experiences with the book to reconstruct the reading. Engagement with letters and sounds may exist but not yet be obvious. Over time, the use of alphabetic knowledge and phonics will be actively assimilated during these reconstructions.

Children also demonstrate **emerging reading** when they notice, hypothesize about, and use print in the environment and other meaningful contexts. For example, using a label with their name on it to find where their belongings should be stored or using a menu to choose what they will have for "lunch" in a socio-dramatic play restaurant scenario. Opportunities to **emergently read** and interact with text encourage children to independently attempt to construct meaning from print, build confidence, and establish a positive disposition toward literacy learning.

8. **Emerging writing**

    The child who begins to use marks, symbols, letter-like forms, or random letters that they imbue with meaning is an **emerging writer**. They have a rudimentary understanding of writing as a process to capture and represent ideas and information. They will expand their use of writing for a number of purposes and increasingly employ concepts of print such as directionality, voice-print match, and page orientation as they observe and recognize the connections between writing and reading. Their writing will begin to look more conventional with time, experience, and instruction, eventually including the sounds they hear in words and their memory of known words.

Children's sense of the reader or audience grows as they use writing for many different purposes. The stop sign they write and put on the bedroom door or their names written in marker on their dinosaurs (or the wall) are explorations of the power of writing. They write to take command, show possession, and communicate with others. Encouraging children to use their *emerging* **reading and writing** in early childhood classrooms creates a positive disposition toward literacy learning across the classroom community and develops many of the other Foundational Anchors on which formal instruction will be built.

9. **Positive dispositions about literacy and literacy learning**

Children's dispositions about literacy and literacy learning include the child's predominant approaches, attitudes, feelings, inclinations, and beliefs about themselves as capable readers, writers, and thinkers. Children who perceive themselves as capable thinkers and literacy users enjoy their interactions with reading and writing and are willing to embrace challenges with the expectation of success. They are open to new ideas from books and scaffolding from instructionally aware adults. Associating literacy with pleasure and purpose helps accelerate learning. Positive dispositions encourage young children to seek opportunities to use reading and writing in their daily lives and in their play. This extends their understanding of the functions (purposes) and forms (concepts and conventions) of print. Children who have expectations of success approach literacy tasks with interest and willingness to persevere and problem-solve, approaches to learning that will serve them well as the tasks of reading and writing become more challenging.

Children who have failed, failed repeatedly, and who struggle to learn as quickly as others are at risk of developing negative dispositions. They may come to see literacy learning as a source of humiliation and frustration. For example, a second grader who is reading at a kindergarten level may reject instruction altogether. When he wraps his arms around his head and puts his face on the desk NOT as a means of opposition, but as a way to avoid another painful experience. Developing the will to learn, recreating attitudes toward reading and writing, or helping the child experience success with literacy is among the most challenging and important work for any teacher.

10. **Executive function**

Executive function is the cognitive action of controlling responses and making decisions. Like other cognitive functions, it can be taught, learned, and increase with successful practice. Paying attention, remembering, organizing and planning, starting and staying focused on tasks, managing emotions to meet the demands of a situation, and keeping track of what they are doing are important cognitive processes. These elements of self-control and flexible thinking are collectively called executive function. They are related to success in and out of school. A child who controls and adjusts their behaviors during challenging situations is able to fully participate in and relish the learning.

When children struggle with executive function, it impacts their entire lives. Just like the development of the rest of the Foundational Anchors of literacy, teachers play a significant role in helping children to gradually learn, practice, and develop executive function (Center on the Developing Child; Harvard University). When expectations are specific, achievable, explicitly stated and explained, modeled, restated as needed and assistance such as reviews and reminders are available in non-punitive interactions, children develop their executive function.

The Interdependency of the Anchors

We have examined each anchor individually for teacher clarity and understanding. However, children's learning about each anchor overlaps and influences learning about the others. In the harsh desert, Navajo peoples plant gardens. Each crop could have its own space but they wisely plant beans, corn, and squash together. The squash vines act as a living mulch, protecting the scant moisture for the corn and beans. The corn stalk acts a trellis for the beans. These three plants are interdependent; they grow more efficiently together. The same is true of the ten Foundational Anchors. As you will see from the examples below, the extension of oral language, vocabulary or background knowledge, causes the others to extend. Each individual Foundational Anchor of literacy develops along a continuum from simple to complex and each is connected to the others. The Foundational Anchors of literacy develop **concurrently and interdependently.** Children do not accomplish one anchor first, before developing another. In fact, as a child develop one, it leads to the development of the others.

Emerging Literacy

Although a child's attempts at literacy may not look exactly like conventional or "real" reading and writing, adults need to become aware of and value young children's emerging attempts. These early attempts are called **approximations** and reflect what the child currently knows about literacy and what they can do independently. For the early childhood teacher, approximations provide a window into the child's thinking about literacy.

When the child emergently reads "Shhhh, the babies are sleeping" on the sign that actually says, "Quiet! Babies sleeping" in the socio-dramatic play center set up as a hospital nursery, they are confident in their approximation and will continue to make future attempts that, over time, will incorporate more conventional print information. A child who writes, "R BZNS IS CLOSD DN" (Our business is closed down), after deciding he wants to leave his play at the "bakery," doesn't expect to be rebuked for his writing attempt. He confidently leaves a critical message for others who might be looking for him. It is important to reinforce children's efforts, their attempts to make meaning, to incorporate what they currently know about print, and the important thinking that is clearly evident as they try out the process. These attempts, like the Foundational Anchors of Emerging Reading and Emerging Writing, are examples of *emerging literacy*. **Emerging literacy** describes the conceptualizations, approximations, behaviors, attempts, and understandings about reading and writing that children demonstrate, beginning in infancy, and continuing until they can independently read unfamiliar accessible text.

Children are eager to use their emerging literacy in a risk-free context where they will not be criticized or corrected **for what they have not yet mastered**. Instead, they will hear recognition and reinforcement of their approximations to strengthen their current level of learning and positive dispositions about literacy. This is what adults will build on the next time children attempt to use reading and writing. For example, when they write, "R BZNS IS CLOSD DN" (Our business is closed down), an adult will notice and reinforce understandings about literacy when they say the following:

- That sign you made will help us remember not to go to the bakery.
- You worked hard on your sign and added a picture to help readers know what you meant.
- You wrote a lot of sounds in your words. That helps us read your sign.
- You thought of the words you needed to tell us, so we would know you were not going to be in the bakery any longer.
- You used the alphabet chart to write that word by yourself.

Criticisms of young children's attempts to use emerging literacy can discourage their future efforts to read and write and create negative dispositions. They will not be inclined to use approximations again, preempting important opportunities for learning and development. Does this mean we do not assist or provide information when children could benefit from it or asks for it? No. But how do we distinguish between criticism and assistance? Unbidden assistance can be interference or criticism (think of the back-seat driver). Engaging a child in a collaborative, assisted effort, however, can lead a child's literacy development forward. Working side by side with the child to achieve the **child's goal** (creating a sign or adding their name to a sign-up list for the computer) is both motivating and empowering the child to use reading and writing for their own endeavors. You increase their sense of confidence and agency around literacy.

The term **emerging literacy** confuses some teachers, administrators, and publishers. They may erroneously presume that emerging literacy experiences are any print, literacy-like activities, or materials that children engage with prior to the time they can read and write conventionally. This confusion often underlies a "hit or miss" incidental curriculum characterized by children reacting to literacy materials without intent or context. These activities are devoid of adequate teacher goal setting, planning, modeling, scaffolding, and instruction for individual learning. This type of emerging literacy curriculum will not construct a solid foundation of the anchors for all children.

Setting out a basket of magnetic letters for children to play with does not ensure any effective literacy learning is taking place. Showing children how to use organized magnetic letters to spell their classmates' names by matching them with name cards can be a very effective activity. Putting pencil and paper into the socio-dramatic play center may or may not be an effective literacy learning opportunity. Introducing the literacy materials first, modelling the possible uses, and discussing why they might be important in the roles children will be playing, such as an airline pilot or cashier at the grocery store. This can be very effective and can encourage children to explore, hypothesize, and stretch their current thinking about the form and function of print. Emerging reading and writing materials and activities should engage children in meaningful uses of literacy under the careful observation of teachers who intentionally analyze and positively support children to solidify their current learning and construct new learning.

From Approximations to Proficiency

How do we move children from approximations to proficiency? In the contextual literacy scenario below, a parent engages with a young child during a risk-free interaction in ways that effectively support her emerging understandings about literacy. Notice how the adult positively **acknowledges** what the child already knows (his approximation) about language and literacy and assists or **scaffolds** new thinking within his range of understanding. The assistance or scaffolding is connected to what the child knows and only includes information that would help the child repeat the task more independently next time. The example in Figure 2.3 is a parent-child exchange that is further explained in Figure 2.4.

Anchor Under Construction

As his mother helped him out of his car seat, almost four-year-old Taylor pointed up at the sign:

Taylor: "S – A – F….. What's the next one, Mom?"

Mom: "E……"

Taylor: "What's the next one?"

Mom: "W"

Taylor: "W – A – Y…….. *Grocery Store!*"

Mom: "You are right, Taylor! It is a Grocery Store. You figured that out by yourself. And the store's name is SAFEWAY. That word says SAFEWAY!"

Figure 2.3 Scaffolding Taylor's Literacy Understandings

Anchor Constructed

Taylor

1. **Alphabet knowledge**

   • Taylor knew that each graphic symbol had a specific name.
   • He recognized and identified an increasing number of letters.

2. **Print concepts**

   • Taylor showed that letters are "read" left to right, demonstrating directionality.
   • He showed he understands that together, the letters represent a meaningful word.

3. **Emerging reading**

   • Taylor demonstrated an understanding that the purpose of reading is to construct meaning from the print and the context (a specific situation).
   • He showed that he knows that print represents a message.
   • He showed that he notices **environmental print** and sees it as a source of information.
   • He demonstrated an increasing awareness of his own thinking about how language works (metacognitive awareness).
   • He constructed a hypothesis about the word on the side of the store (grocery store).

4. **Positive dispositions toward literacy and literacy learning**

   • Taylor demonstrated a positive approach to learning more about reading.
   • He clearly perceived himself as capable of reading and acknowledged that his current understanding was incomplete ("What's the next one, Mom?").

Figure 2.4 Supporting Taylor's Foundations of Literacy

Taylor is emergently reading, not "reading" in the conventional sense, but pieces of his literacy foundation are actively under construction. He knows that print carries a message and that it consists of letters. Let's consider the additional **Foundational Anchors** Taylor has begun to develop.

Supporting and Scaffolding Children's Literacy Understandings

But how did four-year-old Taylor develop this foundational literacy? How did he know that symbols on the front of a building were meaningful? One clue is the response to his emerging reading that he received from his mother. Taylor's mother positively acknowledged his hypothesis about the sign. "*You are right! It is a grocery store!*" She reinforced Taylor's effort and then scaffolded his learning by adding to his understanding of how print can be used in the environment. She connected to what Taylor already knew—*Print on the front of a store is meaningful*—to a new concept. *It can be the store's name as well as its purpose.* The delight in his mother's voice as she responded to and elaborated on his approximation of reading the world around him will increase Taylor's desire to repeat the behavior and hypothesize new understandings with his mother. This is an example of a **high-quality** contextual literacy opportunity because of the insightful adult scaffolding.

Noticing and hypothesizing about **environmental print** is an example of **Emerging Reading**. When children "read" environmental print, they may be actually recognizing the information around the print rather than the print itself (Kassow, 2006). Initially, children recognize the entire word as a logogram, a symbol or sign that represents one word or phrase such as Target or McDonalds, rather than looking at individual letters. The more frequently adults point out meaningful environmental print to a child, the more environmental print the child notices independently (Baader-Meinhof reference). It is evident that adults have previously pointed out print in the environment to Taylor as he recognizes its function; he is very confident in his reading attempt and is not afraid to admit he still has information to learn ("What's the next one?"). Noticing, using available information, and interpreting environmental print are the acts of making meaning from text, the goal of reading.

In the scenario above, Taylor **assimilated** new information about letter names. In other words, he wove new information into his current understanding. He **accommodated** or revised his current understanding by learning that the word on the front of the store could be the *name*, as well as the *purpose* of a store ("It *is* a grocery store. And the store's name is SAFEWAY. That word says SAFEWAY."). When we observe learners actively processing information and settling on new understandings, we recognize this as learning. As you read Figure 2.5, identify which anchors are being intentionally addressed by the teacher.

The multiple exchanges in this conversation create many **high-quality opportunities** for Luke to use and think about literacy. Besides the obvious example of building on and expanding Lukes' vocabulary, using print for a meaningful purpose is likely to encourage him to write independently in the future. Every time he uses his approximations to write a personal message, he gains additional confidence and control of the process. When he participates in supportive conversation with a more literate other, his understandings are reinforced, and he can learn something new about how written language works.

Luke's teacher helped him **assimilate** new vocabulary, such as *taxi* and *runway,* into his airport **schema**, background knowledge specific to the airport. When Luke started to write from right to left, and Ms. G patiently showed him how and **why** to start on the left, Luke **accommodated** his understanding of where to start writing. Luke's teacher is **intentionally and strategically** building on and extending several Foundational Anchors. This is called **scaffolding**.

Anchor Under Construction

In her Head Start classroom, Ms. G kneeled down to watch four-year-old Luke intently building blocks and playing with small toy airplanes.

Ms. G: Luke, tell me about your block building.

Luke: It's a airport. Here's where the plane drives and then goes up in the air.

Ms. G: Oh, that's the runway. The plane taxis on the runway and then takes off into the air?

Luke: Yeah, and no people can be here. Where the plane taxis.

Ms. G: I see. No people can walk on the runway.

Luke: Uh huh. And no pets either. On the runway.

Ms. G: Oh, so they don't get hurt?

Luke: Uh huh. The plane might hit them. When it taxis and then takes off.

Ms. G: Do you think you should make a sign so that people will know not to walk or bring their pets on the runway?

Luke: Yeah, I wanna make a sign so everybody knows.

Ms. G: (She gets a notecard, black marker, and a sign holder she keeps in the block area for children to use). Do you want to write it or do you want me to?

Luke: I want to.

Ms. G: OK. What are you going to write?

Luke: No people or pets can go here.

Ms. G: OK. (Luke takes the materials. He starts to write a letter but starts on the right side of the card).

Ms. G: Mrs. G points to the left side of the card. "Start your writing over here, Luke. You will have more room." Luke changed his starting point and began to write "NoPP CGH."

teacher is teaching in an area of play + interest

Figure 2.5 Scaffolding Literacy during Play

But the sign was not spelled correctly. Should Ms. G have corrected it? Let's consider what Luke was thinking when we wrote his sign (see Figure 2.6). Luke used a sight word he knew (No) and then represented the initial consonant of each of the other words. Listening for the sounds in a word and representing them with their corresponding letters is called **phonemic spelling**, **sound spelling**, or **invented spelling**. It is a mature stage of emerging writing development. In his blog, Timothy Shanahan, a national literacy expert, acknowledges his support for children's use of phonemic spelling as it "provides such extensive and supportive practice with sounds." He would note that Luke had to analyze and record seven phonemes (the discrete sounds in words), a fair number for any phonemic awareness lesson, "so encouraging this kind of writing is **smart teaching**" (Shanahan, 2020) (bold print added). Figure 2.6 further illuminates this interaction.

Anchor Constructed

Luke and Ms. G

1. Oral language

- Luke participated in a reciprocal conversation with Ms. G. He responded to her open-ended questions and extended the conversation, assimilating new information and positively responding to suggestions.

2. Vocabulary and background knowledge

- Luke increased his background knowledge (schema) about an airport as a result of contextual learning and language interactions with a "more literate other."
- He expanded his *receptive* language (runway, taxi).
- He integrated the new information about airports and related vocabulary into his *expressive* language.

3. Alphabet knowledge and alphabetic principle

- Luke demonstrated he knows how to make various letter forms.
- He demonstrated that he understands the alphabetic principle, that written letters represent spoken sounds, and there are predictable, consistent relationships between them.
- Luke demonstrated that he correctly knew the names of several letters and their corresponding sounds.

4. Phonological awareness and phonics

- Luke used early phonemic spelling, also called sound spelling or invented spelling.
- He demonstrated that he could isolate the first letter of the most prominent and important words in his message.
- He indicated that he could correctly associate four letters with their appropriate sounds. Luke wrote: NoPP CGH (P = pets and people, C = can, G = go, H = here).

5. Print concepts

- Luke noticed that print is organized in various ways (genres), depending on its purpose. He created a sign.
- Based on Ms. G's previous observations, Luke demonstrates left-to-right directionality when he emergently rereads his dictated stories. He did not, however, consistently transfer this understanding to his emergent writing.

  Ms. G mediated this understanding of writing directionality with Luke and he started his writing correctly on the left. This does not mean that Luke will use directionality correctly the next time he writes, or that this is the first time it has been brought to Luke's attention. However, with additional opportunities to use writing in contextual situations during which a more literate other mediates, he will move closer to using directionality consistently in his writing.

Figure 2.6 Developing the Foundational Anchors of Literacy through Play *(Continued)*

6. **Emergent writing**

- Luke understood that writing can be a means to communicate.
- He understood the power of writing to inform others.
- He demonstrated familiarity, confidence, and experience using writing tools.
- He demonstrated familiarity, confidence, and experience with the writing process.
- He used a word he already knew how to write, a known word (No).
- He easily used his emerging phonemic awareness in his writing.

7. **Positive dispositions toward literacy and literacy learning**

- Luke confidently engaged in oral conversation with Ms. G
- He demonstrated a positive attitude and inclination toward using writing for meaningful purposes in his play.
- He tried out new vocabulary without hesitation.
- He demonstrated that he perceived himself as a capable learner, a capable writer, and so on and that he considered the other children to be capable readers.

8. **Executive function**

- Luke demonstrated perseverance to remain focused on an activity for a sustained period of time, adding detail and complexity.
- He demonstrated the ability to put himself in another person's experience, a foundation for developing empathy.
- He demonstrated the ability to control his emotions when he integrated instructional comments from Ms. G. He stopped to think and changed his attempt rather than giving up or expressing frustration.

Figure 2.6 (Continued)

The scenarios of both Taylor and Luke describe high-quality language and literacy environments and verbal exchanges with **instructionally aware** adults. Children in limited language and literacy environments, at home and/or in their education and care settings, might also have opportunities to build an airport and talk about it. If children lack the encouragement and scaffolded verbal interactions that were so important to Taylor and Luke's construction of literacy, these experiences represent literacy **opportunities lost**. High-quality opportunities to engage with language and literacy must include interactions with instructionally aware teachers.

The differences nationally and locally in young children's depth and strength of foundational literacy are enormous. Literacy does not emerge easily for children in non-literate societies or from limited language homes and early childhood settings. It emerges from foundations that are intentionally constructed and reinforced with literate adults and peers in the child's world.

Building a strong, deep foundation from which literacy proficiencies can emerge is dedicated, important work. Consider how different the outcome of this altered interaction with Luke would be without an instructionally aware teacher.

The literacy learning that is lost in the scenario in Figure 2.7 is significant, despite the interaction seeming positive. Engagement and pleasure are

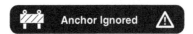

In Ms. R's preschool classroom, she kneeled down to watch four-year-old Luke intently building blocks and playing with small toy airplanes.

Ms. R: Luke, what are you building?

Luke: It's a airport. Here's where the plane drives and then goes up in the air.

Ms. R: Wow. Your airport is really neat. What else will you add?

Luke: A truck and people.

Ms. R: Good idea. Where are the people going?

Luke: California.

Ms. R: Great! They will have fun. We are going to clean up in about 5 minutes.

Luke: OK

Figure 2.7 When Opportunities for Scaffolding Literacy Development Are Ignored

important co-requisites to young children's learning; however, they do not ensure that literacy learning is actually taking place. This is true across disciplines and activities. In this altered scenario, the teacher is instructionally **unaware** of the high-quality opportunities available for Luke to construct and strengthen his Foundational Anchors of literacy. Conversation with a more literate other is a powerful means to develop children's literacy. Expanding vocabulary and background knowledge is at the forefront for Ms. G, but for Ms. R, it is not. In addition, Ms. R does nothing to develop Luke's written language. While both teachers are providing a well-stocked block center in accordance with best practices, the literacy outcomes of their implementation of curriculum are very different. This scenario is explained further in Figure 2.8.

Bridges to Literacy for Multi-Language Learners

Children who speak dual or multiple languages are present in most classrooms and require thoughtful consideration as teachers help them build their understanding about classroom language and literacy and secure it with Foundational Anchors. These children are actually building their ten Foundational Anchors in two languages, which although takes more time but increases their intellectual capacity. If a child lacks the word for elephant in the classroom language of English, it does not indicate that they lack funds of knowledge about elephants. Indeed, a recent immigrant from Cambodia may have seen working elephants, calves, and know about the habits of elephants.

Opportunities Lost

1. **Oral language**

   • The expansion of conversational abilities was not offered.

2. **Vocabulary, and background knowledge**

   • Luke was not introduced to any new concepts or related vocabulary.

3. **Alphabet knowledge and alphabetic principle**

   • Luke sees no need to use writing and try out his understanding of letters and words.

4. **Phonological awareness and phonics**

   • With no writing context, Luke had no reason or opportunity to develop phonological awareness, sound segmentation, or sound-letter relationships.

5. **Print concepts**

   • Luke was not able to hypothesize and approximate the process of writing, preventing an opportunity for reinforcement of concepts and forward development.
   • He did not have an opportunity to transfer his knowledge of print concepts from one aspect of literacy (reading) to another (writing).
   • Without a writing experience to observe, Ms. R was not aware that Luke may write from right to left, missing an instructional opportunity to scaffold new understanding.

6. **Emergent writing**

   • Luke did not perceive a need to use writing. Therefore, he did not have an opportunity to use writing for personal purposes.
   • He remained unaware of the environmental print that might exist at an airport.
   • There was no opportunity to develop familiarity, comfort, and experience with writing tools.
   • There was no opportunity to assimilate and accommodate new understandings about writing and print.

7. **Positive dispositions toward literacy and literacy learning**

   • Luke did not engage in a complex conversation. Therefore, his perception of himself as a capable thinker and oral language user was not supported.
   • Literacy was not connected with a pleasurable activity, a significant missed opportunity.

8. **Executive function**

   • There was no opportunity to respond to a challenge to his thinking about literacy and help him develop resilience.

Figure 2.8 Opportunities for Developing Foundational Anchors of Literacy are Missed

Teachers must recognize that having the words for ideas in one language can be a bridge to a second language.

Not all languages are alphabetic or are read from left to right. The grammatical organization (syntax) of a child's primary language may be different from English. It may have genders assigned to nouns.

As children of all ages work through the stages of acquiring a second or third language (see Chapter 8), there is often a high level of stress and frustration that may accompany that process. This level of stress increases the production of the stress hormone, cortisol, which impacts the prefrontal cortex. The prefrontal cortex is the area of the brain that directly impacts the ability to focus, pay attention, make clear decisions, and learn new information. This is the executive functioning headquarters of the brain. Under chronic stress, a multi-language learner's behavior in the classroom may look identical to an executive functioning disorder when it actually may be stress induced. The teacher must become aware of the linguistic circumstances of each child so that their responses and instructional decisions will be effective, supportive, and appropriate.

Spotlight

It is critical to children's future academic and social success that they develop a strong foundation of literacy in the early childhood years. The specific knowledge, skills, and understandings that comprise a strong foundation are not nebulous or vague. They have been identified by the National Early Literacy Panel (2008), and esteemed researchers such as Snow et al. (1998), Sulzby (1985), Gambrell et al. (1996), Cordova and Lepper (1996), Iyengar and Lepper (1999), Bodrova and Leong (2007),Worthy and McKool (1996), Guthrie et al. (2000), and Sesma et al. (2009). This specific knowledge, skills, and understandings have been organized by the authors into **ten Foundational Anchors of literacy**.

As introduced in Chapter 1, teachers must consider what multi-language learners can transfer from one language to another. Being literate in a first language supports becoming literate in a second (or third or fourth) language. Because the goal for multi-language learners is for them to become literate in two or more languages, knowledge of a child's Foundational Anchors in their primary language will help a teacher to support their literacy learning in English.

Emerging literacies for both single- and multi-language learners move from approximations to proficiency with instruction, scaffolding, encouragement, support, and lots of contextual practice. It is the responsibility of the teacher to fully develop and interweave all ten anchors to help children construct a strong foundation of literacy in the early years. When teachers set up opportunities for children to use literacy in meaningful contexts, they have choices to make. Will they observe carefully, helping children reinforce what they already know, and scaffolding new learning? Or will they just observe for time on task? Will children's anchors be actively under construction or ignored? <u>The outcomes for children always rest on the teacher</u>. As ✳ a result, the necessity for all teachers to become knowledgeable about the Foundational Anchors of literacy and how they are interconnected AND teachers who know how to support and scaffold children's learning accordingly cannot be overestimated.

References

Bodrova, E., & Leong, D. J. (2007). *Play and early literacy: A Vygotskian approach in tools of the mind: The Vygotskian approach to early childhood education.* Pearson.

Center on the Developing Child. (2020). *Executive function: Skills for life and learning.* Center on the Developing Child (@http://Developingchild.Harvard.edu/resources/multimedia/video/inbrief_series/. Retrieved October 12, 2021, from https://developingchild.harvard.edu/resources/inbrief-executive-function-skills-for-life-and-learning/

Clay, M. M. (2017). *Concepts about print: What has a child learned about the way we print language?* Heinemann.

Cordova, D. I., & Lepper, M. R. (1996). Intrinsic motivation and the process of learning: Beneficial effects of contextualization, personalization, and choice. *Journal of Educational Psychology, 88*(4), 715–730. https://doi.org/10.1037/0022-0663.88.4.715

Gambrell, L. B., Palmer, B. M., Codling, R. M., & Mazzoni, S. A. (1996). Assessing motivation to read. *The Reading Teacher, 49*(7), 518–533. http://www.jstor.org/stable/20201660

Guthrie, J. T., Wigfield, A., & VonSecker, C. (2000). Effects of integrated instruction on motivation and strategy use in reading. *Journal of Educational Psychology, 92*(2), 331–341. https://doi.org/10.1037/0022-0663.92.2.331

Hagen, Å. M., Melby-Lervåg, M., & Lervåg, A. (2017). Improving language comprehension in preschool children with language difficulties: A cluster randomized trial. *Journal of Child Psychology and Psychiatry, 58*(10), 1132–1140. https://doi.org/10.1111/jcpp.12762

Iyengar, S. S., & Lepper, M. R. (1999). Rethinking the value of choice: A cultural perspective on intrinsic motivation. *Journal of Personality and Social Psychology, 76*(3), 349–366. https://doi.org/10.1037/0022-3514.76.3.349

Kassow, D. (2006). Environmental print awareness in young children. *Talaris Research Institute, 1*(3), 1–8.

Lonigan, C. J., & Shanahan, T. (2009) *Developing early literacy: Report of the National Early Literacy Panel. Executive summary. A scientific synthesis of early literacy development and implications for intervention.* National Institute for Literacy.

National Early Literacy Panel. (2008). *Developing early literacy: Report of the National Early Literacy Panel.* Washington, D.C.: *National Institute for Literacy*

National Reading Panel. (2000). *Teaching children to read: An evidence-based assessment of the scientific research literature on reading and its implications for reading instruction.* Government Printing Office.

Sesma, H., Mahone, E., Levine, T., Eason, S., & Cutting, L. (2009). *The contribution of executive skills to reading comprehension. Child Neuropsychology: A Journal on Normal and Abnormal Development in Childhood and Adolescence, 15*(3), 232–246. https://doi.org/10.1080/09297040802220029

Shanahan, T. (2020). *How can we take advantage of reading-writing relationships?* Reading-Writing Relationships | Shanahan on Literacy. Retrieved October 27, 2021, from https://www.shanahanonliteracy.com/blog

Snow, C. E., Burns, M. S., & Griffin, P. (1998). *Preventing reading difficulties in young children.* National Academy Press.

Sulzby, E. (1985). Children's emergent reading of favorite storybooks: A developmental study. *Reading Research Quarterly, 20*(4), 458–481. http://www.jstor.org/stable/747854

Sulzby, E., & Teale, W. H. (1985). Writing development in early childhood. *Educational Horizons, 64*(1), 8–12. http://www.jstor.org/stable/42925853

Vukelich, C., Enz, B. J., Roskos, K. A., & Christie, J. (2020). *Helping young children learn language and literacy: Birth through kindergarten.* Pearson.

Worthy, J., & McKool, S. S. (1996). *Students who say they hate to read: The importance of opportunity, choice, and access.* National Reading Conference Yearbook, 45, 245-256. https://www.readingrockets.org/article/speech-and-language-developmental-milestones

- when there are literacy opp. available in a play setting, teach them instead of ignoring them.
- 10 Foundational Anchors of Literacy + examples
- scaffolding w/ assistance. not over-doing it & confusing the child

3 Learning to Read

The Beginnings of Reading

What causes the human brain to go from not reading to reading and how can we assist that process? Researchers come to this topic from many perspectives. They create models (visual representations) of how we learn to read, descriptions of the components of reading, necessary content of a reading curriculum, and definite thoughts about what teachers should be doing in order to cause reading to begin and to increase reading proficiency. Proficiency may be defined as test scores for individual reading components such as letter identification or segmenting syllables. It may be defined as the level of performance a child achieves in speed, accuracy, and/or comprehension. Regardless of any differences educators may have in their current knowledge base or instructional methodologies, most likely agree on the following desired outcomes or goals:

- We want all children to learn to read and write with ease.
- We want all children to enjoy and use reading and writing **proficiently** for pleasure and other purposes in their current and future lives.

There are many different models of the reading process, views on how it is best acquired, and how it should be taught. Cognitive researchers, reading specialists, special education advocates, classroom teachers and others have each put forward their views and the teaching methods that they believe should be adopted. This has frequently been referred to as the "reading wars," inferring that there are winners and losers instead of contributions from multiple perspectives, multiple sources, and multiple models. In this

DOI: 10.4324/9780429284021-3

chapter, we will examine several models from the perspective of their contributions to the understanding of reading and how children become proficient readers. What do they tell us about what a young child must know and be able to do in order to benefit from reading instruction and become a reader?

Proficient literacy includes habits of thinking, understanding of application, as well as personal expectations of oneself as a reader and writer. For example, breaking words into parts, reading known words fluently, and remembering what you have read are all important to proficient reading. If the child only uses some of the information, for example, looking for word parts, then reading is slow and laborious. Comprehension is negatively impacted. The same is true if the child only uses their memory of the text and does not use the word parts or known words. The reading may sound expressive and fluid but may not be accurate. By and large, knowledge and skills that are memorized but not truly understood, including how and when to apply them, do students little good.

Figure 3.1 A child Rereads a Familiar Book Independently.

Stages of Reading Development

Harvard professor, Jeanne Chall, was among the first educators to describe learning to read as a developmental progression. In her 1983 seminal work, *Stages of Reading Development*, Chall described six broad stages of learning to read. These stages describe general expectations for age, developmental stage, and/or grade level, helping teachers to set goals, inform planning, and make instructional decisions. At each stage, teachers help children construct the foundation that will support new learning in the next stage. For the very young child, this developmental progression helps educators, parents, and administrators clarify developmentally appropriate and effective literacy understandings and instruction for children ages six months to six years.

The First Three Stages of Reading Development (Chall, 1983)

Stage 0: Digging Deep to Build Tall

According to Chall, reading development starts with **Stage 0**, the **Pre-reading** stage (Chall, 1983) (see Figure 3.2). It begins around six months and extends to about age six (first grade), when Chall recommends formal reading instruction begin. Stage 0 encompasses a greater period of time and facilitates more new understandings than any other stage of reading development (Bissex, 1980; Kalantzis & Cope, 2021). "From birth until the beginning of formal education, children living in a literate culture with an alphabetic writing system accumulate a fund of knowledge about letters, words, and books. The children grow in their control over various aspects of language—syntax (*grammar*) and words (*meaning*). And they gain some insights into the nature of words: that some sound the same at their ends or beginnings (rhyme and alliteration), that they can be broken into parts, and that the parts can be put together (synthesized, blended) to form whole words" (Kalantzis & Cope, 2021).

Stage 0 encompasses such a broad range of development that it is divided into two substages, Acclimation and Early Competence. **Acclimation** is the phase during which young children become familiar with and accustomed to

---

Stage 0: Pre-reading, birth to age 6 (Foundational Anchor building)

Stage 1: Initial reading and decoding, grades 1–2.5

Stage 2: Confirmation, fluency, ungluing from print, grades 2–3

For a complete list of Chall's stages: https://journal.imse.com/stages-of-reading-development

---

Figure 3.2 The First Three Stages of Reading Development (Chall, 1983)

literacy. This learning occurs in the home and early care environments. For example, a young child acclimated to reading aloud associates book reading with quiet time in the lap of a trusted adult; they know to snuggle in, stay quiet, listen carefully, and to gaze at the pages. During this phase, children develop general, very basic attitudes about literacy and understandings about the routines, materials, and the purposes for which adults read and write.

Following an Acclimation phase, children begin to construct more advanced understandings about the purposes, forms, conventions, and personal value of using literacy. This is Chall's **Early Competence** stage. During this stage, teachers bring children's attention to concepts of print and the patterns of oral language. They model the process of reading and writing within authentic contexts and guide children to use print in their play and in the classroom environment. Children begin to "try out" reading and writing for themselves. Teachers of preschool children should focus classroom time on providing intentional high-quality opportunities for children to notice, use and engage with literacy in authentic and developmentally appropriate instructional contexts so that they can continue to build on what they know. The knowledge, skills, and dispositions about literacy that children construct in the Early Competent stage should align with and support their future introduction to the more abstract components of written language that will be introduced in the next stage, **Initial reading and decoding**.

The work of Chall has remained important and influential into the 21st century. The name of the first stage, however, seems to minimize the complexity of the beginnings of literacy. In the same way that a skyscraper's foundation is not a pre-building, this stage of reading is not pre-reading. It is **early reading development**. The authors refer to this stage as the **Foundation Stage**.

Interaction with adults reading, writing, speaking, and listening contributes to the child's awareness of all literacy modalities, even if the child is not yet accessing books or crayons. During this time period, the teacher's role of **foundation builder** has a profound effect. Some three-year-old children arrive at the classroom door with a strong control of speaking and listening, thus picking up new vocabulary daily. Others will have had little experience with conversation and new words. Effort and planning to develop all aspects of speaking and listening underlies school success. Building and anchoring children's oral language foundation supports the emergence of reading and writing, the more abstract modes of literacy.

Foundation building does not look like reading instruction so much as rich, meaningful language development. Not lessons on language, but extensive opportunities for language use. This includes the exploration of print, both through emerging attempts to read and write, and the inclusion of reading and writing in play. The teacher models reading and writing along with conversing. Bringing attention to print during Assisted Writing or Shared Reading (see Chapters 14 and 15) connects the stages and makes the transition from Stage 0 to Stage 1 fluid.

The **Foundation Stage**, or what is sometimes called *school readiness* or the *reading readiness stage* for that matter, should be intentionally planned to provide high-quality opportunities for children to build a strong foundational understanding of literacy, both oral and written language. One would not launch a rocket into space without first making certain all systems (foundations) were in place. Similarly, a deep foundation of early literacy is critically important in order to support children's ease and confidence in learning to read and write, as well as positive dispositions toward formal literacy instruction when it is introduced. If the time offered during this Foundation Stage is not used wisely, the future introduction of more abstract, isolated, word recognition, and decoding skills can be confusing, uninterpretable, and frustrating to children. This, unfortunately, can start children on a trajectory of negative dispositions toward literacy; discomfort, hopelessness, and a feeling of failure when engaged in reading and writing tasks. The result may be a child who avoids participating in any task that looks like literacy.

Models of Reading

Each model of reading discussed below is represented by *a visual diagram* in order to aid the understanding of how children become proficient readers. Visual models of reading attempt to simplify and explain a complex, nuanced process by identifying its components. However, components are to *reading* what ingredients are to *cake*. Teaching children each component does not cause them to become readers. We will explain and compare some of the models of reading that are currently employed by state departments of education, reading researchers, school districts, advocacy groups, and teachers to provide curriculum and instruction to children across the country.

The Simple View of Reading

The Simple View of Reading (SVOR), a formula developed by Gough and Tunmer (1986), represents a widely accepted view of proficient reading. In the SVOR, **reading comprehension**, the goal of reading, is viewed as an integration of two separate but equally important components: Decoding and Language Comprehension. In other words, a reader must be able to say the word by recognizing it or sounding it out AND the reader must know what the word means within the context and language structure it is being used. The word *down* in the next sentence must be recognized (**decoding**) and understood (**language comprehension**) in three different ways. *Whenever he felt down, he sat down by the fire and wrapped himself in his down comforter.* **Language comprehension** allows the reader to understand (1) He felt sad, (2) He assumed a sitting position, and (3) He had a blanket filled with tiny feathers. The Simple View of Reading is represented by the equation in Figure 3.3.

D X LC = RC

Decoding x Language Comprehension = Reading Comprehension

The equation of the Simple View of Reading is represented as a multiplication equation. When a component is absent or insufficient, it is represented by a zero. Therefore, if either Decoding or Language Comprehension is zero, then Reading Comprehension is absent or insufficient. Making up more of one cannot make up for less of another. Both adequate decoding and language comprehension are required for sufficient reading comprehension.

D x 0 = 0   LC x 0 = 0

Figure 3.3 Equation for the Simple View of Reading

Scarborough's Reading Rope

This **Simple View of Reading** was expanded upon by Hollis Scarborough (2001) when she used the strands of a rope to illustrate the complex process of proficient reading. The "**Reading Rope**," as it is frequently called, divides Gough and Tunmer's two categories (Language Comprehension and Decoding) into strands, each of which represents important sources of information (see Figure 3.4). The model illustrates how the components of reading begin with loose connections between each of these strands. The information becomes tightly woven together into a single rope as readers learn, practice, and

The Many Strands That Are Woven Into Skilled Reading

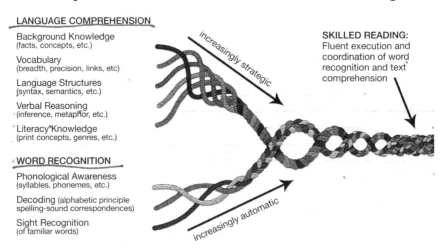

Figure 3.4 Reading Rope

become proficient. This model of reading has been adopted by advocates of the Science of Reading and the International Dyslexia Association.

Take a moment to consider the attributes of a rope. Each strand must be continuous and twisted tightly with all the other strands to create a strong, useful rope. Thus, each component of reading must be carefully considered in teaching and learning. Scarborough's Rope consists of lower and upper strands. The **Word-Recognition** strands (phonological awareness, decoding, and sight recognition of familiar words) work together as the reader becomes accurate, fluent, and increasingly able to automatically read words as a result of instruction, repetition, and practice. At the same time, the **Language Comprehension** strands (background knowledge, vocabulary, language structures, verbal reasoning, and literacy knowledge) become another major part of the rope to support the reader's attempts at understanding the words. Over time, and with instruction and practice, the two large parts (Word Recognition and Language Comprehension) must weave together to produce a proficient reader.

Becoming a reader is a complex cognitive task and this model leads to many questions. If the list of components is neither sequential nor hierarchical, where does one begin to assist the beginning reader? The implementation by many advocates is a phonics first approach and children spend most of their instructional time learning decoding skills. The curriculum often underemphasizes or ignores many other strands that are essential and of equal importance.

The limited number of sound-symbol combinations in the English language can be easily sorted into a hierarchy or continuum for teaching and testing and sorting children into instructional groups. Assessing and teaching verbal reasoning or vocabulary in a meaningful way is unfortunately not common practice.

The Five Pillars of Reading Instruction

The United States Department of Education developed a federal literacy policy over two decades ago. In 1997, Congress requested the National Institute of Child Health and Human Development (NICHHD) to appoint a National Reading Panel (NRP) to review research on reading and determine the most effective methods for teaching it. The result of this work is known as The Five Pillars of Reading Instruction illustrated in Figure 3.5. The 14-member panel included educators such as school administrators, classroom teachers, and scientists involved in reading research. The NRP analyzed over 100,000 quantitative research studies. These studies had to meet the criteria for scientifically based reading research established by NICHHD. These quantitative studies used random-controlled experimental methodology to gather data in numerical form, usually over a short period of time. The panel did not examine or review qualitative research studies such as natural experimental studies, design-based inquiry, correlational studies, case studies, ethnographies, or best practices of successful teachers (Pearson, 2019).

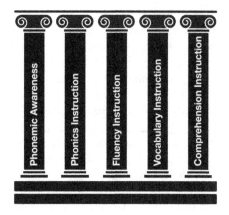

Figure 3.5 The Five Pillars

In 2000, the NRP completed its work and presented the findings. They concluded that the most effective methods for teaching reading were based on direct instruction of five components of reading:

- phonemic awareness instruction,
- phonics instruction,
- fluency instruction,
- vocabulary instruction, and
- comprehension instruction.

The infographic in Figure 3.5 is often referred to as the Five Pillars of Reading Instruction. This federal policy has informed recommendations and mandates to state departments of education and, therefore, district and school administrators and classroom teachers for a generation.

While the importance of these five pillars is not disputed, *how* an aligned curriculum is implemented (pedagogy) does influence outcomes. The easiest pillar to directly teach and systematically assess is phonics instruction. As a result, it is often overemphasized, leaving vocabulary and comprehension to develop more haphazardly. Teaching and assessing vocabulary development is a different kind of challenge and thus, often overlooked. The contents of the pillars, represented as equally important to success, are not often taught with equal time or focus. As with Scarborough's rope, HOW children access, combine, and transfer information from each pillar in order to read proficiently was not clarified. As a result of this lack of clarity to teachers and administrators, the implementation and results looked very different in different hands.

Three Cueing Systems of Reading

The **cueing systems** refer to three sources of information that readers access and manipulate to comprehend text. These sources of information are Meaning (Semantic) information, Structure (Syntactic) information,

Three Reading Cueing Systems

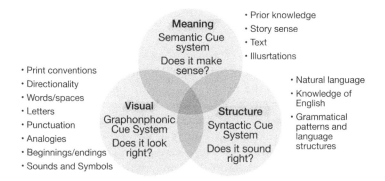

Figure 3.6 Three Cueing Systems

and Visual (Graphophonic) information (see Figure 3.6). These sources of information, the cueing systems, are intentionally taught and their use reinforced by the teacher during both reading and writing instruction. The goal of accurate fluent decoding and language comprehension from text is supported by instruction in encoding and explicit attention to transfer between reading and writing.

- **Meaning information** includes the child's background knowledge and vocabulary. The beginning comes from home and the teaching builds on what the child knows. It also reflects the child's experience with books at home and in the classroom.
- **Structure information** is the grammar that the child brings from home as well as their familiarity with literary language. Home conversation and book reading may be limited or extensive. Learning to read in one's primary language is supported by the child's innate sense of how language is put together. Young children do not know why language is constructed as it is, but they know how it should sound when spoken, and they bring that information to the text. Instruction is built around literary language and increasingly complex oral language use.
- **Visual information** is the print, letters and words, and the child's control of phonemic awareness and phonics. The child may bring rudimentary phonemic awareness but few preschool children bring an understanding of the use of phonics from their early literacy experiences. How and when the use of visual information is taught can vary.

Most commonly, a three circle Venn diagram is used to represent this model. As with the other models, the quality and effectiveness of implementation is varied. Some teachers implementing this model focus on meaning and structure first and often see the visual information as an add-on. A child cannot fully understand a text, however, if they cannot accurately use the letters and words to decode. All three circles are of equal size and importance and work together during reading.

Completing the Model

Regardless of the model, successful application requires teachers to have a deep understanding of the model, along with understanding how to use assessment as a tool for effective teaching. Instructional misapplication has been noted in every model of reading. Having a helpful weight loss guide does not prevent one from eating a quart of ice cream. The problem is not necessarily solved by choosing the correct weight loss guide. Choosing which model of reading is less important than understanding and teaching all the components of the chosen model and providing time for children to practice using these components during emergent reading. Further, one must recognize the missing pieces in the model in order to be both an effective and efficient teacher.

What are the missing pieces in each of the models? The SVOR has two equal strands of Word Recognition and Language Comprehension that are often treated as unequal, with an almost singular focus on decoding. Some teachers implementing the science of reading diagnose every reading problem as one that a systematic phonics program can fix. The Five Pillars of Reading Instruction has led to many separate instructional routines with daily phonics and daily vocabulary lessons that seem to have no connection, and children work on increasing their reading speed as a measure of fluency, even if it is devoid of comprehension. Some children can transfer information from isolated lessons to the context of reading, but others are confused. The Three Cueing Systems model has also been misapplied and instruction has provided inadequate graphophonic information. There is much to learn and apply from examining these models and exploring their implementation. These infographics tell us quite a lot about the complexity of the ideas. And yet none really illustrates all the skills, knowledge, and understandings that children need to become proficient readers.

The Anchored Approach

Let's examine these models and look for commonalities. Is there a component missing that children need to become readers? What assumptions were made about what children bring to the task? Young children must develop skills, strategies, understandings, dispositions, and abilities that support beginning reading and writing and prepare them for formal instruction. They deepen and strengthen their literacy foundation through learning that begins and develops long before anyone is thinking about their development as readers and writers. All the models acknowledge that proficient reading depends on the reader's orchestration of information and must result in the **comprehension** of the text. They all acknowledge that <u>readers must be able to decode the words and understand the word meanings and structures in order to comprehend.</u>

The commonalities among the models informed the authors' development of the ten Foundational Anchors of Literacy and a model called the **Anchored Literacy Curriculum** (see Figure 3.7) that requires the teacher to look closely at the literacy learning of children from three to six years of age. By implementing this model, we see the potential for teachers to enhance learning in such a way as to (1) build on what children already know and create a successful trajectory toward proficiency and (2) both identify and intervene with students at risk for future reading problems.

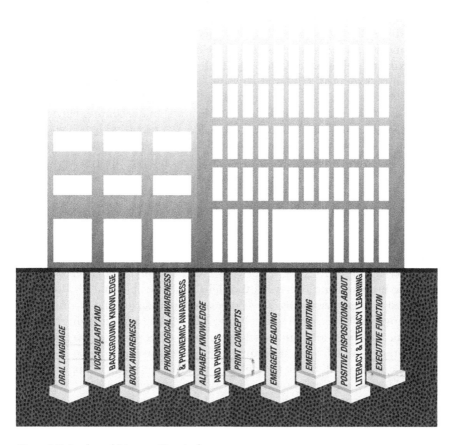

Figure 3.7 Anchored Literacy Curriculum

What's Missing?

The reading models described above, the SVOR, Scarborough's Rope, the Five Pillars of Reading Instruction, and the Three Cueing Systems, represent the current predominant views of reading instruction in the United States. Despite being supported by evidence, missing in all these models are the following critical components.

- **Emerging reading and writing** in which children have opportunities to independently practice and apply their understandings and teachers have opportunities to observe and scaffold children's understandings.
- **Positive dispositions toward literacy and literacy learning** in which children construct positive attitudes and motivation about literacy.
- **Executive function** in which children develop self-regulation such as remaining focused and engaged in learning.

The two Foundational Anchors, **Emerging Reading** and **Emerging Writing,** provide opportunities for children to use, practice, and consolidate all they have learned in order to approximate reading and writing from the naivest beginnings and as they develop toward proficient reading. By approximating reading and writing, children's understandings are cemented and can be extended. Children develop a sense of agency over their learning. The sound/letter correspondences are practiced as the child begins to make marks on paper, using Emerging Writing, and becoming participants in many Assisted Writing routines. The letters or groups of letters and their corresponding sounds are learned to proficiency through explicit instruction and scaffolding. Children use, try out, develop, and practice this knowledge when they approximate reading and engage in reading-like behaviors called Emerging Reading. They must hold the story in their mind while turning pages front to back and narrating pictures. The joy and sense of agency allow children to take risks and add new skills.

Four-year-old Carter makes scribble-like marks and reads, "*I love my mom.*" Here, he has to consciously try out and apply print concepts such as page orientation and directionality. Over time, with instruction and feedback, he will use his phonemic awareness, the alphabetic principle, and his alphabetic knowledge to encode words. This process of sounding out and recording letters is invaluable literacy practice. Emerging Reading and Emerging Writing are critical parts of early childhood curriculum. Choosing to make books and write stories of their own, rereading familiar text, or creating an ice cream store menu they will use in their play scenario are examples of opportunities for children to use Emerging Reading and Emerging Writing.

While **Positive Dispositions about Literacy and Literacy Learning** are not represented in the commonly used models of reading, the authors assert that these are essential to timely and efficacious literacy learning and must be part of planning literacy lessons and experiences for all children. Learning to love reading and writing, seeing reading and writing as part of play, valuing reading and writing as a means to communicate to self and others, and perceiving oneself as a reader and writer ease children into formal instruction and must be intentionally included in each experience. Providing for children with extensive home reading and writing experience to continue joyful associations with literacy will add to their foundation. Children with limited home experiences rely on teachers and educational settings to discover, over and over, the joy of reading and writing books, stories, and informational texts. This discovery is facilitated by each positive, successful, and meaningful literacy experience. While it has been shown that children can learn decoding skills even when they are not interested or enthused, they cannot be forced to read and write for pleasure or to satisfy interests. In addition, positive dispositions toward literacy and literacy learning will increase children's perseverance when literacy instruction becomes more complex and challenging.

Executive function is the set of cognitive functions (thinking) that allow children to control their own behavior and to monitor and change their behaviors to fit a variety of situations. Executive function supports focused attention and inhibits impulsive and reactive behavior. Clear, comprehensible expectations, explicitly taught, prompted for, and reinforced support the development of Executive Function and should be taught and reinforced with young children and beginning readers. Excluding children who have not developed Executive Function further delays their development (see Figure 3.8) Both positive dispositions and executive function play a critical role in any learning humans engage in throughout their lives. Executive function has a high predictive power of learning and academic success in the early childhood years and good predictive power for ages 6–12 (Pascual, Muñoz, & Robres, 2019). Once again, we see and can support their beginnings in early childhood.

Anchor Ignored

Mr. R has three children in his kindergarten class who have not had home read-aloud experiences. During Read-Aloud time, they touch other children, make noises, giggle, and yell out their ideas and questions. Mr. R redirects them often and after three reminders, the children are sent away from the activity. A day when all three hear the whole book is rare. These boys have not had 1:1 read-aloud experiences and so are not able to transfer listening and focusing behaviors to a group reading situation. They have not yet developed the Executive Function needed to attend to an extended story, inhibit their reactive behaviors, or to control and change their behavior. While the other children are practicing and extending their listening comprehension, vocabulary and background knowledge, executive function, and positive dispositions toward literacy learning, the three boys who desperately need to develop these anchors are excluded.

Figure 3.8 Executive Functioning

Spotlight

Choosing a side in the reading wars does little to change reading outcomes for our children (NAEP). The Foundational Anchors of Literacy is an inclusive model that recognizes the true complexity of becoming a proficient reader and writer. As a teacher, one must learn from both the failures and successes of the past and create a pathway for each child. Some begin at the starting line, others begin a mile behind or a mile ahead. The challenges are huge and take all the expertise we can access. As teachers, we can lead children to literacy, draw them in, support and encourage them, and assist their efforts. This is an intensely powerful role. We are setting up future relationships to reading and writing that may last a lifetime.

References

Bissex, G. L. (1980). *GNYS AT WRK: A child learns to write and read.* Harvard University Press.

Chall, J. S. (1983). *Stages of reading development* (pp. 10–24). McGraw Hill.

Chall, J. S. (1996). *Stages of reading development.* Harcourt Brace College.

Gough, P. B., & Tunmer, W. E. (1986). Decoding, reading, and reading disability. First Published January 1, 1986. Research Article. https://doi.org/10.1177/074193258600700104

Kalantzis & Cope. (2021). Common ground scholar: e-text. Works and days. Retrieved December 15, 2021, from https://newlearningonline.com/kalantzis-and-cope/works-and-days

Pascual, A. C., Muñoz, N. M., & Robres, A. Q. (2019). The relationship between executive functions and academic performance in primary education: Review and meta-analysis. *Frontiers in Psychology.* 10:1582. pp. 1–18. doi.org/10.3389/fpsyg.2019.01582

Scarborough, H.S. (2001). Connecting early language and literacy to later reading (dis) abilities: Evidence, theory, and practice. In S. Newman & D. Dickinson (eds., *Handbook for research in early literacy* (pp 97–119). Guilford Press.

4 Effective Curriculum for Young Children

Focus and Big Ideas

- Organizing curriculum around a topic of interest
  - Theme-based curriculum
  - Investigation curriculum
- Integrating the foundational anchors
- Anchored literacy curriculum

Making Decisions about Curriculum for Young Children

What do we mean by curriculum? Educators across grades, ages, and institutions express different perspectives of curriculum. In considering our own definition of curriculum, we emphatically resist referring to the notebooks passed out at the beginning of the school year with "Curriculum" printed on the front. Research and experience have taught us that **everything** that happens in the classroom, planned or unplanned, is curriculum. All the classroom materials, the environment, the opportunities, the activities, the instruction, and the interactions children engage in with other children and with their teacher have the potential to support the goals of an effective early literacy curriculum. From learning how to replace marker tops (an executive function), to learning how to hear the first sound of a word (phonemic awareness), to learning and using the vocabulary associated with an investigation about sea animals (oral language, vocabulary, and background knowledge), everything we do and say has the potential to support children's learning.

To benefit from any curriculum, young children must find it appealing, engaging, and relevant. It must be aligned with appropriate outcomes. Teachers must plan and implement learning contexts for children to meet those outcomes. The most engaging curriculum for young children is one that helps them make sense of their world. Preschool and kindergarten children are fascinated by the natural world and the world of adults. Teachers must plan an early childhood curriculum that takes advantage of and builds on this curiosity.

DOI: 10.4324/9780429284021-4

Literacy learning does not occur incidentally for most children. Regardless of how engaging, most children will not sufficiently develop the ten anchors of literacy through a curriculum that does not include frequent intentional events for children to (1) develop literacy concepts and (2) authentic opportunities to apply them.

Organizing Curriculum around a Topic of Interest

This chapter will introduce an effective and engaging early childhood curriculum that includes intentional instruction of literacy skills, knowledge, and dispositions. It begins with a classroom study of a topic of interest through a theme (ages three to early four) or investigation (ages four to six). This type of curriculum requires that teachers have a strong knowledge of literacy development and the Foundational Anchors of literacy. In this way, they can approach children's literacy learning from multiple angles, both directly and indirectly (see Chapters 5–7). Regardless of the early childhood curriculum being used, however, embedding intentional teaching and learning of the ten Foundational Anchors of literacy is what gives it the power to support future learning.

Educators have long used a topic of interest to weave in children's development and learning across developmental domains and subject disciplines. Two specific early childhood curriculum models that are frequently used are a **Theme-based** and an **Investigation** curriculum. Both have specific purposes and value and are appropriate for children of a specific age.

Theme-Based Curriculum

A theme-based curriculum ties early childhood disciplines, subject areas such as math, literacy, oral language, science, social-studies, music and art, to a specific topic. A typical topic might be bugs, transportation, families, apples and pumpkins, or the five senses. Once a topic has been determined, teachers plan connected learning events such as independent centers, a socio-dramatic play center, crafts, whole and small group instruction, songs, fingerplays, a listening center, and books for read-alouds and independent browsing. Each learning event represents an early childhood discipline (subject area).

A theme-based curriculum is an *awareness* curriculum. The goal is to go very wide with the learning, but not very deep. While sometimes used with older children, it is most appropriate for **younger preschool children, specifically three-year olds**. It helps these children become aware that while the world is large, learning can be connected and fun. The topic of a theme-based curriculum changes frequently, typically every one to two weeks.

As an example, a theme-based curriculum on "homes" could involve making houses out of boxes, reading aloud *The House that Jack Built*, using little houses as counting manipulatives in math and setting up the classroom dollhouse.

A theme-based unit on birds might include learning events in which children:

- use pattern strips with die cut paper birds to create and match patterns; (math)
- listen to books such as *Are You My Mother?*, *Owl Babies*, *There is a Bird on Your Head*, and *Make Way for Ducklings* (literacy);
- paint with feathers (art);
- write alphabet letters in bird seed (literacy);
- use a paper bag and packing strips to craft a nest (art);
- sing along to the nursery rhyme, "*Sing a Song of Sixpence*" (literacy);
- match birds on a branch that have the same letters printed on them (literacy);
- match pipe cleaner (chenille) worms of the same color (sensory);
- learn playful fingerplays such as *Three Little Birds* (literacy);
- explore cages and plastic birds placed in the block center (math and science);
- make binoculars to take on a planned walk around the neighborhood (art and science).

While this curriculum is engaging, it provides limited meaningful learning about birds, and few contextual authentic opportunities for children to use literacy (and other disciplines) as tools to learn about birds. While that is appropriate for three-year-old children, it is not sufficient for fours. Vocabulary and background knowledge are incidental to a theme-based curriculum rather than a planned outcome. Most children are unable to transfer understandings about the theme from one activity to the next or to make connections with their own life. How these activities are connected to each other and what they are learning are questions the children are left to answer on their own. For example, in the bird theme above, the children might hear a Pigeon book by Mo Willems (Willems, M. 2009) at read-aloud time and the next day examine and draw feathers. The connection may seem obvious to the adult, but the child may not realize a pigeon is a bird or that pigeons, like all birds, have feathers. Once again, this type of curriculum is most appropriate for three-year-old children.

Investigation Curriculum

An **Investigation Curriculum** also provides learning events for children to learn about a topic through an integration of subject areas. It directly builds on children's natural inquisitiveness about the world. Children get excited about learning, by *going deep*. An investigative curriculum is more of a **study** of a topic, rather than a broad awareness. Various interpretations and implementations of an investigation curriculum specifically developed for preschool children include the Project Approach (Katz & Chard, 2000), the

Figure 4.1 Preschool Investigates Worms

Reggio Emilia Approach (Gandini, 1993), Investigations—A project-based preschool curriculum developed at Eastern Connecticut University Child Family Development Research Center, and Tools of the Mind (Bodrova & Leong, 2007). It is used with older preschoolers through high schoolers by Expeditionary Learning schools (Expeditionary Learning Brochure 2011.)

The selected topic of an investigation should reflect children's concerns, interests, prior experiences, culture, and environments. An investigation can be as broad as *Changes in Winter* or as narrow as *Pets*. As an example, an investigation about *homes* can help children realize the many ways people use the environment (geography and climate) to determine what kind of a home they will need, what materials they will use to build them, and who will live with them. Children are guided to think deeply about the topic. Why do some people live in house boats and other people live in yurts? Why does each child live in the home they have? What are common elements in homes? Doors? Windows?

Once a topic for an investigation is determined, teachers plan for children to learn about it over time, typically from four to six weeks. To start their learning journey, teachers guide children to discuss and document what they think they already know about the topic, what they wonder about the topic, and how they might go about learning it. The less children actually know about a topic, the fewer and less specific questions they will have. Children don't know what they want to learn about what they don't know. For example, Ms. C's kindergarten class shared a common interest in germs. They didn't ask questions about viruses and antibiotics because they didn't know very much about germs. The teacher helped this information become part of their investigation.

Investigation curriculum has the potential to expand many of the classroom community's Foundational Anchors of literacy as children investigate the topic of study. For example, children can develop significant background knowledge, vocabulary, habits of learning, and dispositions toward literacy learning. Throughout an investigation, teachers provide ongoing opportunities for children to construct concepts about the world (background knowledge) **and** to engage in positive and productive habits of thinking and learning. Background knowledge cannot be teased apart from habits of thinking and learning (Eastern Connecticut University, Child Family Development Research Center, n.d.). All are critical for children's brains to grow and change. For example, children can find out about the source(s) of heat in their own home, then draw a picture of and label the furnace, radiator, fireplace, or space heater. Encouraging children to discuss the topic with an adult at home can expand the conversation beyond the classroom. Gathering information about the number of doors, the size of windows or the colors of the bathtub in their home will help children find similarities and differences that they can document (literacy) and explain (oral language). Teachers intentionally help children develop broader understandings about the world and encourage them to identify connections between phenomena. They initiate thoughtful inferences and higher level thinking. In a study of homes, four-year-old children in one preschool classroom began to predict what kind of a home you would need if you lived in a cold versus a hot climate, a forest versus a seashore.

Integrating the Foundational Anchors of Literacy

A teacher using an **investigation curriculum** for children ages four to six would first set goals and establish a baseline of information they want children to learn about the topic, bears, for example. This includes the **background knowledge** and **vocabulary** that will be an outcome for all children. Overarching goals and broader understandings might include how animals' physical characteristics are related to the geographical area in which they live, i.e., polar bears are white and live in snow covered areas; we can hypothesize that a white fox lives in a snowy area and that an animal with fins lives at least part of the time in water. In an investigation curriculum, specific connections, understandings, higher level thinking, and outcomes are an integral part of the curriculum.

A teacher's **baseline** for the background knowledge and vocabulary they want all children to learn about birds might include the following:

- there are different kinds of birds; they have names related to how they look or sound (bluebird, chickadee);
- birds have common body parts adapted for them to be able to eat their food;
- we can compare and contrast different birds;
- birds come in all sizes, so eggs come in all sizes;
- birds live in different ecosystems around the world;
- some birds live in Colorado;
- we can learn about the different habitats of birds;
- not all birds fly;
- real-world professions related to birds include ornithologists, veterinarians, and park rangers;
- some birds are protected in wildlife refuges that can be visited.

Unlike a theme curriculum, this is not a list of activities but rather factual and conceptual information (baseline background knowledge) that children are intended to learn over the course of the investigation. Learning and literacy events to support and connect this learning will be designed with these goals in mind.

An investigation curriculum offers children interesting, exciting, and personally meaningful content as they engage in both actual and vicarious experiences. These include field trips, guest speakers, read-aloud and resource books, videos, topic-aligned socio-dramatic play centers, website explorations, and actual props and artifacts. Teachers use these events to build background knowledge and provoke children to ask questions; to puzzle, inquire, connect, and stretch children's thinking in a way that an awareness theme-related curriculum cannot (Eastern Connecticut University, Child Family Development Research Center, n.d., Katz & Chard, 1989). Other Foundational Anchors of literacy are developed as teachers guide them to authentically use literacy to explore, organize, communicate, extend, and share their learning.

Anchored Literacy Curriculum

Both theme and investigative curricula offer a means for children to learn about a topic through active events and language. While a theme is a superficial exploration for most four-year-olds, it can be used effectively with three-year-old children. Children, four to six years old, are better served by a more in-depth investigative approach. Importantly, neither approach guarantees the significant early literacy foundation building that those children ultimately rely on for school success. That is where the teacher's knowledge and planning for the Foundational Anchors of literacy makes the difference.

While investigating bears or birds or houses around the world is engaging for young children and builds background knowledge and vocabulary, the specific information children learn about a topic contributes to but will not be essential for success in reading and writing. Developing all of the ten Foundational Anchors is the **essential learning** that will underlie future learning. All ten anchors are literacy concepts, skills, dispositions, and habits of learning that children can carry forward. An investigative curriculum that intentionally incorporates effective literacy learning of the ten Foundational Anchors is an **Anchored Literacy Curriculum**. An Anchored Literacy Curriculum must include both the teaching and learning of literacy through an investigation of a topic **and** through direct differentiated literacy instruction.

Investigation-Related Literacy Learning

During an investigation, literacy is used for much more than just reading aloud about the topic. Teachers provide intentional events for children to use literacy authentically in their daily learning about a topic of interest. Conversation, speaking, and listening are facilitated and extended in both the whole group and small group. Making a scientific drawing with labels that identify the parts of a bird helps children make use of and develop Foundational Anchors of literacy such as executive function, emerging reading and writing, concepts of print, phonemic awareness, and alphabet and phonics knowledge. Children learn to use the various forms of literacy, such as diagrams, lists, or timelines. For example, children are guided by the teacher to use emerging reading and writing to organize, record, analyze, communicate, and share their learning.

Extending children's learning in the socio-dramatic play center helps children integrate literacy in an authentic, engaging way. Children learn that literacy is critical in the world of adults to get things done, to be productive. Children observe, learn, and experience what pizza restaurant workers do and how they use and depend on literacy in the course of their work. Through emergently trying out the functional use of literacy, children notice and expand their understanding of the forms of print and the processes of reading and writing.

An Anchored Literacy Curriculum is interesting to children, intentionally planned, authentically integrates literacy throughout, and supports the development of all the Foundational Anchors of literacy. Because all ten Foundational Anchors of literacy develop concurrently, children transfer skills across contexts and disciplines. The teacher maintains an awareness of how children can accelerate their learning through transfer or use what they have learned in one context to solve new problems in another. For example, how does making a scientific diagram of a bird help us look for differences between birds? Or to make a diagram showing the parts of a snowman? How can our study of birds help us think about our study of plants?

Figure 4.2 Kindergarten Investigates Bugs; When this Bug Sucks Your Blood Out, It Spits in Your Arm. That's Why there's a Bump.

Direct Differentiated Literacy Instruction

As stated previously, a strong literacy foundation does not develop incidentally for most children nor do all children begin with the same levels of competency. Therefore, in addition to the literacy learning embedded in an investigation, teachers plan for direct differentiated instruction based on individual children's current understandings of the ten Foundational Anchors of literacy. Individual children's foundations of literacy are assessed to determine what skills, knowledge, and dispositions need to be directly taught and to determine the appropriate type of instruction to facilitate effective learning. Instructional contexts will be further discussed in Chapters 5–7.

Spotlight

Curriculum is the total package; it is everything that happens in the classroom every day. The teacher is in charge of, responsible for, and accountable for the curriculum outcomes. Implementing an **Anchored Literacy Curriculum** includes planning intentional events for children to learn about and use literacy across contexts as they investigate a topic of classroom interest. Teachers recognize that the anchors that secure children's literacy foundation are interwoven and complex. They plan for children to develop literacy as they learn, apply, connect, and transfer knowledge throughout the day, week, and year. Belonging to a supportive classroom learning community encourages children to try out literacy skills they watch the teacher model and see peers use.

In addition to embedded literacy learning, an Anchored Literacy Curriculum includes explicit differentiated literacy instruction for all children. Teachers determine what each child knows and understands about each of the Foundational Anchors and plans teacher-led instruction accordingly. As a result of this composite of teaching and learning contexts, teachers intentionally diminish barriers to learning and support long-term school success. It must be noted that the **Anchored Literacy Curriculum** is the opposite of finding cute topic-related activities on-line that we implement and from which we **hope** children will learn. Hope is not a teaching strategy, and the outcome is scattered at best.

References

Bodrova, E., & Leong, D. J. (2007). *Tools of the mind: The Vygotskian approach to early childhood education* (2nd ed.). Merrill/Prentice Hall.

Eastern Connecticut University, Child Family Development Research Center. (n.d.). *Investigations—A project-based preschool curriculum.* https://www.easternct.edu/center-for-early-childhood-education/investigating/index.html

Expeditionary Learning. (n.d.). *Expeditionary learning [brochure].* Retrieved April 18, 2011, from http://elschools.org/our-approach

Gandini, L. (1993). Fundamentals of the Reggio Emilia approach to early childhood education. *Young Children, 1*(49); 4–8.

Katz, L. G., & Chard, S. C. (2000). *Engaging children's minds: The project approach* (2nd ed.). Greenwood Publishing Group.

Malaguzzi, L. (1950). Reggio Emilia Approach. *Obtenido de Reggio Emilia Approach:* https://www.reggiochildren.it/en/reggio-emilia-approach/100-linguaggien

Wishon, P., Crabtree, K., & Jones, M. (1998). *Curriculum in the primary years: An integrative approach.* Merrill-Prentice Hall.

Reference for Children's Literature

Willems, M. (2009). *Pigeon series: 7 book set.* Hyperion books for children.

5 Assessment and Instruction
Critical Connections

Focus and Big Ideas
- Evaluating children's early literacy knowledge, skills, and dispositions
- Literacy anchor status
- Literacy learning contexts: direct and indirect
- Helping children make connections between direct and indirect learning contexts

Where Should the Foundation Building Begin?

Teaching blindly, such as doing what the teacher guide says to do next, is guessing or wishing that the lessons actually address the foundational learning needs of all children. No curriculum writer knows the children in a specific classroom. They are assuming, often incorrectly, that the lessons are building on a stable literacy foundation. When four children in the whole group know all their letter names and sounds, having them participate in the daily letter lesson may be inefficient and cause them to lose interest in literacy learning. They are not gaining new information. Having a child who does not know the letters in their own name participate in an alphabetic awareness activity about a jumping jellybean from Jamaica, adds little to their stores of knowledge either. They, too, become frustrated and discouraged about literacy learning. The goals of teaching are for instruction to be both effective and efficient. This means that the instruction is accessible (comprehensible) to the child, builds on what the child knows, and moves the child forward along the path to proficient literacy.

Evaluating Children's Competencies

Planning effective literacy learning contexts that will help each child construct a strong foundation of literacy requires that teachers first determine what each child **knows** about literacy and the concepts and understandings they can **apply**. In an Anchored Literacy Curriculum, literacy assessment and evaluation occurs **directly** and **indirectly, formally** and **informally** throughout the day. Children's understandings across multiple literacy activities are observed

DOI: 10.4324/9780429284021-5

by teachers as they participate in focused literacy assessment sessions, literacy routines, and small group focused early literacy instruction.

Teachers analyze this information to determine individual children's strengths and instructional needs. In an Anchored Literacy Curriculum, there is a need for both **initial assessment** as children join the classroom and **ongoing assessment** as children participate in whole group, small group, one-to-one, and independent activities.

An alphabet screening can tell us about a child's number of known letters at a particular time. Phonemic awareness screenings can inform us whether a child can hear sounds in words. Knowledge like oral language development and vocabulary are more difficult to assess. The number of exchanges in a conversation can be counted, but the words a child knows, while vitally important, are not something one can count.

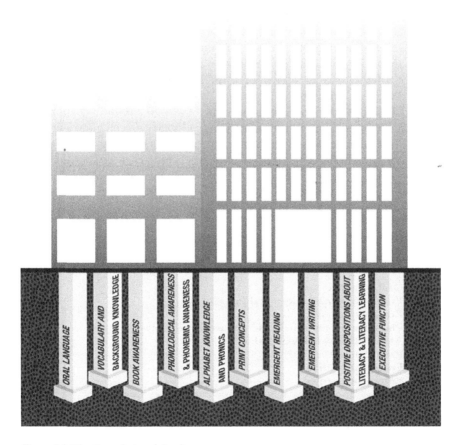

Figure 5.1 The Foundational Anchors

Teachers must assess and consider assessment performances that are easy to count and provide a number score, and the observations that reveal the literacy understandings, skills, and dispositions that cannot be counted. Examining what a child understands and can demonstrate on all ten Foundational Anchors of literacy provides actionable information to make teaching efficient and effective.

Anchor Status

During the first few weeks of the school year, teachers plan and provide an array of literacy events during which they carefully observe and record individual children's demonstration of each of the Foundational Anchors of literacy. Some opportunities encourage children to independently engage with print, others will be teacher-guided (performance sampling) so that children's performance on specific anchors can be observed and analyzed. Some opportunities are unplanned, such as when the child engages the teacher in conversation about what they have built in the block area.

Teachers use their professional knowledge of literacy development, informal checklists, and developmental continuums to guide their observations and analysis. In addition, teachers may use specific assessments to analyze children's demonstration of anchors such as phonological awareness. They make notes detailing each child's *anchor status in literacy*. **Anchor status** is defined as the understanding and performance a child currently demonstrates for each of the ten Foundational Anchors of literacy (see Figure 5.2). This teacher observation, assessment, and analysis opens a window into what the child knows and understands, what they are just beginning to try out, and what they are ready to learn. This is not a child's ability level. It is the sum of their learning experiences and an indication of the learning experiences the teacher must provide in order to build a strong, reliable foundation.

The Ten Foundational Anchors of Literacy

1. **Oral language**
2. **Vocabulary and background knowledge**
3. **Book awareness**
4. **Phonological awareness and phonemic awareness**
5. **Alphabet knowledge and phonics**
6. **Print concepts**
7. **Emergent reading**
8. **Emergent writing**
9. **Positive dispositions about literacy and literacy learning**
10. **Executive function**

Figure 5.2 The Ten Foundational Anchors of Literacy

Example: Determining a Child's Anchor Status

Marissa's preschool teacher-planned opportunities throughout the first several weeks of school to observe the status of her and every child's Foundational Anchors of literacy. This is the foundation on which the teacher will help them build throughout the year. Notice how one activity can provide information on several Foundational Anchors.

Assessing Marissa's Foundational Anchors

1. **Oral language (receptive and expressive), executive function, emerging writing,**
2. **Concepts of print, emerging reading** (Tuesday, Sept. 8, 9:30 am). Performance sample assessment.
   - The teacher asked Marissa to talk about her "show and tell" teddy bear. Marissa said that she loved it and that she got it when she was a baby. Marissa answered questions but seemed reluctant to engage in extended conversation with her teacher.
   - Marissa was asked to draw a picture of her bear. She carefully chose several colors of crayons and drew a picture that included the bear's face, tail, and paws. She was silent as she drew, despite the teacher encouraging her to talk about it. Her executive function was developed enough for her to focus and remain on task for 7 minutes. The teacher asked, "What do you call your bear?" Marissa responded, "I call her Marissa Bear" and she began to write her own name from memory next to the picture. When the teacher asked her to write the rest of Marissa Bear's name, she said, "I can't write. My big sister said I can't." The teacher said, "OK, today I'll write it for you."
   - The teacher asked Marissa what she wanted to tell her about the bear. She said, "She sleeps on my pillow. I hold her leg."
   - The teacher repeated Marissa's words as she wrote them under the picture. She then reread the entire text, pointing with her finger to every word as she read it. She then invited Marissa to reread it, using her finger to point at the text. Marissa emergently read, "My Marissa Bear is asleep. I love her." She demonstrated left-to-right directionality as she pointed. She moved her hand over the text but didn't point to individual words or demonstrate voice-print match. Her emerging reading did not match the words the teacher had written.
3. **Alphabet knowledge and phonics knowledge** (Wednesday, Sept. 9, 9:15 am). Formal assessment.
   - The teacher sat with Marissa and used a letter identification screening tool to determine the capital and lowercase letters that Marissa was able to correctly name in isolation.
   - When asked what sounds specific letters represented, Marissa appeared confused by the question.

4. **Book awareness and emergent reading** (Wednesday, Sept. 9, 1 pm). Performance sample assessment.
   - When handed a **familiar** book upside down and backward, Marissa turned the book over correctly. When asked, she correctly pointed to the title. She did not understand the terms author or illustrator. When asked to read the story to the teacher, Marissa started at the beginning and emergently read from front to back. Although familiar with the book, she told a loosely connected story, describing what was going on in each of the pictures. She did not use character names or provide detail. She did not use vocabulary from the book.
5. **Phonological and phonemic awareness** (Sept. 7–11). Group Routine.
   - Marissa enjoys participating in group songs and chants. She caught on quickly to counting words in sentences and clapping syllables in names and words. An additional phonological assessment tool will be used to assess further understandings 9/15.

After Marissa's teacher determines her current status for each of the anchors, she will consolidate what she has learned into a chart for further analysis. This will enable her to consider and plan **learning goals.** During the first few weeks of school, Marissa's teacher began a chart (see Figure 5.3) for each child. She will continue to use this type of chart as she observes progress throughout the school year.

Literacy Learning Contexts

Literacy learning contexts are intentionally planned teaching and learning literacy events that help children construct a strong foundation of literacy. They are designed to provide instruction, opportunities, activities, and strategies that support children's development of the ten Foundational Anchors of literacy. Critical to an effective early literacy curriculum are opportunities for children to (1) **learn new information** about literacy as well as opportunities to (2) **practice and apply** that learning. Literacy learning contexts are organized into **direct** learning and **indirect** learning events.

Direct Learning Contexts

Teachers use **direct learning** contexts to teach children **new** information about literacy. They determine the learning events based on observations of children's anchor status of each of the ten Foundational Anchors. This includes whole group, small group, and one-to-one instruction to meet children's needs. Teachers help children connect new information to known information, introduce and demonstrate new concepts, skills and strategies, provide feedback to individual children, reinforce both cognitive behaviors and content acquisition, and extend children's learning. The children follow the teacher's modeling and look to the teacher for support and assistance. This type of learning is teacher-led and the teacher is always present.

Chart: Literacy Anchor Status

Name: Marissa   Date: 9/13

Age: Years _4____

Months___5___

Literacy anchor	Literacy anchor status	Observation notes
1. Oral language	✓ Sentence length **4–5 words** • Asks questions • Combines sentences with: and, but, then • Number of conversational exchanges _____ • Willing to converse with adults • Confident in conversing with adults	Discussion was limited. Short sentences dictated. M. was reluctant to engage in back-and-forth conversation with T (Teacher) Reticent to talk with adults and some children. Very watchful in play
2. Vocabulary and background knowledge	• Range of word choice (small or large) • Uses two or more Tier 2 words	Does not actively participate in shared book read-alouds. Did not use the vocabulary from the familiar book during emerging reading
3. Book awareness	• Title • Author • Illustrator ✓ Front to back ✓ Attention to pictures • Attention to print • Can tell if story is real or make-believe	Correct understanding of front to back. Used pictures to tell a disjointed story Unfamiliar with terms author and illustrator
4. Phonological awareness and phonemic awareness	• Hears beginning sounds • Hears ending sounds • Hears onset and rhyme • Rhyming—identify ✓ Counts words in a sentence • Count syllables in a word • Counts sounds in a word	Phonological awareness: Established: Differentiated words in sentences, syllables in words and names TBA (to be assessed) 9/15
5. Alphabet knowledge and phonics	✓ Names_**10**__ out of 26 caps • Names____out of 26 lower case ✓ Can form some letters • Understands alphabetic principle • Writes or names beginning with sounds • Can create a rhyme • Connects some sounds with letters • Connects some letter with sounds	Recognized ten individual capital letters, including those in her name, and correctly sang the alphabet song. She does not point one to one to the letters when singing the ABC song

Figure 5.3 Marissa's Anchor Status Chart *(Continued)*

Name: Marissa	Date: 9/13
Age: Years _4_____	
Months___5___	

Literacy anchor	Literacy anchor status	Observation notes
6. Print concepts	✓ Uses directionality • Return sweep • Voice-print match (one-to-one matching) • First word • Last word • Capital letter • Lowercase letter • Period • Question mark?	Appropriately used directionality with return sweep to emergently reread the sentences she dictated about her Marissa Bear. Does not demonstrate voice-print match
7. Emergent reading	✓ Willing to "read" • Uses pictures • Repeats familiar book • Reads own books • Uses familiar book vocabulary • Looks at print	Attempted to read dictation Does not choose reading on her own during center time (predictable books, charts, etc.) M. emergently read the familiar book by using pictures. She labeled each picture but did not tell a connected story. She did not use character names or provide plot details
8. Emergent writing	• Willing to "write" • Starts at an appropriate place • Left to right • Random letter strings • Phonemic writing • Some known words	Resistant to trying out emergent writing. She said *she can't write and doesn't want to try. Her big sister told her so*
9. Positive dispositions about literacy and literacy learning	• Confident to read emergently • Confident to write emergently ✓ Participates in read-aloud ✓ Participates in songs and rhymes • Enjoys small group literacy work	Positive: Whole group phonological awareness games and songs Shared book read-aloud Emergent reading
10. Executive function	• Minutes on task: **7 minutes** • Focused attention in small group ✓ Focused attention in a large group ✓ Follows steps in procedures ✓ Minimally distracted • Perseveres through literacy challenges	M. showed good focus and attention to drawing (7 minutes. Could have continued).Very compliant with requests but did not display interest in the other tasks

Figure 5.3 (Continued)

Indirect Learning Contexts

The teacher also plans daily **indirect learning** contexts for children to **apply** and **extend** their learning as they engage in child-led events (see Figure 5.4). Children practice, integrate, approximate, problem-solve, and reinforce their literacy understandings. Indirect learning contexts are teacher-planned but child-led. The teacher is not necessarily present, but plans, provides materials and tools, creates the environment, teaches procedures, and supports understanding if needed.

Learning contexts

← Most teacher support   **Less teacher support →**

Direct learning contexts	Indirect learning contexts
Teachers: Provide instruction to help children connect new information to known information, introduce, demonstrate, provide feedback, reinforce, and extend children's learning **Children:** Follow teacher modeling and look to the teacher for support and assistance	**Children:** Apply, problem-solve, reinforce, and extend their learning **Teachers:** Plan, provide materials and tools, create the environment, teach procedures, and support understanding if needed
Guided group learning *Purpose:* To introduce, extend, and reinforce specific aspects of children's Foundational Anchors of literacy as they engage their classroom in whole or small group **contextual** activities.	**Socio-dramatic play** *Purpose:* For children to use, experiment with, apply and extend their knowledge of the Foundational Anchors of literacy during high-level socio-dramatic play.
Explicit anchor building *Purpose:* To introduce and reinforce specific aspects of Foundational Anchors of literacy that require explicit, systematic instruction for effective learning. This includes whole group, small group, and one-to-one activities	**Literacy learning centers and areas** *Purpose:* For children to practice their current Foundational Anchors of literacy as they engage in literacy learning areas or centers. Materials suggest the activities and their purpose
Literacy activities and games *Purpose:* To reinforce and extend children's literacy understandings as they engage in activities and games with teacher direction and support	**Literacy learning activities and games** *Purpose:* For children to practice and extend their current understandings of foundational literacy through independent engagement in child-led small group or independent activities and games

Figure 5.4 Direct and Indirect Learning Contexts

Direct and Indirect Contexts Are Used throughout the Day

Effective literacy programs provide all children with direct and indirect contexts throughout the day. The literacy outcome that each context is designed to provide complements one another and supports the development of a strong foundation of literacy.

A visitor on a typical day might see the teacher engage with children in teacher-led **direct** learning contexts as they:

- sing phonological awareness songs, clap out syllables in a word (Chapter 13);
- make a list of ingredients and steps for making paper;
- engage in a shared book read-aloud (see Chapter 11);
- dictate a Story Picture (Chapter 16);
- learn phoneme blending through explicit instruction (Chapter 13).

On the same day, the visitor would see the results of the teacher's carefully planned **indirect learning contexts** as children independently and collaboratively:

- use emergent reading and writing to act out their roles as customers and employees of a dramatic play grocery store (Chapters 9, 15, 16);
- use felt figures and a flannel board to retell the story of *The Three Billy Goats Gruff*;
- follow along with a book at the Listening Center (Chapter 7);
- play an alphabet matching card game (Chapter 14);
- make a book about their favorite and least favorite vegetables in the writing center (Chapter 15).

Transfer between Direct and Indirect Learning Contexts

The need for teachers to ensure children are making strong connections between content learned during direct learning and indirect learning events cannot be overstated (see Figure 5.5).

When Teachers Do Not Teach for Transfer Between Direct and Indirect Learning Events

Casey used a pointer to reread the familiar nursery rhyme, Hickory, Dickory, Dock on a chart in the classroom library, an indirect learning context. His eyes wandered briefly to the wall and the alphabet chart they had been chanting and singing all year. "Hey!" he said. "These are kind of like the ABCs up there!" He pointed to the chart and felt he had discovered something new for everyone. The teacher had assumed that Casey had made that connection for himself and wondered how many other children needed her to help them make that connection. **Connections between indirect learning opportunities and direct learning should always be part of the teacher's thinking.** Learning where and how information is useful to children increases the amount of time a child will practice using the information in indirect learning events. Connections between the many contexts in which information matters are not always obvious to a naive learner. Ensuring that children make these connections and transfer knowledge to new contexts is part of a teacher's critical work.

Figure 5.5 When Teachers Do Not Teach for Transfer

Spotlight

When teachers make sound decisions about early literacy curriculum, they assess what individual children already know and can do independently. This helps them determine what knowledge, skills, and dispositions about literacy children are ready to learn. Children come to the literacy learning environment with a wide array of strengths and needs that must be observed and documented in order to determine their anchor status. Teachers use this anchor status information to intentionally plan appropriate **direct** and **indirect learning contexts.** The desired outcome is to help each child connect with and build upon what they already know and to strengthen their Foundational Anchors of literacy.

> - initial & ongoing assessments help tell a studen'ts progress + where they stand academically
> - anchor status ↑ w/ 10 Found. Anchors of Lit.
> - direct vs. indirect learning

6 Direct Learning Contexts

Focus and Big Ideas

- Instructional learning contexts
- Grouping for direct learning contexts
- Explicit anchor building
- Implementing explicit instruction

Instructional Learning Contexts

Direct Learning is what most observers consider *teaching* because it is teacher-directed. With the direct assistance of the teacher, children connect new information to known information. The teacher introduces and demonstrates new concepts, skills, and strategies and provides feedback and reinforcement of both cognitive behaviors and content acquisition. The children follow the teacher's modeling and look to the teacher for support and assistance.

During direct learning contexts, (see Figure 6.1) **the teacher remains present** and directs the children's attention, thinking, and responses throughout the instruction or activity. This type of instruction is also called **teacher-led**. Teachers provide constructive verbal feedback to children's attempts, clarifying, reinforcing, or expanding their learning. This is called **scaffolding.** Scaffolding is very teacher controlled, and as the learner's understanding grows, the teacher withdraws or changes the type of scaffolding. The thinking and performance of the skill is gradually released from the teacher to the child.

Grouping for Direct (Teacher–Led) Learning Contexts

Teachers determine group size for direct learning contexts based on the instructional needs of individual children and pre-planned outcomes. Group size can consist of a whole group, small group, or a single individual.

Direct (Teacher–Led) Whole Group Learning

Teachers guide children's understanding of specific Foundational Anchors of literacy by engaging them in whole group direct learning that includes

DOI: 10.4324/9780429284021-6

Direct Learning Contexts
TEACHERS: **introduce, demonstrate, provide feedback, reinforce, and extend** **children's learning** **CHILDREN:** **follow teacher modeling, connect new information to known information,** **and look to the teacher for support and assistance**
• **Direct (Teacher-led): Meaningful contexts**   *Purpose:* To introduce, extend, and reinforce aspects of children's Foundational Anchors of literacy as they engage their classroom community in meaningful contextual activities. Examples include: Morning Messages or Class News, Assisted Writing, and shared book read-aloud. These learning contexts are **typically whole group and always teacher-led**.
• **Direct (Teacher-led): Explicit anchor building**   *Purpose:* To introduce and reinforce specific aspects of the interdependent Foundational Anchors of literacy that require explicit, systematic instruction for effective learning. This includes phonemic awareness and phonics instruction. **Small instructional groups** are the most effective context for this type of learning.
• **Direct (Teacher-led): Literacy activities and games.**   *Purpose:* To reinforce and extend children's literacy understandings as they engage children in activities and games with teacher direction and support. Examples include alphabet lotto, extended vocabulary building during hands-on activities such as baking and art, and Interactive Writing. **Small instructional or social groups** are used, depending on the desired outcomes.

Figure 6.1 Direct Learning Contexts

reading, writing, speaking (talking), and listening. The teacher observes their participation, reminds them of what they currently know that connects to the new learning, and helps them to build on this, providing feedback and coaching to ensure learning.

Whole group direct (teacher-led) learning can be used throughout the day (see Figure 6.2). It can be used for various purposes, including literacy routines. During circle or morning gathering time, routines might include a shared book read-aloud (See Chapter 11), a Morning Message, and a phonological awareness game. These activities build classroom community, provide enjoyable and predictable learning contexts, and help develop common understandings about language and literacy. The specific Foundational Anchors that teachers focus on during whole group time

---

Interacting Whole Group Direct Literacy Learning Events

- writing and/or reading a Morning Message together,
- construction of a learning web for the class to plan an investigation of a topic of interest,
- teacher use of a document camera to demonstrate the process of phoneme (sound) spelling during an Assisted Writing activity,
- composing a list of the things and people children expect to see on a field trip,
- participating in a Shared Reading of a predictable text,
- engaging actively in an shared book read-aloud,
- gathering information about the ocean from a website projected on a large screen,
- creating or adding to a KWL chart (what I know or think I know, what I want to learn, and what I learned throughout an investigation)

Figure 6.2 Direct Literacy Learning Events

are sequenced to build toward developmental and age appropriate expectations and outcomes. All children are encouraged to participate in the group instruction to the extent that they can and without fear of reprisal for an incorrect response. This is an intentional form of **differentiation** or meeting the varied instructional needs of each child. Differentiation during group learning is crucial to developing children's positive literacy dispositions and shared understandings, ensuring all children will participate in the future.

During whole group, teachers choose children to respond and contribute in a differentiated manner based on what specific children already know and are ready to practice or learn. Children observe the contributions of their classmates, which reinforces and introduces new learning. Because children arrive at the classroom with large individual differences in their anchor status, whole group instruction should not be used to teach critical concepts that will not be pretaught or revisited in small groups or 1:1. Teachers cannot fully observe or support individual learning to the degree required for independent application in whole group settings.

During these whole group direct learning contexts, teachers help children develop understandings such as what goes on in the minds of readers and writers before, during and after they read and write, the different forms literacy takes (lists, webs, narratives, charts, letters, expository pieces, etc.), and the concepts and conventions of print (directionality, voice-print match, capital and lowercase letters, punctuation, etc.). In this way, children learn the why, what, and how of literacy, while developing motivation to engage in literacy for themselves. Some teachers would not perceive a read-aloud as direct teaching, however, it should be as purposeful and well-planned as all direct learning contexts.

Direct (Teacher–Led) Small Group Learning

How do teachers determine which children should be part of a group? Small groups are used by teachers to ensure all children actively engage with the instruction and effectively benefit. In addition, teachers use small groups as opportunities to observe, scaffold, and assess children's individual understandings and control of specific concepts. Small groups can be used for a variety of purposes and can intentionally align with a classroom context, investigation, or theme. DeShawn, the teacher in Figure 6.3, uses a small group with his least experienced children to reinforce content and vocabulary as well as checking for understanding.

Depending on the Foundational Anchors and learning needs being addressed, teachers decide whether to use **instructional** or **social** grouping. **Instructional groups**, also called homogeneous groups, include children who have the same instructional needs and rate of learning. For example, a teacher may decide that several children are not yet demonstrating specific concepts of print such as voice-print match (wordness). The context for an instructional group may be a personal Story Picture about the class's field trip to the farm. Each child contributes to a group discussion about the trip and selects the part about which they will draw and dictate. Children emergently reread their own text with the teacher and to a partner. These groups remain fluid, disbanded, and reconstructed, to allow for individual rates of learning and instructional purposes. It should be noted that continuously grouping low language or multi-language learners together for instruction both limits their learning and isolates these children.

Social groups, also called heterogeneous groups, include children who may have different instructional needs but who can benefit from being part of a diverse group of children for a specific purpose. Socially grouping children with different instructional needs can be used to support children's development of specific Foundational Anchors of literacy. For example, a teacher might group children with diverse oral language, vocabulary, and background knowledge experiences when the focus is on expanding oral language. During the activity of printing vegetables or making butter, children benefit from interaction across social groups but still require a small group to fully participate, discuss, and question. During this small group time, the teacher would guide and scaffold each child's language development as they learned the names of the vegetables, used their language to describe and compare them, and connected them to what they eat at home or have seen at a market. Children learn at various rates and benefit from collaborating with children of different background experiences, language, cultures, and with varying degrees of literacy learning.

Individual learning can be used effectively with children who have not experienced high-quality language and literacy environments. The purpose of 1:1 teaching is to provide pre-requisite experiences on which the child will build and/or to accelerate a child's demonstration of various Foundational

 Anchor Under Construction

An Investigation about Firefighters

Beginning an investigation of firefighters

The first few weeks
DeShawn and his preschool class were investigating firefighters. During their first two weeks of the study, they had read several books and watched videos. One of the books DeShawn had planned to read the following week was a preschool informational book called, "Let's meet a firefighter," (Bellisaria, 2013).

Monday
Before reading: After introducing the book, connecting it with what they had learned so far about firefighters, DeShawn wrote new vocabulary in clear, manuscript print on a big piece of chart paper. He planned to use child-friendly definitions to explain *first responders, medical emergencies,* and *wildfires.*

During reading: DeShawn read the first chapter, stopping to restate the meaning of the new words. After they discussed the first chapter, several children dictated sentences about what they had learned and DeShawn wrote them with a blue marker on another large piece of chart paper. He said each word as he wrote it.

Afterwards, DeShawn and the children reread their dictation as DeShawn used a pointer to point to the words. He then encouraged three children to come to the chart one at a time and use the pointer to reread a sentence. This type of dictation and rereading of children's own words is known as a Shared Writing activity (see Chapter 16). It is a **direct literacy learning** context.

DeShawn had intentionally planned to use this direct instructional context (the read-aloud **and** the related Shared Writing) to develop and reinforce several of the children's Foundational Anchors of literacy. The anchors he planned to focus on included:

* oral language, as children carefully listened to the text and engaged in meaningful discussion;
* book awareness, as they became more familiar with the genre of informational books;
* content knowledge and vocabulary about firefighters;
* concepts about print such as directionality and voice-print match;
* positive approaches to literacy through active and enjoyable engagement;
* executive function as children regulated their behavior during the read-aloud, dictation, and rereading by individual children.

Tuesday morning
The following morning, a small group of the least experienced children met with DeShawn to reread the language experience chart and look again at the pictures in the previous day's reading. They suggested pictures (icons) for DeShawn to add to the chart to help everyone remember what they had learned. He drew quick line drawings and had the children name the parts as he drew.

Figure 6.3 An Investigation about Firefighters *(Continued)*

Later the same morning
DeShawn again used the pointer to reread the children's dictation with the whole class. He then introduced the next section of the book about firefighter's tools. He explained that they would once again hear new words and learn new information about firefighters. Before reading aloud, DeShawn explicitly introduced three new vocabulary words from the new section and added them to the vocabulary list. He had chosen these words intentionally. He knew that these children would probably need teacher support to understand and assimilate them into their receptive and expressive language. These words included *bunker gear, air pack,* and *a hook and ladder truck.* DeShawn introduced each word to the children, careful to use a pre-planned child-friendly definition, an explanation that connected the new word to their previous learning about firefighters. He used pictures in the book to reinforce the meanings.

As DeShawn began to read the section on firefighter's tools, he paused at the new words, quickly reminding children of their meaning and how each tool was used. After they read and discussed the new section, De Shawn returned to the Shared Writing chart started the previous day. DeShawn indicated that they would add new information they had just learned. The children dictated several sentences and DeShawn continued to write in blue marker. Everything in blue would be the information they learned about firefighters from the book. As he discussed the new learning with the children, De Shawn encouraged them to use the new vocabulary words in the dictation and he put highlight tape over each one. Afterwards, the class reread the dictation together, with another child pointing as they read.

The following week
The following week, DeShawn's preschool class went on a field trip to a fire station. DeShawn visited with the firefighters on a previous day to discuss the management of the trip and the concepts and vocabulary he wanted the children to hear and learn. When they returned, the children joined De Shawn on the rug to revisit their chart. With DeShawn's help, they eagerly provided new information and vocabulary they had learned during their field trip. DeShawn recorded the new learning in purple! How exciting it was for them to see how much they had learned! The class reread the entire Shared Writing chart. This chart would remain in the library area as an indirect learning context. Children would be encouraged to reread the dictation independently or collaboratively during independent Choice Time. Each time they emergently read it, they added to their Foundational Anchors of literacy.

Integrating play into their investigation
Included in DeShawn's class's investigation of firefighters were opportunities for children to use literacy in play. DeShawn planned for a fire station to be the theme of the socio-dramatic play center. Literacy props (maps, message pads, pencils, names, and addresses of the children in the class and the school, a firefighter sign-in book) were included and demonstrated so that children knew how and why they were used. The most effective investigation combines both Direct and Indirect literacy learning experiences.

Figure 6.3 (Continued)

Anchors of literacy. Children who have not experienced frequent lap and 1:1 reading, for example, may not understand how to successfully pay attention and engage with a story being read aloud to the group. To help them develop book awareness, the cognitive processes used for listening to a story, and the expectations and routines of a read–aloud, time should be planned daily for the teacher, volunteer, or assistant to read aloud to the child. Purposes of 1:1 instruction other than addressing specific Foundational Anchors of literacy include supporting social and emotional needs, speech and language difficulties, and building rapport between the child and teacher.

Explicit Anchor Building

The steps of explicit instruction are used to teach specific literacy concepts, knowledge, and skills and the Foundational Anchors of literacy. They are also effective and efficient for teaching learning routines and behaviors that enhance school success. The term **explicit instruction** indicates that the teaching will result in children's unambiguous learning. The target learning goal and the steps for achieving that goal are clearly stated in detail and demonstrated by the teacher, leaving no room for children to be confused or in doubt. Explicit instruction is **systematic,** signifying that acquiring the knowledge and skills proceeds along a continuum, and that teachers introduce them by breaking lessons and activities into sequential, manageable steps. This ordered sequence guides learning from concrete and simple to the more complex and abstract. Prerequisite knowledge or skills must be solidly in place before the new knowledge or skill should be taught.

Explicit Anchor Building requires that teachers astutely observe and evaluate children's developmental understandings of each of the anchors. They determine where, along a continuum, individual children's instruction should begin and ensure that new learning is connected to and built on a solid understanding that children already possess. Explicit anchor building is used to **teach literacy skills** such as:

- **encoding during emerging writing**: listening for the first sound in a word and writing the appropriate letter;
- **phonological awareness:** counting the number of syllables in a word, clapping the number of words in a sentence, or blending individual sounds into a word;
- **alphabet knowledge and phonics:** learning letter names and their corresponding shapes, developing the alphabetic principle, and mapping letters to sounds.

Implementing Explicit Instruction

The steps of explicit instruction follow a sequence in which the teacher gradually hands the responsibility for demonstrating knowledge and/or application of the skill to the children. These steps are frequently described using the familiar **I Do, We Do, You Do** sequence (Pearson & Gallagher, 1983). *explicit instruction*

- **I Do:** (The Teacher) Thinking aloud, explaining, demonstrating, modeling:

In the introduction of the concept or skill, the teacher first helps children recall the prerequisite knowledge on which they will help the children connect and extend. To begin the new instruction, the teacher tells the children what they will be learning. They explain why it is an important skill or concept for them to learn. For example, a teacher tells the group of children that they will want to use their knowledge of letters and sounds to represent words in their emerging writing. They will be showing children how to do that at the appropriate developmental level.

In another example, a teacher may want children to extend their understanding of compound words by being able to blend two words together to form a compound word. She will remind them of their previous thinking about compound words and explain that they will be listening for them in a story she will later read. She demonstrates the process of sliding the two words together to make a new word with red and green blocks. For a word such as *sandbox*, the children will discuss how the meaning of the two words supports understanding the meaning of the new word.

During the **I DO** stage of explicit instruction, a teacher demonstrates proficiency of the skill so that children see what competent performance of the skill looks like and the thinking that goes into doing it correctly. In this way, children can be certain of what they are trying to accomplish, how to accomplish it, and to recognize what proficiency looks like when they do.

Teachers ensure this clarity by precisely demonstrating and modeling the skill. They "think aloud" in front of children as they make decisions or solve problems to reach the desired outcome. Teachers must plan ahead to ensure they use unambiguous, clear, and concise language called **intentional talk** with the children. It should be succinct and mirror the exact thinking and language they want children to remember and use. To avoid possible confusion, the complexity of a teacher's speech (vocabulary and sentence structure) should be based on the students' oral language comprehension. Checking for children's understanding and watching for (and interrupting) confusion or frustration supports the child in staying engaged. Do not use unknown concepts or words to explain new learning. It is always a best practice to separate teaching information, skills, and strategies that are similar and, therefore, may generate confusion.

In the explicit anchor building lesson in Figure 6.4, children learn to represent the first sound with the corresponding letter. This is their introduction to phoneme (sound) spelling.

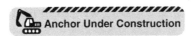
Anchor Under Construction

I DO
Target learning goals:

- *Listening for the first sound in a word; using a sound chart to match the sound to the corresponding letter.* This phoneme awareness skill will start children on their journey to encoding print, i.e., writing/composing by mapping sounds to letters. The teacher is using an instructional context known as Scaffolded Writing (Bodrova & Leong, 1998).
- Reinforcing phonological awareness and concepts of print, e.g., wordness.

Procedure: Using a document camera so that all children can see and hear the demonstration, the teacher, Margo, talks to the children about a mishap she had with her dog, Rex, that morning. She draws a picture that includes herself and her dog. She explains that she wants to write about her experience and will start her story with the following sentence.

Teacher: *Today, I was looking for my dog, Rex. Let me count the number of words in my sentence. 1, 2, 3, 4, 5, 6, 7, 8! There are 8 words in my sentence. I am going to draw a line for each word in my sentence.* The teacher made eight lines to represent the words, leaving clear spaces between words. (This is an Assisted Writing routine that the children have used many times.)

———————— —— ——— —————————— ———— ——— ————

Margo repeated the sentence slowly, verbally mapping each spoken word to a line.

Teacher: *Now, I am going to write each word of my sentence.*

Today, What do I hear at the beginning of the word "today"... /t/ today /t/ today /t/ today. I hear the /t/ sound at the beginning of today? Make that sound with me. /t/ Today.

The letter T makes the /t/ sound, so I am going to write it here on the first line. If I don't know what letter makes the /t/ sound, I can look at my sound chart. See, I am looking at my sound chart, finding the /t/ for tiger, so I know it is the letter T.

Margo writes the rest of the word without comment. Stretching out words to hear middle and ending sounds is not part of this lesson. Hearing beginning sounds is the prerequisite skill for being able to hear middle and ending sounds.

Teacher: *I am going to say my sentence again. Today, I was looking for my dog, Rex.*

The next word is I. We all know how to spell I. Margo writes the I. She then says, *I is saying its own name. I.*

Margo again reads the whole sentence and some of the children join in.

The next word is was. /w/ /w/ Was. Make that sound with me. I hear /w/ at the beginning of was. I'm going to look for the /w/ sound on my sound chart. The letter W makes the /w/ sound like in whale, so I am going to put the letter W right here for was.

Margo then writes the remaining two letters of the word <u>was</u>.

Figure 6.4 An Explicit Anchor Lesson: Introduction to Phoneme Spelling *(Continued)*

> **Teacher:** *We are using "sound spelling" to write our sentences. We're all going to start using sound spelling in our writing. It helps us and other people reread what we wrote and to understand more about our stories.*
>
> Margo completes the lesson with the other words using the same steps. Altogether, Margo writes eight letters that correspond to the sounds of the eight words in the sentence, thinking aloud and demonstrating how she determines the letter by making the beginning sound and using the sound chart. The children are starting to respond in unison during the teacher's decision-making process so she determines that it is time to move on to the next stage of explicit instruction, Guided Practice (We Do).

Figure 6.4 (Continued)

- **We do:** (Teacher and children) Trying out the skill with adult guidance and support   *time before test taking (ex. math)*

After explaining and demonstrating the new learning, the teacher will provide intentionally planned opportunities for the children to immediately try out the skill <u>with adult guidance</u>. This is the **We Do** stage of explicit instruction. It begins when the teacher observes that most of the children are making the sounds and naming the letters. During the We Do stage, the teacher invites the children to participate, in unison or individually, and observe signs of understanding and confusion. The teacher <u>interacts with</u> individual children at the <u>appropriate level of support.</u> This support is called **guided practice**. Several guided practice opportunities should be provided before determining readiness for the next stage of explicit instruction.

Children are not expected to independently apply the concept or skill until the teacher has observed and confirmed that they can apply it successfully on their own. As teachers provide guided practice, they may determine that some children will need additional instruction or mediation to apply the skill independently and reach competence. Teachers need to continually evaluate the effectiveness of their instructional interactions. Are they able to successfully help children connect new information with what they already know? Are they using succinct, clear explanations? Did an explanation support children's learning or confuse them? <u>Self-awareness of the results and impact of instruction will help teachers fine-tune their delivery over time.</u>

The **We Do** stage is often a process that can and should extend over many days or weeks. For example, consider children learning a physical skill such as tying their shoes. In preschool and kindergarten, **We Do** occurs over <u>and over before a child begins to independently take it on.</u> The same is true of the Foundational Anchors of literacy. Guided practice happens across instructional contexts over and over. <u>As each child grows in competence, the **We Do** occurs at a higher level with less explicitness.</u>

Unfortunately, the **We Do** step is sometimes left out of instruction. Teachers demonstrate a skill or concept and send children off to complete the task independently. When this step is overlooked, the result is often frustration, failure, and negative dispositions toward literacy teaching and learning in both children and teachers. The teacher explains and demonstrates, for example, how to fold the paper in quarters and put an alphabet letter in each box so the child can draw pictures of objects beginning with the letter. After the demonstration, the teacher hands out the paper and children return to their tables. Many children end up upset and crying. Why? They cannot fold their paper correctly. They needed the **We Do** when the skill was introduced and will probably require it for the next few times they do this type of activity. Then, the teacher can hand it off to almost all the children. The teacher still may, however, have a few that need assistance for longer.

- **You do** (Children) Independent practice and application

Once a concept or skill has been sufficiently introduced, modeled with think aloud (I Do) and children are guided to try it out with teacher support (We Do) those who have demonstrated clear understanding proceed to the next stage of explicit instruction, **You Do**, or independent application (see Figure 6.5). Students who are not yet able to successfully apply the skill on their own may need additional guided practice before trying it out without teacher support. This step by step process embeds intentional differentiation

---

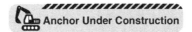
Anchor Under Construction

You Do

Target learning goals:

- **Children will independently segment and produce the first sound in a word.**
- **Children will use a sound chart to match the sound to the corresponding letter.**
- **Children will write the correct letter.**

The children in Margo's class have a daily scheduled writing time. After several days of **I Do** and **We Do** instruction, she suggests that they use their letters and sounds when they draw and then write independently. She observes both children's products and the process of their work to inform her future instruction. She makes notes of their understandings, confusions, and future learning goals, including a need for some clarification. She scaffolds individual children's attempts within their range of understanding.

Figure 6.5 The "You Do" Step of Explicit Instruction

of instruction so that children are not required to learn more complex materials or skills without grasping the pre-requisites.

Explicit Anchor Building: Whole Group

Systematic anchor building can use instructional groupings of whole group,
small group, or 1:1, depending on the purpose and instructional strengths
and needs of the children. Whole group instruction should not be used in a
non-differentiated way or to teach critical concepts that will not be pretaught
or revisited in small groups or 1:1.

In addition to academic knowledge and skills, whole group explicit
instruction is frequently used to help children learn and independently follow
classroom management routines. This type of direct instruction of children's
Executive Function can help ensure that the entire classroom community runs smoothly and predictably, learning and implementing the steps of a
teacher determined classroom routine. For example:

- **classroom management routines** such as engaging actively and appropriately during a shared book read-aloud, buddy reading, independent
  reading, or transitioning to a new activity or learning sequence;
- **the appropriate use and organization of materials** such as putting
  books away in their correct tubs, carefully using construction and art
  materials, and storing personal belongings;
- **the use of literacy props in theme-designated socio-dramatic
  play centers.** This may include learning how to "read" lists of menu
  items in a pizza restaurant or a bakery, finding students' names and
  addresses on a map in the fire station, deciding on services and using
  corresponding price lists for a hair salon or auto mechanic's garage, or
  following directions to navigate the security of an airport;
- **instructions** for using a pointer to reread Interactive Charts, or to use
  equipment in a listening center.

Explicit Anchor Building: Small Group

A small instructional group could be used, for example, to explicitly teach
a phonological awareness activity where a teacher demonstrates and then
guides children to identify and sort objects by their initial sounds (see
Figure 6.6). After children can proficiently demonstrate the concepts and
directions of an activity, the materials can be placed in learning centers
for independent or collaborative practice of the learning. Grouping is fluid
and based on individual children's instructional needs, previous experiences
with literacy, and learning rate.

Anchor Under Construction

The teacher, Mr. Brandon (Mr. B) observed several children whose emerging writing is a continuous string of letters. Despite the children recording two to three letters per word, there is no space between words. He checks to make sure they can hear and clap single words, the pre-requisite skill. Here is Cameron's sentence.

MIMOMIZAGUDCUCR (My mom is a good cooker.)

(I DO) In this small instructional group, Mr. B will teach the children to place a penny on the page after each word to help the reader. He shows them two sentences and asks them which is easier for a reader to read:

Ilovepepperonipizza I love pepperoni pizza.

In exuberant unison, they choose the sentence with spaces. Mr. B says it's even easier for HIM to read and he was the writer!

Mr. B demonstrates the strategy on a dry erase easel by saying a sentence, clapping each word in the sentence, and writing the sentence word by word, putting a sticky note after each word. **When he removes all the sticky notes, the sentence is conventionally spaced.**

(We do) Next, Mr. B dictates a sentence for the children to write and supports each of them to place a penny after each word. He does not correct or fix words written with only a few sounds because he is focused on the skill of wordness and spacing. A future lesson might be to teach these children how to listen for and represent the corresponding letter of the medial sound in a word.

Here is Cameron's work.

i (penny) lv (penny) to (penny) pt (penny) mi (penny) dg (penny) afr (penny) dnr (penny)

I love to pet my dog after dinner.

Mr. B asks the children to put their pennies in a jar and read their sentences. The writing appears conventionally spaced without any **visual interference**. There are no dashes or dots between words. The children read their sentences together and individually.

(We do) Now Mr. B asks the children to write a sentence about their favorite food. Each child says their sentence aloud and claps the words as they say them. He gives them pennies. Mr. B is still supporting each child in the group, carefully observing how close each is to independence. He assists when needed so that each child has correctly placed spaces. He decides if he needs to plan another **We Do** task for the following day or for several days. He will encourage the children to approximate using pennies during independent writing time.

Figure 6.6 Explicit Instruction of Word Boundaries

Saad is a multi-language learner with limited vocabulary in both English and Arabic. In order for him to benefit from whole-group read-alouds, he first needs time to get the gist of the story, look at and name the pictures, and use the words he knows in both languages before hearing the story with the class. Ms. Christie points to an ice cream cone in the picture and says *Ice cream cone.* Saad repeats the words. She asks him, "What is it in Arabic?" He says makhrut alayaskrim. Ms. Christie tries to repeat and they laugh. She uses **wordhippo.com** to find and play audio of words in Arabic like delicious, hungry, demand, as she shows the picture of the boy wanting the ice cream cone and reads the words in English. They act out parts of the story and talk in English about what he thinks. When it is time for the whole group read-aloud, Saad will have information to comprehend the story. If his attention drifts, Ms. Christie has points to re-engage him.

Figure 6.7 One-to-One Instruction

Explicit Anchor Building: One-to-One

Independent systematic anchor building can be planned for any Foundational Anchor for which a child needs focused, systematic skill introduction or practice. A child may need one-to-one assistance to understand a new concept or to accelerate their control of a previously taught concept. One-to-one grouping allows a teacher to carefully observe children's response to instruction. It can also provide the teacher with additional information as to whether insufficient progress is potentially due to lack of literacy experience, a cognitive challenge, or another factor. A teacher can observe the type and rate of instruction the child requires to proficiently demonstrate specific literacy concepts and skills. This type of grouping is also fluid and based on a child's current instructional needs (see Figure 6.7).

Teacher-Led Literacy Activities and Games

Teacher-led activities and games are designed to reinforce and extend children's understanding of a specific or combined use of specific Foundational Anchors. Teachers **remain present** during these instructional contexts. Examples include supporting children's literacy learning through an alphabet naming board game, small world objects matched to the correct first letter and sound, and sets of zoo or farm animals, which encourages children to develop vocabulary and knowledge related to a specific organizing concept. Teachers introduce the purpose of the game and the instructions if the children are unfamiliar with them. The directions should be introduced **explicitly** to ensure a child's understanding. Confusion about the rules can impact their understanding and practice of the skill.

Spotlight

Children's Foundational Anchors of literacy develop along continua. Therefore, knowledge, concepts, and skills are introduced and reinforced along a sequence, from concrete and simple to the more complex and abstract. Teachers strategically use the Anchored Curriculum to identify each child's anchor status. They use this information to plan, create, demonstrate, instruct, and scaffold literacy learning events that help each child develop a strong foundation from which proficient literacy can emerge and grow.

An Anchored Curriculum includes both Direct and Indirect instructional contexts. Direct contexts are facilitated by the teacher in groups of various sizes. Group size is determined by children's anchor status, the identified purpose or outcome, and the level of required teacher support. Direct Learning Contexts include teacher-led whole group literacy instruction, teacher-led explicit anchor building, and teacher-led literacy activities and games.

In conjunction with a teacher's thorough knowledge of literacy development, a carefully planned use of the Anchored Curriculum can facilitate a high-quality early literacy curriculum. The focus of this work is to co-construct with each child, strong Foundational Anchors needed for long-term school success in **literacy and content learning**, regardless of the anchor status with which a child arrives in the classroom.

Besides **Direct Teacher-led** literacy events, young children also need opportunities to use, practice, and apply literacy in **Indirect** literacy contexts. This includes high-level socio-dramatic play in which children use literacy for functional purposes. The next chapter will provide support for early childhood teachers to thoughtfully plan **Indirect Instructional Contexts** as part of an Anchored Curriculum.

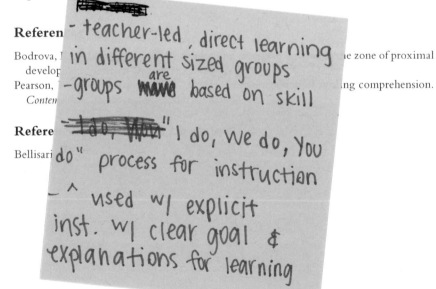

Referen

Bodrova, ... develop ... e zone of proximal

Pearson, ... ing comprehension.
   Conten...

Refere

Bellisari ...

Saad is a multi-language learner with limited vocabulary in both English and Arabic. In order for him to benefit from whole-group read-alouds, he first needs time to get the gist of the story, look at and name the pictures, and use the words he knows in both languages before hearing the story with the class. Ms. Christie points to an ice cream cone in the picture and says *Ice cream cone*. Saad repeats the words. She asks him, "What is it in Arabic?" He says makhrut alayaskrim. Ms. Christie tries to repeat and they laugh. She uses **wordhippo.com** to find and play audio of words in Arabic like delicious, hungry, demand, as she shows the picture of the boy wanting the ice cream cone and reads the words in English. They act out parts of the story and talk in English about what he thinks. When it is time for the whole group read-aloud, Saad will have information to comprehend the story. If his attention drifts, Ms. Christie has points to re-engage him.

Figure 6.7 One-to-One Instruction

Explicit Anchor Building: One-to-One

Independent systematic anchor building can be planned for any Foundational Anchor for which a child needs focused, systematic skill introduction or practice. A child may need one-to-one assistance to understand a new concept or to accelerate their control of a previously taught concept. One-to-one grouping allows a teacher to carefully observe children's response to instruction. It can also provide the teacher with additional information as to whether insufficient progress is potentially due to lack of literacy experience, a cognitive challenge, or another factor. A teacher can observe the type and rate of instruction the child requires to proficiently demonstrate specific literacy concepts and skills. This type of grouping is also fluid and based on a child's current instructional needs (see Figure 6.7).

Teacher-Led Literacy Activities and Games

Teacher-led activities and games are designed to reinforce and extend children's understanding of a specific or combined use of specific Foundational Anchors. Teachers **remain present** during these instructional contexts. Examples include supporting children's literacy learning through an alphabet naming board game, small world objects matched to the correct first letter and sound, and sets of zoo or farm animals, which encourages children to develop vocabulary and knowledge related to a specific organizing concept. Teachers introduce the purpose of the game and the instructions if the children are unfamiliar with them. The directions should be introduced **explicitly** to ensure a child's understanding. Confusion about the rules can impact their understanding and practice of the skill.

Spotlight

Children's Foundational Anchors of literacy develop along continua. Therefore, knowledge, concepts, and skills are introduced and reinforced along a sequence, from concrete and simple to the more complex and abstract. Teachers strategically use the Anchored Curriculum to identify each child's anchor status. They use this information to plan, create, demonstrate, instruct, and scaffold literacy learning events that help each child develop a strong foundation from which proficient literacy can emerge and grow.

An Anchored Curriculum includes both Direct and Indirect instructional contexts. Direct contexts are facilitated by the teacher in groups of various sizes. Group size is determined by children's anchor status, the identified purpose or outcome, and the level of required teacher support. Direct Learning Contexts include teacher-led whole group literacy instruction, teacher-led explicit anchor building, and teacher-led literacy activities and games.

In conjunction with a teacher's thorough knowledge of literacy development, a carefully planned use of the Anchored Curriculum can facilitate a high-quality early literacy curriculum. The focus of this work is to co-construct with each child, strong Foundational Anchors needed for long-term school success in **literacy and content learning**, regardless of the anchor status with which a child arrives in the classroom.

Besides **Direct Teacher-led** literacy events, young children also need opportunities to use, practice, and apply literacy in **Indirect** literacy contexts. This includes high-level socio-dramatic play in which children use literacy for functional purposes. The next chapter will provide support for early childhood teachers to thoughtfully plan **Indirect Instructional Contexts** as part of an Anchored Curriculum.

References

Bodrova, E., & Leong, D. J. (1998). Scaffolding emergent writing in the zone of proximal development. *Literacy Teaching and Learning, 3*(2), 1–18.

Pearson, P. D., & Gallagher, M. C. (1983). The instruction of reading comprehension. *Contemporary Educational Psychology, 8*, 317–344.

Reference for Children's Literature

Bellisaria, G. (2013). *Let's meet a fire-fighter.* Cloverleaf Books.

7 Indirect Learning Contexts

Focus and Big Ideas

- Different learning contexts lead to different learning outcomes
- Indirect learning contexts
- Designing the environment
- Transitions that build executive function

Different Learning Contexts Lead to Different Learning Outcomes

Effective literacy programs provide all children with both direct and indirect contexts for learning on a daily basis. The literacy outcomes that each context is designed to provide are intended to complement one another and support the development of a strong foundation of literacy.

Direct learning contexts facilitate instruction directed by and provided by the teacher to lead children toward a known outcome. Explained in Chapter 6, this instruction is determined by a teacher's observation and analysis of individual children's literacy strengths and instructional needs, their current anchor status. Instruction is focused, effective, and efficient. Direct instruction allows the teacher to shine a light on a concept and check for understanding. During the **I do-We do-You do** cycle, also called Gradual Release of Responsibility (Pearson & Gallagher, 1983), the teacher provides assistance and can move to more or less assistance as needed by the children to be successful.

Indirect learning contexts, in contrast, are child-led learning events that are planned by the teacher although the teacher is not present while the children are learning. The teacher is often occupied with observing or teaching other children, while children engaged in indirect learning events are practicing their literacy learning on their own.

Indirect Learning Contexts

Teachers create **indirect learning contexts** by

- shaping the environment to support children's independent engagement,
- providing discrete areas that lead children to interact with materials and one another, and

DOI: 10.4324/9780429284021-7

- center-based activities that guide children to apply, practice, integrate, approximate, problem-solve, reinforce, and extend their literacy learning.

Indirect learning contexts can spring from children's learning during prior direct instruction or as a result of a teacher's decisions about centers and room arrangement. Indirect learning contexts can provide extensions of learning and practice of recent learning. In these ways, the teacher provides time for the child to strengthen and integrate the Foundational Anchors. Attention to planning well-designed indirect contexts makes the teacher's job easier. It accelerates children's learning by allowing them ample time to practice what they know in meaningful contexts. It supports socio-emotional development and collaboration skills. It extends their executive function; their ability to focus on and complete a task on their own. When we consider the time spent in a piano player's lesson compared to the hours to the hours of practice needed to master the piano, the need for independent practice of direct learning becomes clear. This practice occurs in Indirect Learning contexts.

The Physical Environment Is an Indirect Learning Context

In the field of early childhood education, it is widely believed that, if carefully planned with appropriate understanding and intention, the classroom environment can positively impact children's learning. When teachers recognize that the physical setting is an active and pervasive influence, they pay careful attention to classroom set-up, materials, organization, and presentation (Vukelich, Enz, Roskos, & Christie, 2020). Reggio Emilia teachers describe the environment as another teacher in the room. Montessori teachers follow strict principles to provide a meticulously prepared environment to maximize children's learning. Unfortunately, many teachers see the classroom's physical environment as unrelated to important learning and instructional goals. Instead, it is frequently designed for the warm, tidy, and inviting atmosphere it can create. While visual esthetics are a very important element of an effective environment, they are not sufficient to support learning.

The physical design of a classroom has been shown to affect children's choice of activities (Jalongo, 2014; Morrow, 2020) and the amount of time they remain interested and engaged. Effective classrooms are strategically organized to support children's learning across all developmental areas; social-emotional, physical, cognitive, language, and literacy development. They are well managed, physically and emotionally safe and secure for children, and developmentally appropriate. They are easily accessible, clean, and well organized, intellectually stimulating, and inviting to young children and their families (Vukelich et al., 2020).

Figure 7.1 A Kindergarten Child Draws Herself with Her Teacher, Including Many Details

Designing the Environment

We assigned our university students to analyze the preschool classroom environments where they had spent the previous semester observing and working.

The results were surprising to them. Many students were agitated and confused as they struggled to interpret what they had observed. They had assumed the preschool classrooms would score high on the assessment they administered, the Environmental Language and Literacy Observation Checklist (ELLCO) (Smith, Brady, & Anastasopoulos, 2008*).*

*The ELLCO is an assessment widely used to evaluate the extent to which a preschool environment effectively supports children's early language and literacy development. Many students were shocked by the low scores they were forced to assign as they closely examined the environment through the lens of the ELLCO. After all, these rooms were attractive and filled with books and had lots of **environmental print**, the print on the walls and around the classroom.*

Unfortunately, early childhood environments that effectively support children's early language and literacy learning are not that common

(McGee, 2007). "While most early childhood educators believe they have print and language-rich classrooms, in reality these teachers provide children with only a basic level of environmental support" (Vukelich et al., 2020) Early childhood teacher's confusion often lies in what they believe constitutes a "literacy-rich environment."

Environmental Print

The *golden nugget* for constructing literacy-rich environments is under-standing that children will only notice and use **environmental print** that is made **meaningful** to them (see Figure 7.2). This means that teachers must model, teach, and guide children to see a need and a purpose for using it. If children do not perceive print in the classroom as serving a personal and relevant purpose, they will ignore it. Therefore, labeling everything in the room, from flag to door to window to sink, does not effectively support children's literacy learning. Children tend to view random print unrelated to a meaningful context as wallpaper, not something interesting and important to ponder and use. For example, the teacher can model how a chart of the children's names can be used to send messages to friends, to take attendance and name children who are missing, and to hear beginning

Anchor Under Construction

Mrs. Alley read to her kindergarten children everyday from carefully chosen pic-ture books. Each book cover was photocopied onto a half sheet of paper and posted on a nearby bulletin board labeled, Books We Have Read. She referred to it daily as part of her read-aloud routine. For example,

- She asked the children if they remembered reading another book by the same author or illustrator.
- She connected the new book to a familiar book during her book introduction.
- She invited children to take turns choosing a book to reread every Friday.
- She connected books by the theme, topic, or characters.
- She showed children where the familiar read-aloud books were in the class-room library.
- She referred to words in books titles for help spelling during Assisted Writing.

In these ways, Mrs. Alley kept the bulletin board meaningful and relevant to the children. This example of environmental print was personally useful to each child. Children were drawn to it and were often observed pointing to and naming the books, emergently reading titles, and matching books from the classroom library with the photocopied covers on display.

Figure 7.2 Meaningful Use of Environmental Print

sounds and syllables. Without the teacher modeling its usefulness again and again, it can hang on the wall and go unnoticed.

Another form of environmental print is the artifacts of the literacy events that children have engaged with and experienced. These might include:

- the emergent writing the children have done;
- color, number, and picture alphabet charts;
- class books that have been created during investigations or as innovations;
- language experience stories;
- morning messages;
- charts composed by the teacher and the children;
- interactive writing examples;
- a display of the read-aloud book covers; and
- a chart indicating what children think they already know about the current topic of investigation and the things they are wondering about (KWL chart).

All of these items of class-made print must be **reread, referred to, and used repeatedly** in reading and writing in order to remain relevant and useful to children. Items should be replaced when no longer used, rather than adding more and more print to the classroom. Current, useful, meaningful print, not just lots of print, makes the environment print-rich. Unused or excessive displays of charts, pictures, and other print material do not enhance learning and can be overstimulating for some children.

Areas and Centers

At some time in our teaching career, we opened up the door to our new classroom and faced a large empty space and four blank walls. At first breath, it can seem overwhelming. At the same time, it is exciting as we begin to imagine the life and learning that will take place there. But where and how to begin?

Areas

We start by making the large open space into smaller designated learning areas. Effective early childhood classrooms require that the space, no matter the size, be broken up into smaller, well-defined areas, and centers. **Areas** are designated learning spaces, the use of which is easily determined by the design and the choice and arrangement of associated materials. Unlike centers, areas are not **task** specific. Defining an area for a useful purpose requires creativity and resourcefulness. Each area should be enclosed on three sides so children feel they are entering a separate room. The teacher must explicitly introduce the purpose of the area to the children, including the materials and the various learning events that can occur there. All areas should be labeled, creating environmental print that helps children know the name and use of each area. The appropriate size of the area is determined partly by the physical logistics of the classroom, and most importantly by the number of children that the teacher decides will best result in positive relationships and collaboration, extended conversation, and effective learning. The combination of enclosing the area on three sides, limiting the size to support effective learning, and introducing the area's purpose and materials facilitates children's focus and meaningful engagement in the area.

The sides of areas can be designated with a variety of furniture. Bookshelves and small file cabinets can be used if their height is not taller than the children. A child's ability to see the teacher and the teacher's ability to observe all of the children at all times is critical to effective management and a safe environment. The goal here is to define the space in a way that makes sense to children.

Areas include a **whole group meeting area** for learning events such as read-alouds, songs, movement, chants, finger-plays, and instruction. This area is very important as children will spend time there several times during the day. It must be large enough that all the children can sit comfortably spaced on the floor. They must have a clear line of sight to the teacher and the materials in use such as charts, whiteboards, and calendars. The area should have minimal distractions. A window to the playground, a set of cubbies filled with math materials, or a door to the hallway can all disrupt children's learning. This area may be multi-use, perhaps serving as the block and building center during centers' time or it may be the classroom library, for example, when not in use for whole group events.

The **classroom library** is one of the most important areas. Low bookshelves with labeled tubs should offer easy accessibility to books. Tubs should be labeled (on all sides) by topics (informational books about real animals, people, or processes) and fictional topics (such as unicorns). Tubs may also contain books with both informational and fictional books about a common topic (mice, for example). Other important features can define a tub of books, such as favorite author, genre (poems and rhymes, fairy tales, fables, joke books), and seasonal or event specific (the lunar landing) so that both children and teachers can access them quickly.

The books in the library area should reflect the children in the classroom as well as children not in the classroom. Multicultural books, multi-ethnic and books that include characters with disabilities are important. Every child should be able to see themselves on the page and in the photo of the author and illustrator. They should also be able to learn about the lives of others who live in different places and do not look like them. At least eight books, per child is the number of books that should be in the classroom library area. There should not be so many that children can't find what they are looking for or put them away. Young children often benefit from putting an adhesive sticker (animal, colored dot, birds, etc.) on the front of the book and the same sticker on the labels of the tub it belongs in. Using the sticker as a procedure to return books to their appropriate tubs must be explicitly taught and practiced. Small copies of Big Books, classroom chants and songs, class-made books, and books read aloud by the teacher should be placed in the library area and be easily accessible.

Other areas include defined spaces for computers, small group instruction, cozy independent and buddy reading, and rereading of Big Books and charts. Areas for storing children's outdoor clothing, parent information displays, and lining up should also be considered in the daily traffic flow.

Centers

Centers offer specific activities that children will engage in individually or with peers that support practice of the Foundational Anchors of literacy. These may include but are not limited to:

- a writing center,
- a block and building center,
- a socio-dramatic play center,
- an art center,
- a listening center,
- an alphabet letter and word play center,
- a math center, and
- a science center.

The size of each center is determined by its purpose and the type of activities with which children will engage. The dramatic play and the block centers are larger than the listening center or the writing center, for example. None of the centers should accommodate more than four children. This is by design as smaller centers have been shown to increase language interactions between children and increase their sustained engagement with the materials and activities. This results in a quieter, more productive classroom atmosphere (Vukelich, Enz, Roskos, & Christie, 2020).

Literacy Centers

Literacy centers provide activities the teacher creates for children to apply and practice the Foundational Anchors of literacy they know and/or have been taught. Children must be able to understand the literacy concepts and the procedures of the activity for it to support effective learning. These activities may be **specific tasks** such as sorting familiar (known) words by the number of letters, putting together an alphabet puzzle, playing a letter-sound lotto game, or using the pointer to reread a nursery rhyme or a Shared Reading Big Book. Center activities may also be **open-ended,** for example, drawing a picture of the topic of their investigation and writing something new that they learned about it, writing signs for the block area, or making Valentine

Questions to Ask Yourself about a Literacy Center Idea
Are the materials familiar to the children?
Have the children learned and practiced the activity with you? (I do, We do BEFORE You do)
How will children know if they are successful?
Is the activity interesting?
What skills will children be applying?
Is there physical or hands-on work required?
Is interaction, oral language, or conversation encouraged?
Can the children 'clean-up' the center for the next group?
Is the activity open ended?
How will it help children who struggle and children who excel?

Figure 7.3 Questions to Ask Yourself about a Literacy Center Idea

cards for a classmate. The activities must be at the children's independent level, what they can do and sustain on their own without the help of an adult. There are many great sources of ideas for literacy centers. Some that look cute yet serve a very superficial learning purpose result in little sustained engagement. The important work for the teacher is to **analyze the center ideas** they locate or create in relation to the group of children they are currently teaching (see Figure 7.3).

Reacting to and playing randomly with materials at literacy centers does not sustain most young children's engagement or scaffold new learning. This means, for example, that they need to understand **what** they are supposed to be doing with the magnetic letters, the clipboards in the dramatic play center, the books in the block area, etc., **why** they are using them, and **how** to use them. Modeling and explaining the purpose and use of literacy materials are much more likely to result in enjoyable, prolonged concentration, engagement, and legitimate literacy learning for young children. Environmental print (labels, directions, icons) can further support the intentional use of the center if it is modeled and explained.

A Close Look at an Effective Center

Mr. Josh's Writing Center is distinct from his Art Center. In the Writing Center, only writing implements (pencils, colorful pens, thin markers) and writing tools (Picture alphabet, Words by Heart, Class list with pictures, topic-related words, and word wall access) are provided. Celebrating writing daily makes the writing center important to the children. Mr. Josh models where each item in the center belongs and how he knows by using the printed label and icon. The children must be able to put things back in an orderly fashion so the next child can also enjoy the center. Not all children have benefited from organized or tidy homes, and Mr. Josh supports the clean-up routine without negative consequences. With practice and support, children will learn the executive function necessary to tidy up.

The Writing Center in Mr. Josh's classroom has baskets for pencils, colored pencils, and fine tip markers. The baskets are labeled with the word and icon or the actual object glued on the label. There is an empty red basket for broken pencils and dried markers. (There is a red basket in each center for things that are broken or torn or used up. This commonality supports children in applying common behaviors.) There is a paper selection with common sizes, lined and unlined, and a few colors. A basket of envelopes is also available. A recycle bin for used paper is handy.

On the wall above, the center are the directions for the task with icons.

1. Think of a person
2. Make a message
3. Deliver the message

Mr. Josh has modeled in both large and small groups what a message is, how to use and take care of the materials, what stopping and cleaning up means and looks like, what the delivery routine is, and how to use the tools to help themselves.

The tools available vary by the age of the children and the time of year. Early in the year, Mr. Josh's writing center includes a chart with every child's first name and picture. The teacher and paraprofessional are also included on the chart. The children have learned to "think of a person" in the class to whom they will send a message, find the name/picture to copy, and then make their message. Children can make a picture only, writing and a picture, or just use writing. The task is open-ended in order to differentiate for more and less competent children. The children at the center will use all the literacy knowledge they have to **make** their message. Mr. Josh has made a decision not to say, "**Write** a message." "Making" things is a low risk, developmentally appropriate activity for young children.

Also in the center are several laminated copies of the picture alphabet chart that is used in the classroom. Children are at various levels of learning to use this as a tool. When the message is finished, it can be placed in an envelope, and the recipient's name written on the outside. Delivery is as straightforward as carrying the message to the recipient who says, "Thank you."

After centers' time, the children gather in a circle to talk about what they did. Mr. Josh begins with, "Who got a message today?" Each recipient gets to name the message sender. This public acknowledgement adds a child-based reward for the message maker and creates a meaningful incentive for message writing.

As the school year progresses, Mr. Josh will add other possible message recipients to the list, including school staff with their names and pictures on the chart. Additional word lists will include frequently requested words such as Mom, Dad, Grandma, and Grandpa with a picture or icon to represent the word's meaning. Additional words are taught to the whole group, and again in small groups so the lists become useful tools. Additional writing center tasks will be introduced over time, for example, related words and suggestions for writing about their investigations. These will also be explained and modeled.

Writing tools are important ONLY if children know how and when to use them. This must be taught and modeled, modeled, modeled. **Transfer** must be taught so that children see that the tool-use in reading is also useful in writing and vice versa. It appears obvious that if a child can use the word Mom in the writing center, they will be able to read it during small group instruction, but for most children connections must be explicitly taught. Teaching for transfer is a powerful practice.

Transitions that Build Executive Function

In the dramatic play center, the theme was birthday parties. There were invitations to write, gift tags for the gift bags, cakes to bake, the words for the birthday song, hats and colorful plastic letters to hang up Happy Birthday on the magnetic white board. Deena was the mom, Ari was the brother, and Ali was the birthday girl. The teacher observed the children prepare for a party, using the class name/picture chart to fill in invitations. She had moved across the room when she heard Deena yell, "Clean up quick. The cops are coming!" This was both heartbreaking and revealing. Deena's background knowledge includes how parties end. She knows how to be the mom and keep everybody out of trouble. She is playing her role in the scenario accurately. She will need support to learn how to stop play and reorganize the socio-dramatic play center.

So what are our expectations for stopping play and reorganizing the center? Stopping, transitioning from play to clean up, is a huge struggle for children who have not had time and opportunity to develop executive function. Moving from one activity to another takes executive function and self-regulation, one of the Foundational Anchors of literacy. Children have to recognize the end of play and step out of the process in which they were involved. They have to manage the emotions that come from being interrupted. They have to move from that emotional response and survey the scene from the point of view of a non-player. *What is out of place? Where does it go? It could fit behind the shelf. Should I put it there? Oh, look at the cake. I can eat some…*as they slip back into play. So often, children like this are seen as uncooperative, when really, they need non-punitive reminders to re-engage their executive function.

Children must also know where things go. It is essential to realize that centers need to be organized. Here again labels and icons help children see the way materials are organized. In the Art Center, for example, a basket for glue, a rack for scissors, a tray for watercolors, and a can for brushes can easily be used by children. They must be able to follow routines for washing brushes so they are ready for use by other children. When materials are added or switched, the children must be taught what the new expectations for cleaning up will be. If the clean-up routine is complex, teachers must either allow adequate time for the children to accomplish the task or simplify the routine.

Cleaning up also depends on providing an appropriate number of materials. A dramatic play center with dress up clothes that suggest a variety of roles, fire fighter, princess, doctor, and cowboy, along with tutus, a workbench and tools, feather boas, and several pairs of glasses, pots and pans, dishes, plastic foods and produce, table and chairs, moon boots, mittens that look like paws, doll beds, dolls, and doll clothes…does not suggest any meaningful scenario. The children will get out lots of materials, and when time is up, they have no idea how to organize them or where to put them. Even if the teacher is able to invent multiple categories, children will be overwhelmed and unable to use executive function. Assisting children in cleaning up after play is reasonable, but if they are not able to manage most of the task on their own, the teacher must reevaluate where the barrier to success lies. A theme, a place for everything, labels, a clear organizational structure (food goes here, clothing goes there), adequate direct instruction on how and where to store things and time to transition and clean up are necessary. If clean-up is frustrating, the teacher must analyze the problem and fix it (see figure 7.4).

Using Direct Instruction to Teach for Independence

Launching successful centers is multifaceted. Teachers will want to consider which Foundational Anchors can be practiced at a center, what materials are essential, what activities are available for children, and how they will know what to do. Providing water paints to a young child who has never seen them before is **not** an opportunity to paint. This is where direct instruction, in small groups, becomes so important.

Carla, an experienced pre-school teacher, knows how much her 4 year olds love to paint. She introduces water color paints to children in small groups using the mantra Water, Color, Paint. She creates a chart with icons to support the children in following the procedure. First you dip your brush in the **water**, then you put your brush on the **color** and stir, stir, stir, then you **paint.** The children are pleased with the resulting color on the paper. They have access to how to use the materials. At clean up, they put their water cups and brushes in a dishpan as Carla decided that traveling to the sink and back is a barrier to success.

Teaching the use of materials is one reason for direct instruction. Another is what the materials can help the children do. At the alphabet center, the

---

Analyzing Your Environment

Use of print

- *Is there evidence of:*
  - thoughtful use of print to indicate the purpose and procedures in the environment and at a center or area?
  - clear and legible teacher handwriting of purposeful print?
  - icons to support children's understanding and use of the print?

Selection of materials:

- *Is there evidence of:*
  - all materials being effective teaching and learning tools rather than decorations?
  - a sufficient number of books in the library. Recommendations by various early childhood groups suggest at least eight books per child?
  - visual representation of all children in the classroom; multiculturalism demonstrated in materials, books, mounted posters, or photographs?
  - multiple genres accessible to children (storybooks, picture books, predictable books, informational books that reflect the vast interests of the children, ABC books, poetry, counting books, biographies and autobiographies, etc.)?
  - books related to specific topics that reflect developmental interests and concerns of young children in general and members of the class specifically (growing up, emotional challenges, social justice, dinosaurs, etc.)?
  - resources for investigations (field guides, atlases, manuals, informational books, etc.)?
  - books to support specific literacy events such as shared book Read Alouds, Shared Reading, emergent reading, and innovations of texts?
  - technology being available, accessible, and supportive of learning goals?

Organization of materials

- *Is there evidence of:*
  - well-organized and accessible materials ensuring that children can find what they need, use them, and replace them appropriately? Have procedures been explicitly taught and practiced?
  - books placed in other centers for purposeful use? Have children been made aware of the connection of the books to the center, the purpose and the potential use of the books?
  - revising room arrangement to meet current needs and to support classroom management?

Figure 7.4 Analyzing Your Environment

children have magnetic letters on cookie trays. Letters are grouped in alphabetical order with two capital and three lower case of each letter. The teacher has taught the children to find their name on the class name chart that has been reproduced and placed in the center, and to make their name with the letters. They can then choose picture/word cards to make other words. She has these word cards sorted by animal or vehicle at this time. During units of study such as learning about space, she will have a set of topic words with pictures that children can emergently read and spell with magnetic letters.

Solving Common Problems during Centers' Time

Teachers sometimes experience problems during centers' time with many of the details of implementation. Some of these are common across classrooms. Some can be prevented with more careful planning, choice of materials, direct instruction of materials and procedures, and management. Here are some issues that are commonly observed.

- **Johnny always picks blocks**
  - Children choose the same center repeatedly for a number of reasons. The teacher begins by observing what is happening for that child as they play. Choosing blocks everyday may show the child exploring many kinds of structures, creating scenes such as zoos or airports, and integrating purposeful literacy. This child is actively learning how these materials work and extending his knowledge. This may be a positive progression in his learning and therefore not a problem.
  - Another child may be laying out a flat block road in the same way day after day. This child may lack confidence to try another center, or not know how to engage in play with other children. This requires teacher assistance for the child to explore how blocks work and to explore other centers. A child who goes to the dramatic play center to rock the babies every day will also require teacher assistance. Careful observation and consideration of factors (refer to Chapter 1) that may be impacting the child's decision-making and learning are critical.
  - This situation also requires a teacher to reflect on the degree of interest and engagement provided in the other centers. Are there high interest materials and activities that provoke the child's interest available at other centers?
  - Create or suggest a center that is related to the center of choice. For example, Legos and other small construction materials may serve as surrogates for the block center. Make sure the child has been introduced to the other center, understands the materials available, can successfully use them, and is confident about what can be accomplished there.
  - Create a system for the equal rotation of children. Using an attendance sheet visible to the children, allow a different group of children to be the first to choose centers each day. Children can see when their turn to choose first will be.
  - Teacher created sign-up sheets placed on a clipboard also help children see that the process is fair and that they will get a turn.

- **Susie doesn't clean up**
  - When a child does not clean up, teachers must remind themselves of the complexity involved. The child has to transition out of the play, deal with the emotions that can come up when play is curtailed, look at the center as a non-player, and determine how to begin clean-up. During clean-up, their executive function is essential in order to focus on the clean-up task and resist reacting to the play materials. What part or parts does the child struggle with and how can the teacher assist the child?

  - Punishment cannot teach a new behavior. Teaching and assistance teach new behavior. If clean-up is a new behavior for some children, teach it explicitly, with **I do-We do-You do.**
  - Practice explicit steps for how to clean up in small group. Create and use consistent reminders. *(1) Stop and thank your friends for playing. (2) Put away five items. Make sure you count. (3) Check and see if you need to put away five more.*
  - Provide non-punitive reminders. *Have you put away five things? Or Please put away five more things.*
  - Have a labeled place for the items.
  - Play a consistent song during clean-up to assist focus and provide a sense of how long clean-up should last.
- **Centers are too noisy**
  - Teach children about voice levels so they know what is meant by outside voice, inside voice, whisper, or silence and when each should be used.
  - Address the noise level *PRIOR TO* center time if this is a frequent problem. *Let's practice using our inside voices today when we are at centers.* Have children said their name using their inside voice? (The teacher is not asking them to *remember* to use their inside voice. She is asking them to *practice*.)
  - Have a consistent signal for unacceptable noise level; a bell, a call and response, a physical response to lights out (children put hands on heads).
- **Tears…not getting the choice you want**
  - Acknowledge disappointment. It is real for the child. *I can see how disappointed you are. Do you want help solving the problem?*
  - Allow the child to cry to express their disappointment. Offer comfort. *You can get the teddy bear or the blue cushion until you feel better.*
  - Offer alternative choices if available.
  - Let the child determine when they are ready to participate. Learning to cope and self-comfort are essential school skills.
  - Your kindness and warmth in recognizing when they have accomplished this, reinforces coping behaviors and executive function. *You took care of yourself and now you are ready. You know how to feel better.*

Spotlight

Indirect literacy learning contexts are child-led learning events planned by the teacher and used by the children to apply and practice their Foundational Anchors of literacy. Indirect learning contexts are as important to a child's literacy learning as Direct or Teacher-led learning opportunities. One way children practice using their Foundational Anchors is by interacting with the **environment and the environmental print** that the teacher has carefully designed. Modeling the use of environmental print ensures that children will use it effectively to accomplish tasks.

The teacher constructs distinct **areas**, designated spaces, the use of which is easily determined by the design, and the choice and arrangement of associated materials. The whole group area and the library area are the most important areas of a classroom. The teacher also constructs **centers**, some of which are specifically **literacy centers**. Literacy centers offer specific activities that children will engage in individually or with peers that support practice of the Foundational Anchors of literacy. Literacy centers can be **open-ended**, giving the child more opportunities to explore materials or processes in a differentiated way. They can also be **task-specific**, providing materials and specific directions for the children to follow in order to complete the task.

Stopping play and cleaning up centers is a complex process that calls for the teaching and practice of executive function, a foundational anchor. Teachers must analyze the organization of their centers to ensure that children will be capable of success. Direct instructions of the process and procedures are often required prior to independence.

References

Jalongo, M. R. (2014). *Early chil*

McGee, L. M. (2007). *Transform* *give all children the opportunity t*

Morrow, L. M. (2020). *Literacy* Pearson Education, Inc.

Pearson, P. D., & Gallagher, G. (Contemporary Educational P*

Smith, M. W., Brady, J. P., & A *room observation: Pre-K tool.* Ed

Vukelich, C., Enz, B. J., Roskos *language and literacy: Birth throu*

[Handwritten note:]
- indirect learning for children to apply material
- areas vs. centers
  · open ended or task specific
- transitioning + clean up, adjusting + how to deal w/ it

8 Oral Language
The Engine of Thinking and Learning

Focus and Big Ideas

- Oral language underlies all literacy
- Background knowledge and vocabulary Educational inequities begin early
- The significant role of the teacher
- Talking Bag lesson
- Multi-language learners: pathways to literacy

Oral Language Underlies All Literacy

Oral language develops in the young child during social give-and-take conversational interactions between the child and others; the words and expressions of the adult that are understood by the child and the response and communication that are shared. From these interactions, the child learns and is able to think about words and concepts. Because of its impact on children's cognitive or thinking skills, **oral language** is often called the "engine" of learning and thinking (Goodson, Layzer, Simon, & Dwyer, 2009). Children actively attempt to use language to represent and make sense of their world, regulate their and others' actions, and solve problems. These attempts allow them to gain greater control of more language. Patiently **listening** to a child talk and **waiting** as they try to compose their ideas into words are important parts of supporting language development. Encouraging the child to persevere in their attempts to communicate meaningfully gives the child important language opportunities. This is one of the reasons for providing opportunities for children to talk, interact, and listen to peers and adults throughout the day. Children who engage more with oral language become more active, engaged listeners. Results of a recent study (Romeo et al., 2018) indicate that young children who engaged in more back-and-forth conversations with adults demonstrated more brain activity while they were listening and processing their understanding of a story being read aloud.

Oral language includes speaking and listening. For children who are deaf or hard of hearing, American Sign Language and other accommodations are used to converse. Communication and learning rely on the use of language.

DOI: 10.4324/9780429284021-8

Spotlight

Indirect literacy learning contexts are child-led learning events planned by the teacher and used by the children to apply and practice their Foundational Anchors of literacy. Indirect learning contexts are as important to a child's literacy learning as Direct or Teacher-led learning opportunities. One way children practice using their Foundational Anchors is by interacting with the **environment and the environmental print** that the teacher has carefully designed. Modeling the use of environmental print ensures that children will use it effectively to accomplish tasks.

The teacher constructs distinct **areas**, designated spaces, the use of which is easily determined by the design, and the choice and arrangement of associated materials. The whole group area and the library area are the most important areas of a classroom. The teacher also constructs **centers**, some of which are specifically **literacy centers**. Literacy centers offer specific activities that children will engage in individually or with peers that support practice of the Foundational Anchors of literacy. Literacy centers can be **open-ended**, giving the child more opportunities to explore materials or processes in a differentiated way. They can also be **task-specific**, providing materials and specific directions for the children to follow in order to complete the task.

Stopping play and cleaning up centers is a complex process that calls for the teaching and practice of executive function, a foundational anchor. Teachers must analyze the organization of their centers to ensure that children will be capable of success. Direct instructions of the process and procedures are often required prior to independence.

References

Jalongo, M. R. (2014). *Early childhood language arts.* Allyn and Bacon.

McGee, L. M. (2007). *Transforming literacy practices in preschool: Research-based practices that give all children the opportunity to reach their potential as learners.* Scholastic.

Morrow, L. M. (2020). *Literacy development in the early years: Helping children read and write.* Pearson Education, Inc.

Pearson, P. D., & Gallagher, G. (1983). *The gradual release of responsibility model of instruction.* Contemporary Educational Psychology.

Smith, M. W., Brady, J. P., & Anastasopoulos, L. (2008). *Early language and literacy classroom observation: Pre-K tool.* Education Development Center, Inc. Brookes Publishing.

Vukelich, C., Enz, B. J., Roskos, K. A., & Christie, J. (2020). *Helping young children learn language and literacy: Birth through kindergarten.* Pearson Education, Inc.

8 Oral Language

The Engine of Thinking and Learning

Focus and Big Ideas

- Oral language underlies all literacy
- Background knowledge and vocabulary Educational inequities begin early
- The significant role of the teacher
- Talking Bag lesson
- Multi-language learners: pathways to literacy

Oral Language Underlies All Literacy

Oral language develops in the young child during social give-and-take conversational interactions between the child and others; the words and expressions of the adult that are understood by the child and the response and communication that are shared. From these interactions, the child learns and is able to think about words and concepts. Because of its impact on children's cognitive or thinking skills, **oral language** is often called the "engine" of learning and thinking (Goodson, Layzer, Simon, & Dwyer, 2009). Children actively attempt to use language to represent and make sense of their world, regulate their and others' actions, and solve problems. These attempts allow them to gain greater control of more language. Patiently **listening** to a child talk and **waiting** as they try to compose their ideas into words are important parts of supporting language development. Encouraging the child to persevere in their attempts to communicate meaningfully gives the child important language opportunities. This is one of the reasons for providing opportunities for children to talk, interact, and listen to peers and adults throughout the day. Children who engage more with oral language become more active, engaged listeners. Results of a recent study (Romeo et al., 2018) indicate that young children who engaged in more back-and-forth conversations with adults demonstrated more brain activity while they were listening and processing their understanding of a story being read aloud.

Oral language includes speaking and listening. For children who are deaf or hard of hearing, American Sign Language and other accommodations are used to converse. Communication and learning rely on the use of language.

DOI: 10.4324/9780429284021-8

"It's how we process information and remember. It's our operating system" (Fisher, Frey, & Rothenberg, 2008). Teacher's understanding of the primacy of oral language supports children's development of cognition. In the classroom, there are many different language needs, including:

- children who are learning multiple languages with an age-appropriate command of their home language and an age-appropriate command of English;
- children who are learning multiple languages with an age-appropriate command of their home language and limited, low, or no English;
- children who are learning multiple languages with a limited or low command of their home language and limited, low, or no English;
- children who speak monolingual English (MLE) with an age-appropriate command of English;
- children who speak English only with limited or low command of English.

All of these young children are oral language learners due to their young age and some have additional learning layers. All of them need support, instruction, and lengthy, connected periods of time to converse. They need teachers who can extend their vocabulary, background knowledge, and use of increasingly complex language structures. They need a response to the meaning of their attempts, feedback in the form of restatement and modeling, experiences that elicit conversation, and **comprehensible input,** language that a child can understand, despite not being able to understand all of the words and grammatical structures.

Background Knowledge

Background knowledge, a Foundational Anchor of literacy, consists of what a child knows and understands about their own world and the world at-large. The background knowledge a child has developed helps them understand a current situation and integrate new learning. The more varied a child's background knowledge, the easier it is for them to listen to, read, understand, and remember the important ideas of a new book or experience. For example, a child who has made cookies at home can understand what is going on in the gingerbread man story more easily than a child who has not had that experience. Background knowledge is both cumulative (it grows over time) and exponential (the more you know about something, the more you can add to your knowledge).

Each child has unique memories and understandings based on their own culture, family, experiences, and opportunities, although there can be significant overlap between children's background knowledge. Most children know what a Happy Meal is, for example. A person's capacity for background knowledge is infinite. As we plan learning opportunities for children, we should be naming, comparing, describing, questioning, and explaining ideas in order to incorporate new words and concepts into their background knowledge. These opportunities occur during direct teaching, where teacher and children work together in and out of the classroom to name, compare, etc., as well as during informal conversations, routines, and child-initiated play activities. Science and social studies (geography, culture, history, civics, and economics) investigations are optimal times to intentionally build background knowledge and embed conversation.

Vocabulary

Vocabulary consists of the words a child understands (**receptive vocabulary**) and the words a child uses to express themselves (**expressive vocabulary**). There is, of course, a large overlap between expressive and receptive vocabulary. This overlap is the body of words that a child owns and controls. It provides them with the ability to label, organize, think, connect, and talk about what they already know (background knowledge) and to express curiosity and pose their own questions about what they do not yet know; processes that increase both their knowledge base and cognitive abilities.

The Interplay between Background Knowledge and Vocabulary

Background knowledge and vocabulary are two important components of children's oral language development. Together, they impact *listening comprehension* and later *reading comprehension*. Both are essential for school success. Read the next paragraph carefully and be prepared to summarize the content.

> Hereditary transthyretin amyloidosis is caused by pathogenic single-nucleotide variants in the gene encoding transthyretin (TTR) that induces transthyretin misfolding and systemic deposition of amyloid. Progressive amyloid accumulation leads to multiorgan dysfunction and death. Inotersen, a 2′-O-methoxyethyl–modified antisense oligonucleotide, inhibits hepatic production of transthyretin.
>
> (Benson, et al., 2018)

Could you summarize what you "read"? Could you understand the main points? Have you added the term *transthyretin misfolding* to your receptive or expressive vocabulary? How about *systematic deposition of amyloid*? Unless you have significant medical training in hereditary diseases, you probably lack the **background knowledge and vocabulary** for this to be comprehensible input. You were decoding the words, you recognized a few words, and you might have even been able to read it fluently with expression. But you were probably not able to comprehend the content. The definition and goal of reading is to construct meaning from print. Therefore, you were probably not reading.

For numerous young children, many of the classroom words and concepts they hear or read about every day are *transthyretin misfoldings*. In other words, they don't have the background knowledge and vocabulary in the classroom language required to understand books read aloud or that they are required to read. Making language input comprehensible allows children to think deeply about new content being shared during science or social studies investigations. The teacher must also make instructions and the navigation of the social and learning requirements of the classroom understandable for everyone, including MLLs (multi-language learners) and those with limited or low language (who speak only English).

In some cases, children may have background knowledge that you can **activate**. When the mom said, "They are as big as cherries," Sammy's prior knowledge of cherries became active or front of mind. Other times, you will be **constructing**, adding to, the child's background knowledge, while connecting it with what they already know. In other words, you are helping children think about things they already know that will help them understand a new concept, word, or text (activating) or you are teaching the children new information that will help them understand a new concept or text (constructing). Often there is a dance of both (see Figure 8.1).

Syntax: Internal Grammar

In order for oral language to be understood, children must follow the rules of the language. These **rules** are called the **language structure, syntax,** or **grammar**. Young children do not learn rules of grammar explicitly but internalize them by repeatedly trying to make sense of and apply the rules as soon as they begin to talk. They follow verb patterns such as *Sing, Sang, Sung, Bring, Brang, Brung,* even though *brung* is not a word. They form superlatives *Good, Gooder, Goodest* again following the pattern they have figured out. Trying out, generalizing, and approximating language structure continues to develop with modeling, feedback, and rewording or adding to the child's message. For example, the child says, "I very miss my mom." The teacher responds to the **content** of the child's message and adds, "Sometimes we do miss our moms very much when we are at school."

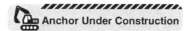
Anchor Under Construction

Sammy saw a basket of cherry tomatoes his mom put in the grocery cart and said, "Look mom, baby tomatoes." She handed him one to examine. He knew that these were tomatoes and that they were smaller than the tomatoes he knew. His background knowledge about tomatoes was limited to the full-size tomatoes he had seen, and he knew the mommy-baby relationship was connected to size. He concluded that these were the baby tomatoes. His mom responded, "These are little tomatoes called cherry tomatoes. They are only as big as cherries."

Figure 8.1 The Interplay Between Background Knowledge and Vocabulary

Anchor Under Construction

Five-year-old Claire came home and told her mom that they had a new child in class and that she "spoke Japan."

Mother: "Was she from Japan?"

Claire: "Yes"

Mother: *"Oh, people from Japan speak Japanese. They come from Japan and they speak Japanese."*

Figure 8.2 Substantive Conversation

Note that the teacher does not correct the child; she models, provides feedback, and rewords the message correctly, while holding onto the meaning first such as in Figure 8.1 and 8.2.

Children's oral language use gives us a window into their experiences and development. Consider the ideas of up and down. These simple directional words are opposites but the variety of language structures in which they occur may not express directions or opposites at all. Consider the following: throw up–throw down, sit up–sit down, think up an idea–write down the idea, speak up–talk down. In order for the use of these simple words to be fully understood, a child has to be able to employ structure and context.

Language Comprehension

Language comprehension is demonstrated by the use of expressive and receptive language as a means to communicate. Background knowledge, vocabulary, verbal reasoning, literacy knowledge, and syntax provide the context for making sense of the language being spoken and heard. A child's language comprehension is the degree of understanding a child demonstrates when listening, speaking, reading, and writing. A child's level of language comprehension is a predictor of later reading comprehension development (Shanahan & Lonigan, 2010).

Educational Inequities Begin Early

Most teachers are aware that children's oral language, vocabulary, syntax (grammar), and background knowledge are important and can be impacted by the quantity and quality of their early experiences and interactions with the wider world, including more literate or knowledgeable adults. Consider how language differences can begin to multiply by reading the following

The jelly bean was blue like the ocean.
It was as small as a finch's egg.
The sweetness of the jelly bean was sweet on my tongue.

A POEM BY TATE.

Figure 8.3 This Kindergarten Child Wrote a Poem Using Comparisons. The Expressive Vocabulary He Uses Is Interesting and Shows His Background Knowledge. The Sentence Structures are More Complex than His Peers, Using Like and as to Clarify Meaning

language interactions of three parents during preparation to eat a meal (adapted from Vukelich).

Parent 1: Okay, Erica, let's eat.

Parent 2: Okay, Ben, it's time to eat our lunch. Let's see what we are having. Yes, let's have carrots.

Parent 3: Okay, Nita. It's lunchtime. Are you hungry? Mommy is so hungry! Let's see what we have today. What's this? It's orange. See the picture on the jar. It's carrots. Yum!

When children's early language experiences and behaviors closely align with the expectations of school, there is an increased likelihood of early school success and academic achievement. When children have limited receptive language and even less expressive language, research indicates they are afforded fewer and shorter conversations with the adults in educational and care settings (Lingard, Hayes, & Mills, 2003), while teachers engage in more frequent and longer conversations with the more verbal, experienced children. Thus, the inequities with which the children arrived at the classroom become ever greater. **Educational equity** means that each child's needs are met even though they are not the same needs of all children. A child with low language needs requires more teacher interaction and conversation to meet their needs in developing language comprehension. As a side note, this difference in interaction time and frequency often affects children's social status in the classroom. The children to whom the teacher pays less attention become less desirable conversational partners with peers. Teachers who serve low SES children are also shown to use more directives (like parent number 1) and are less likely to support sustained verbal exchanges and interactions with and between these children and adults (Lingard, Hayes, & Mills, 2003). One might look closely at the school behavior management policy from the perspective of language development. Policies designed to keep the teacher in control of verbal interaction (no talking without hand raising, no talking at lunch, etc.) decrease the amount of thought to language cognitive activity for every child. Deficiencies in a child's oral language can, and often do, persist or even increase over time (Garcia & Weiss, 2017).

In the recognizable pattern of "those who have more, get more," children who start school with large and diverse **vocabularies** and who can understand and use more complex **syntax** (sentence structures and grammar) have a significant advantage in learning to read and write compared to those children with less developed language proficiency (Vasilyeva & Waterfall, 2011). They can learn with greater ease because the oral language and language comprehension they bring to school align well with what they are being asked to learn. Children with less receptive language absorb less of the new learning, especially when it is presented without a meaningful context of real experiences. Awareness of the need to support children's language development is not sufficient. "When children's vocabularies are not large on entering school, children's prospects for reading success **depend on the richness of their school experiences**" (Hiebert, 2020). Let's think about the important role the teacher can play from this same perspective.

The Significant Role of the Teacher

After parents, early childhood teachers are the first line of identification and support to change a trajectory of limited language and language comprehension. "Her parents didn't read to her, take her to the zoo, talk to and listen to her …" may explain to us how a child arrives at preschool without names for colors, baby animals, or common vegetables. It does not explain, or excuse, however, how a child can spend extended time in our educational settings and continue to struggle with these limitations. Teachers are the most important model and source of language input for young children. Unfortunately, preschool teachers et al. 2020 "have a history of using language in ways that may not be consistent with the interactions found by research to be conducive to language learning" (Shanahan & Lonigan, 2010). Providing appropriate and accessible instructional opportunities for all children to develop and expand their oral language and language comprehension needed for both short-term and long-term school success **must become a daily part of an early childhood teacher's work.**

Each decision a teacher makes can change the amount of language that the child can access. For example, in a lesson about baking cookies, the teacher plans both a read-aloud and a baking activity. When the baking experience comes first, **with intentional language use**, a hook is created for the language and content of the book to attach. The lower language children will have a greater opportunities to build background knowledge. When the book is presented first, these same children may not be able to imagine the activity at all. Their background knowledge may be limited. What seems like a small curriculum decision is actually very consequential for learning. Providing real experiences, while talking with children about what is happening, is the most effective and efficient means for building language. Abstract or vicarious experiences should follow firsthand experiences when possible.

During both the baking activity and the read-aloud, the effective teacher will facilitate a **substantive conversation** with the children (see Figure 8.2 & 8.4). "Substantive conversation is a form of talk between

Anchor Under Construction

During a small group language lesson, three- and four-year-old looked at and talked about real tools the teacher had brought. She encouraged them to talk about the hammer, asking them what it is used for and who uses one. "Bang, bang," Amal, a three-year-old child, yelled as he got up to jump, demonstrating the noise.

"Yes, it goes bang when I hit a nail. And look, the hammer has a *handle* and a *head*," the teacher said as she showed the children the parts. She would use the word *handle* for many of the tools. Although the children could not name all the tools or parts of the tools independently, the vocabulary and concepts were within their range of understanding. They could name them with assistance from the teacher. The pretend tools in the workshop area now had names and parts and connected to the real tools that the children had seen.

Later in the morning, Amal brought a toy saucepan to show the teacher and pointed to the handle. "Handle!" he said. He had learned a new word and generalized the concept.

Figure 8.4 Substantive Conversation about Tools

adults and children that informs, explains, and elaborates on ideas. It includes teachable moments when adults have the opportunity to provide background knowledge on topics. It involves expanding the amount of child talk in a conversation and stretching the conversation to add details, new words, and new language structures, such as adjectives and adverbs, idioms, and figurative language" (Morrow, Roskos, & Gambrell, 2016).

Building Tiers of Vocabulary

A common framework for thinking about vocabulary development is the three-tier model (Beck, McKeown, & Kucan, 2013). Vocabulary words and language can be categorized as follows:

- **Tier 1** (everyday words and language)
- **Tier 2** (academic words and literary language)
- **Tier 3** (content-area-specific words and language, technical words)

Tier 1 words are basic words that children typically learn in their early years through conversation with adults and peers and during read-alouds. These words rarely need to be explained. Words like **dog, big, run, car,** and **funny** are common and commonly used. MLLs often know these words in their primary language and these are the first words they understand in English.

Tier 2 words are the language of school and books. They consist of the words and language teachers use to model, explain, coach, organize, and encourage effective thinking and appropriate classroom behaviors. It includes **academic language**. The instructional emphasis in most schools is on this middle tier rather than the everyday words of Tier 1 or the content-area-specific words and language of Tier 3. Instruction is often intentionally planned and facilitated through shared book read-alouds from quality picture and informational books. It includes figurative and literary language, and abstract concepts that are not explicitly defined within the text of a book. Children must understand and use Tier 2 words and language in order to participate in classroom learning. For example, *once upon a time, cover, author, equal, compare, similar, illustration,* and *actually* are part of academic conversations and read-alouds that may require explanation.

During the morning meeting, the teacher asks the children to "pay attention" to the daily schedule while she names the day's activities. "Before we eat lunch, we have recess." Both the prepositions (before, after, around, below, etc.) and the school terms (recess, art, drama, centers) are words that require more conceptual understanding. We often assume our children understand or can use context to figure out Tier 2 words but this is not always the case. Carefully expressing school terms and checking for understanding can support young children as they continue to develop Tier 2 vocabulary.

Careful consideration of an existing gap between what we are saying and what children are comprehending helps us support their understanding. Teachers should mindfully consider their word choice and provide many opportunities for all children to engage in conversation that encourages Tier 2 language use. The length of a child's utterance is one aspect of language development and the complexity of vocabulary is equally important. Both are developed through repeated opportunities to listen and express one's ideas. There is no replacement for conversation.

Tier 3 words are specific to a content area such as science, math, social studies, and history. They are often called **Advanced Vocabulary** and become an integral part of a child's background knowledge. A preschool investigation about winter might include words such as hibernate, freeze, thaw, blizzard, and precipitation – words that are specific to the topic of study. Children learn and internalize these words **when teachers use and explain them within meaningful and contextual experiences**, such as read-alouds and investigations of high-interest subjects. Teachers must then provide multiple opportunities and indirect learning contexts for children to **use** these words in their own talk and in their play in order for children to "own" them.

All teachers must assume that there are some children in a group who will need explanation and context more frequently than other children. Teachers need to be constantly observing each child's language comprehension, their ability to understand and follow directions, and their use of Tier 2 and Tier 3 words in their own conversations. Observing and noting a child's knowledge and use of multi-tiered language provides the teacher with a baseline from which to engage verbally with them and plan oral language opportunities (see figures 8.5 and 8.6).

Anchor Under Construction

As part of an author study on Denise Fleming, Riley involved her kindergarten children in papermaking. She showed the children the fiber and the pulp. They felt and examined the two substances and talked about how they were different, although they were both parts of paper. As the children worked through the process, they shredded and blended, they used a deckle, a mold, and dye. The Tier 3 vocabulary that was used is both specific to the papermaking process and can be transferred for use in other contexts. The class then created a shared writing entitled "How to Make Paper." This provided another opportunity to use and understand the meaning of the Tier 3 words.

Figure 8.5 The Tier 3 Vocabulary of Papermaking

Anchor Ignored

Ms. G makes playdough at center time every Monday. She allows the children at the playdough center to watch. She puts flour, salt, and oil in a bowl, adds hot water and food coloring, and stirs. Then she kneads the dough until it is smooth and gives some to each child. The dough still feels warm and the children hold it before they begin to roll and flatten it.

The language she uses is limited to, "Stand back, Be careful, No touching," and other short reminders. **She could have**:

–narrated her process, "I'm going to check the recipe." "First I put in the flour ...."

–asked questions, "What else can you make with flour?" "What's our next ingredient?"

–listened and responded to children's reactions and questions, *"Look it's pink!"* "Can we eat it?" "Why do you think it turned pink?" "No, it's so full of salt it will make you very sick."

–thought out loud, "Now that I'm getting the hot water, I'm going to be extra careful."

–included sensory labels, "At first it will feel very warm. Feel it."

–increased vocabulary, "Watch me knead the dough. Here, you try kneading it."

Figure 8.6 Substantive Conversation While Making Playdough.

Daily Language Learning

Building Tier 1 Vocabulary

All of our interactions with children include Tier 1 words and can add to the child's repertoire. Supporting children in their use of Tier 1 words includes strategies as follows:

- **Listening patiently as the child talks**. A soft smile and eye contact are important.
- **Responding with words.** Shaking your head or pointing don't meet these criteria.
- **Responding to the meaning of the child's utterance**. For example, the child says, "I gots to use it." Teacher responds, "OK. Go to the bathroom."

- **Responding and expanding.** For example, the child says, "I gots to use it." Teacher responds, "Oh, you need to use the toilet. Thank you for telling me."
- **Persevering to understanding.**Patience is important for all children and particularly for children who are difficult for the teacher to understand due to limited vocabulary, language differences, or articulation. They need the teacher to stick with the interaction until the child can make himself understood. For example:

Child: "I want a pie do book."
Teacher: "Can you tell me again what you want?"
Child: "The pie do book."
Teacher, thinking of the recent read-alouds: "Can you show me the book? Then I can get it for you."
Child: "Here, the pie do. I see it," pointing to a spider on the cover.
Teacher: "Oh yes, the spider book. Here you go."

Building Tier 2 Vocabulary

The language of school, also called **academic language**, is built into many of our daily interactions and conversations with children. "Read, write, draw, line up, pay attention, no talking, crisscross, first, last, same, different, letter, number, word, sentence …." All have meanings that the child needs to understand to succeed in school. Considering the words and the meanings as we use them, noticing and checking for understanding helps us to be clear to all children about what we are expecting and supports them in developing the necessary concepts and vocabulary.

Another rich source of Tier 2 words is labels for feelings. Recognizing and naming feelings of happy, sad, angry, scared/frightened, brave, proud, frustrated, etc. and having the words to tell another person how they feel supports the child in gaining control of their responses (executive function). When Mike yelled loudly, "Weece, I am vewee, vewee angwy!" his teacher saw him able to stop himself from hitting. That was language in the service of executive function.

Unfortunately, research indicates that preschool teachers rarely intentionally develop rich academic language with children (Dickinson, Darrow, & Timubu, 2008; Michael Luna, 2017). Teachers often talk without thinking about and using rich academic vocabulary. For example, while it may be common to count hot and cold lunch, if one thinks about it, the temperatures do not accurately describe the meal. However, it is an opportunity to use accurate language that expands children's vocabulary. "Who brought a *lunch box* or *lunch bag* from home today? Who will be eating the lunch *prepared* in the *cafeteria*?". Using accurate vocabulary to express ideas, using vocabulary repeatedly, and thinking about what you are hoping children will understand should become a teacher's habit of mind (see Figure 8.7).

Anchor Under Construction

In Brad's four-year-old Head Start classroom, he offered a soft start to the day, which included children writing their name on a strip of paper to put in the attendance basket. Some children copied from a model **(Aliah)**. Some children used a partial model (_ _ _ **a h**), and others wrote from memory. Brad had brief interactions, using Tier 2 vocabulary in context, with a few of the children as they signed in.

Brad: Eli, what are you *writing*?

Eli: My name.

Brad: Yes, that *word* is your name. Will you *point to* it and *read* it to me? (Eli does).

Brad: (Brad points to Natee's name). Natee, will you *read* this to me?

Natee: I can't read.

Brad: You can *read* this *word*. It says Natee. (Brad points and reads.) Natee smiles, points at the word and reads, "Natee."

Brad: Yes, you *read* that *word*!

Rosa: Look, Brad. I **drawed** mine, too.

Brad: You **wrote** the *letters* in your name. (He points and spells, R-O-S-A) Those *letters* make the *word*, Rosa! Let's *read* it together. (She puts her hand over his to point together and they read her name.)

Brad interacts with various children until everyone is finished and moves to the rug. He then sits with the attendance basket, draws each name out of the basket and encourages the children to help him read the names aloud. These simple interactions emphasized the use of Tier 2 vocabulary such as *word*, *letter*, *writing*, *wrote*, *read*, and *point*, essential to understanding future literacy instruction.

Figure 8.7 Building Tier 2 Vocabulary.

Building Tier 3

Developmentally appropriate **content vocabulary** should be intentionally identified by the teacher and embedded in curriculum investigations about concepts interesting to children (see Chapter 4). Young children love to learn about the world around them. Anchored Literacy Curriculum provides opportunities for learning and using Tier 3 language. These words become part of children's background knowledge, supportive of future reading comprehension.

Tier 3 words are often called **Advanced Vocabulary** and become an integral part of a child's background knowledge. Tier 3 vocabulary includes the following:

- **Content vocabulary** – words and concepts related to learning in the content areas of science, history, civics, etc. (i.e. astronomy, astronomer, constellation, planet, moon, satellite, space shuttle)
- **Metaphors and figurative language** – one word or phrase that represents a bigger idea (i.e. raining cats and dogs; quiet as a mouse)
- **Abstract ideas** – concepts that cannot be concretely described (i.e. freedom, victory, truth, pity)

Building Tier 3 vocabulary takes repeated, meaningful experiences and use. Exploring science and social studies with young children, while being mindful of the importance of vocabulary, is powerful practice. Consider the preschool teacher who creates a doctor's office for high-level socio-dramatic play. This offers the teacher the chance to introduce and use words like appointment, receptionist, injection, examination, scrubs, prescription, healthy, unhealthy, germs, and bandage. Children will happily play their roles and use the new vocabulary when the teacher provides the experiences, read-alouds, and substantive conversations to introduce the words and support them. Without this support, children will use the Tier 1 vocabulary they already have in their play, shots, sick, doctor and nurse, and the opportunity for further developing the Foundational Anchors is lost. If supported, children's understanding of complex words will continue to grow as they progress through school, encounter the words in their reading, use the words in writing and conversation, and add new words to better explain ideas.

In Chapter 11, Reading Aloud to Children, you will find information on **text sets**. This refers to a set of fiction and informational books that explore a similar topic, idea, concept, or person. Using text sets is an effective format for developing Tier 3 vocabulary. A deeper dive into a topic, a genre, or a feature of a story or informational book gives children the chance to repeatedly hear, use, and remember new vocabulary. A text set may be five books with rabbits as the main character or main topic. It may be stories set on a farm or that happen in the winter. It may be stories,in which the main character is afraid of something. Using text sets allows children to see and connect ideas and vocabulary between books. What are the winter words the authors used? What are the names of animals, outbuildings, and equipment on a farm? With a focus on using Tier 3 words from books where ideas are connected, children have a chance to play with the language and practice during a structured, supportive lesson.

"Hands-On/Words-On" Learning

Collecting snow and seeing how it melts, how long it takes a quart and a teaspoon to melt, **having conversations** about what the children see happening, what they think about it, and what it makes them wonder about. *Words-On,* in addition to *Hands-On*, learning facilitates use of vocabulary such as melting and thawing, introduces the labels for states of matter (solid and liquid) and lengths of time, and opens up other questions. Hands-On/Words-On is the focus. It is not enough for children to participate in hands-on activities; there must be words attached through explanations, labeling, describing through child and teacher interactions. Some hands-on experiences are not replicable in a school setting but a YouTube virtual field trip to a sled run or pictures of hibernating animals can support the talk that has to happen. Adding toy replicas or realia can clarify meaning. Using a stuffed bear and having it hibernate in the classroom are both possible and preferable to inviting in a grizzly. Both MLLs and English-speaking preschool children lack a mastery of English needed to access daily classroom information. At 4, 5, and 6, all children are immature speakers of the language(s) they will later master. Creating picture boards for daily activities such as using the bathroom, handwashing, and lining up can be very helpful.

When we include manipulatives and **realia** (real objects and materials from everyday life) in children's lessons and experiences, we provide hands-on opportunities for children to use symbolic and real items to construct background knowledge and vocabulary about their world. Hands-on learning creates an experience that the child cannot necessarily explain; however, intentionally adding **Words-On** learning creates a strong learning context for language development. Retelling the Hands-On/Words-On experience creates another context for using new words. For example, a child puts a puzzle together and the teacher begins Hands-On/Words-On. The teacher asks questions or makes statements as follows:

- What picture did you make with your puzzle? I can see a man repairing a pothole in the street.
- How did you know that piece went there? You matched the parts of the worker's uniform.

These questions can begin a conversation with the child, allowing you to model more complex vocabulary than "Wow! Good job." Adding words to the child's activity, having conversations, and using Tier 2 and 3 words are the goals of the Hands-On/Words-On strategy. Hands-On/Words-Onlearning is a higher level of **pedagogy** (method and practice of teaching) intentionally included by the thoughtful, informed teacher. When a child sorts buttons, they have done the **"hands-on"** work. Talking together to name each category adds the **"words-on"** part. The teacher may begin by modeling, "I see that the **large** buttons are in this pile. What size of buttons are here?" The language expands the possibilities for categories. Buttons can be sorted by color, size, number of holes, prettiness, or any other idea that can be **talked** about. Giving children the chance to discuss real items, to tell what they know and compare items, has the capacity to expand children's vocabulary, understandings, and thinking. A child can use words to

Anchor Under Construction

The teacher in a low SES kindergarten provided many experiences around which talk could happen. These hands-on/words-on activities included making playdough with small groups. The ingredients, tools, and process were discussed. "What do you think we will need this food coloring for? Etc." As Anthony kneaded his dough, the lack of experience was clear. "If your dough is sticking to your fingers, you need more flour," the teacher offered. Anthony responded, "I need more powder!" The teacher said, "This is called flour." He replied, "I need more flowder." Flour was clearly new vocabulary to Anthony. His teacher would continue to use the new words as they worked, providing opportunities for Anthony to use them as well.

Figure 8.8 Hands-On/Words-On Activities

describe an object they are holding more easily than describing the same object in the abstract (see Figure 8.8).

This teacher will provide many other Hands-On/Words-On activities so that her children can talk about them, connect one activity to another, relate dough to batter, printing vegetables to printing fish, making candles, and melting snow. Her children enjoyed risk-free, content-rich oral language development. In an effective early literacy curriculum, teachers plan direct and indirect opportunities for learning vocabulary. The following lesson is a direct teacher-led small group lesson specifically for a set of children who would benefit from this language support. This included MLLs and limited English speakers. As you read the following lesson, the Talking Bag, (see Figure 8.9) imagine the teacher with a bag containing a variety of items that all belong to the same category: shoes. The bag contained a baby shoe, a sandal, a hiking boot, a high heel, and a soccer shoe.

A focus on a category of objects helps children make connections that expand their understandings and background knowledge (see Figure 8.9). Children should be encouraged to make the following connections in conversation.

- **-object-to-object** connections (apples and bananas are both fruits),
- **-object-to-self connections** (I have apples at my house), and
- **-object-to-world** connections (people can grow and eat fruits)

Multi-Language Learners: Pathways to Literacy

The pathway from beginning language to proficient literacy is fairly straightforward for many children, particularly for those whose primary language is the predominant language spoken in the classroom (English across most of the United States). They learn to talk from others in their home and community. They begin with baby talk and over time, with input, become more

The Talking Bag
An Oral Language Lesson

Goal of the lesson:

- to increase use and understanding of Tier 1 and 2 words;
- to name and describe a series of items in a category;
- to involve the children in a conversation to reinforce the following words *same, similar, compare, contrast, part,* and *whole.*

Materials:

- a total of five to seven items in the same common *category* (for example, tools, shoes, spoons, flowers, kinds of cups, fruit, musical instruments, tools to write with, toy animals, types of candy);
- a large basket or bag that the children cannot see through;
- Chart paper, markers.

Sequence:

1. **Today I have many items in my Talking Bag and the items in it all go together.**
   Let's see what the first thing is.
2. Remove the first item and ask, **What's this? What do you know about this?** (Encourage children to speak out instead of hand raising/turn taking. You want children to put their ideas into their own words to create a reduced-risk setting.)
3. **Does it have parts? Can you name the parts? This has a lot of parts. Let's talk about the parts we see.**
4. **I wonder. Where do we find these? What do people do with these?**
5. **Let's write the name of this object.** (Write it on the chart.)
6. **What else could be in the bag that might go with this? How would that go with this?**
7. Remove the next item and ask, **"What's this?"**
8. **What are some ways it goes with (item 1)? Is it the same, similar, or different? Describe how they are (same, similar, different)?**
9. **Does it have parts? Name the parts.**
10. **I wonder … Where do we find these? What do people do with these?**
11. **Let's write the name of this object.**
12. **What else could go with item 1 and item 2?**
13. Repeat with each item, extending and expanding the talk.
14. Finally, add to the written list other items that could have been in the bag. (For example, other fruits that you didn't bring). Reread the list together.

This lesson can conclude with children using emergent writing about the topic or adding pictures to the chart or expanding the category of things. You can revisit charts if there is something new to add.

Figure 8.9 The Talking Bag: An Oral Language Lesson

competent oral language users. They use both expressive and receptive language to interact with the world around them. As that world expands, it includes school experiences in the same language, which leads the child to written language, reading, and writing.

Oral language and written language grow together and as a result of one another. If the child arrives at the school setting with limited oral language, the teacher must consciously support the development of more complex oral language through the many avenues presented in this chapter. The pressure to go directly from limited language to reading and writing instruction often ignores language development, leaving the child at a disadvantage for developing a strong foundation of literacy. Taking the extra time needed to develop oral language does not appear to delay reading performance (Soodla et al., 2015).

But what if the child speaks a language at home that is not the same as the language of instruction at school. A strong dual language program recognizes this as a strength that requires nurturing and respect. Children who expand their oral language in their native language and learn written language in their native language have a distinct pathway to literacy in both languages. They simultaneously gain literacy in their home language and literacy in the language of instruction. The school, and the teacher, must support the child's native language as well for as long as possible. Transferring from the language spoken at home to school language is made easier when the home language development has been well supported. For a child whose primary language is not that of the classroom language, it is important for the teacher to determine the child's breadth and depth of vocabulary in the primary language.

"That poor guy in the front office speaks 4 languages," said NO ONE EVER. Multilingualism in adults is admired and respected. It creates greater cognitive flexibility and decreases the occurrence of dementia in older adults. How is it that beginning multi-language learners are so often seen as lacking English, rather than future multilingual adults?

Even when teachers are not speakers of the child's home language/s, they can make children feel welcome, acknowledged, and respected. Learning the child's name and how to correctly pronounce it is basic to the child's sense of belonging. The teacher should learn key phrases in the children's languages and use them frequently. The teacher's use of the child's language establishes safety and inclusion.

Renowned researcher, Stephen Krashen, developed the Language Acquisition Hypothesis (1981) that explains how children learn language (see Figure 8.10). This continuum is widely recognized in the field of multilingual education and adapted in the chart below. The acquisition is divided into stages, although not all children move sequentially through each stage. They may move fluidly, back-and-forth from one stage to another. The timeline is an approximation. Each child, with their unique linguistic and cultural perspectives, will move through these developmental stages at their own pace. The language acquisition process, whether for native English speakers or MLLs, is dependent upon the quality of home literacy experiences, instruction, appropriate exposure to comprehensible input, and various sociocultural and other factors that impact learning.

Stephen Krashen's Language Acquisition Hypothesis (1981)

Silent/receptive stage: Appropriate for the first six months of exposure to a new language.

The child does not verbally respond to communication in the new language, although there is receptive processing. The child should be actively included in all class activities but not forced to speak. Teachers should give children sufficient time and clues to encourage participation. Students are likely to respond best through nonverbal interaction with peers, being included in general activities and games, and interacting with manipulatives, pictures, audiovisuals, and "hands-on materials." As children progress, they will provide one-word verbal responses.

Early production stage: This stage may take six months to one year to accomplish.

The children begin to respond verbally using one or two words and develop the ability to get some meaning from what is said to them. They continue to develop listening skills and build up a large vocabulary. As they progress through this stage, they may say two or three words together in short phrases to express an idea.

Speech emergent stage: This stage typically takes one to three years to accomplish.

MLL children begin to respond in simple sentences if they are comfortable with the classroom community and are engaged in activities in which they receive large amounts of comprehensible input. The children's attempts to communicate (i.e. gestures, attentiveness, following directions) should be warmly received and encouraged by the teacher and peers. It is especially important that neither the teacher nor peers make fun of, mimic, or discourage the child's attempts at speech as this can be a stressful task for young MLLs.

Intermediate fluency stage: This stage typically takes three to five years to accomplish.

Children gradually transition to more elaborate speech as a result of comprehensible input. Using stock phrases, children begin to generate sentences. Increasing comprehensible input is accomplished as teachers help children develop and extend their vocabulary and provide opportunities to engage in substantive conversations in comfortable situations.

Advanced fluency stage: This stage typically takes five to seven years to accomplish.

Children begin to initiate sustained conversation and tell their own stories. This is an appropriate time to introduce grammar instruction focusing on idiomatic expressions and reading comprehension skills. Activities that develop higher levels of thinking, vocabulary skills, and cognitive skills, especially in reading and writing, are appropriate at this time. This is the phase in which MLLs successfully perform age-appropriate, academic skills as compared to heritage speakers of English.

Adapted from Krashen (1981); Krashen and Terrell (1983).

Figure 8.10 Adapted from Stephen Krashen's Language Acquisition Hypothesis (1981).

Teachers working with MLL's must understand and share with families the importance of children's continued use of the primary language of the home. When a child continues to advance in their primary language, they become more proficient listeners, speakers, readers, writers, and problem-solvers in that language. The great news is that those skills fully developed in their primary language WILL transfer to the second or third languages they attempt to learn.

Federal Requirements and Guidelines for MLLs

In many private, non-profit, and corporate-owned early childhood programs, there are no distinct requirements or programs for MLLs. Multilingual children are integrated into the regular English-speaking classroom. Federal law, however, protects the educational rights of MLL students who attend schools that receive public funds. This is to help ensure educational equity across ethnic and cultural student populations and improve the education of MLLs with becoming proficient in English. Most states have additional legal requirements for MLL programs, but all states are required to follow the four important components established by the federal government. These requirements should inform all teachers involved in educating young MLL children, regardless of whether or not the program is a public school or receives public funds. It is the responsibility of all educators to understand and support the intent of these requirements established to ensure all children are given access to the best possible education.

1. *Identification:* A home language survey is given to parents in all public school environments to determine if a language other than English is spoken in the home.
2. *Language assessment:* If it has been established that a language other than English is spoken at home, it is a federal requirement that all students be assessed in English. Parent permission is not required. Analysis of the assessment is used to establish the English language learning needs of each child and the most effective type of program.
3. *Diagnostic prescriptive process:* After a child has been assessed in English, their current level of English language proficiency is determined. Many states, including the state of Colorado, use World-Class Instructional Design and Assessment (WIDA) standards to determine the child's current level. Learning opportunities appropriate to each WIDA level are required to be provided at all schools for all children. Programs can be designed based on the unique student population they serve.
4. *Exit criteria:* As with all federally supported programs, criteria for students to leave a program must be established. Each district can determine its own criteria but having criteria is a federal mandate.

Public schools in the United States typically offer MLLs some or all of their literacy instruction in their primary language, based on their WIDA levels.

These programs are typically of two types: **Transitional bilingual programs**, in which native speakers of Spanish, for example, are instructed entirely in Spanish for a period of time before transitioning into English instruction or **Dual language programs**, in which approximately half of the students are native Spanish speakers and the rest are native English speakers. Students receive instruction in both languages, with the goal of all students becoming fully bilingual.

In addition, some families choose for children who are native English speakers to receive all of their instruction in Spanish (or another language) so that they can become fluent in the language. These are called **Immersion programs** (Ford & Palacios, 2015).

Because all programs do not receive the assessments provided to schools that receive public funds, the following is an example of an assessment used to evaluate young children's proficiency in English.

- *Observing Children Learning English (OCLE):* (Tabors, 2008). This checklist is a tool for keeping track of the progress of young children learning English as a second language **over time**. In the checklist, *understand* means that the child responds nonverbally to a word or phrase, *repeats* means the child repeats a word or phrase used by another person, and *uses* means that the child produces a word or phrase without anyone having recently used the same word or phrase. This tool can be used informally and formally as teachers observe children's progress from recognition to utilization of words. https://brookespublishing.com/wp-content/uploads/2021/06/Tabors-children-learning-english.pdf

Spotlight

Acquiring oral language is not passive learning. Young children **cannot** develop vocabulary, background knowledge, and syntax by just listening to the teacher talk, any more than they can by watching television, Netflix, or YouTube. The more limited the child's early oral language, the more obstacles the child is likely to encounter in the classroom. (Juel, Biancarosa, Coker, & Deffes, 2003). This is true whether those early language experiences are in English or in another language. Language comprehension is highly correlated to future proficient reading and academic success.

Educational equity, therefore, depends upon teachers ensuring that all children's language comprehension is a primary focus. Despite the degree of economic resources and prior language interactions children have experienced, **all** young children, including MLLs, can make significant gains in the Foundational Anchors of literacy as the result of intentional and effective teacher interactions.

References

Benson, M., Waddington-Cruz, M., Berk, J., Polydefkis, M., Dyck, P., Wang, A., Plante'-Bordeneuve, V., Barroso, F., Merlini, G., Obici, L., Scheinberg, M., Brannagan, T., Adams, D., Heitner, S., Conceicao, I., Schmidt, H., Vita, G., Campistol, J., Gamez, J., ... Coelho, T. (2018). Inotersen treatment for patients with hereditary transthyretin amyloidosis. *New England Journal of Medicine, 379*(1), 22–31. doi: 10.1056/NEJMoa1716793

Beck, I. L., McKeown, M. G., & Kucan, L. (2013). *Bringing words to life: Robust vocabulary instruction* (2nd ed.). The Guilford Press. NY, NY.

Dickinson, D., Darrow, C., & Tinubu, T. (2008). Patterns of teacher–child conversations in head classrooms: Implications for an empirically grounded approach to professional development. *Early Education and Development, 19*(3), 396–429. doi:10.1080/10409280802065403

Fisher, D., Frey, N., & Rothenberg, C. (2008). *Content-area conversations*. Association for Supervision and Curriculum Development.

Ford, K., & Palacios, R. (2015). Early literacy instruction in Spanish: Teaching the beginning reader. Colorin Colorado: A bilingual site for educators and families of English language learners.

Garcia, E., & Weiss, E. (2017). *Education inequalities at the school starting gate: Gaps, trends, and strategies to address them*. Economic Policy Institute. Washington, DC.

Goodson, B., Layzer, C., Simon, P., & Dwyer, C. (2009). *Learning to talk and listen: An oral language resource for early childhood caregivers*. National Institute for Literacy. https://doi.org/10.1037/e529992011-001

Hiebert, E. H. (2020). The core vocabulary: The foundation of proficient comprehension. *The Reading Teacher, 73*(6), 757–768.

Juel, C., Biancarosa, G., Coker, D., & Deffes, R. (2003). Walking with Rosie: A cautionary tale of early reading instruction. *Educational Leadership, 60*(7), 12–18.

Krashen, S. D. (1981). *Second language acquisition and second language learning* (7th ed.). Pergamon Press. Elmsford, N.Y.

Krashen, S. D., & Terrell, T. (1983). *Natural approach*. Pergamon Press.

Lingard, B., Hayes, D., & Mills, M. (2003). Teachers and productive pedagogies: Contextualising, conceptualising, utilising. *Pedagogy, Culture and Society, 11*(3), 399–424.

Michael Luna, S. (2017). Academic language in preschool: Research and context. *The Reading Teacher, 71*(1), 89–93.

Morrow, L. M., Roskos, K., & Gambrell, L. B. (2016). *Oral language and comprehension in preschool: Teaching the essentials*. The Guilford Press. NY, NY.

Romeo, R., Leonard, J., Robinson, S., West, M., Mackey, A., Rowe, M., & Gabrieli, J. (2018). Beyond the 30-million-word gap: Children's conversational exposure is associate with language-related brain function. *Psychological Science, 29*(5), 700–710.

Shanahan, T., & Lonigan, C. J. (2010). The National Early Literacy Panel: A summary of the process and the report. *Educational Researcher, 39*(4), 279–285.

Soodla, P., Lerkkanen, M., Niemi, P., Kikas, E., Silinskas, G., & Nurmi, J. (2015). Does early reading instruction promote the rate of acquisition? A comparison of two transparent orthographies. *Learning and Instruction, 38*, 14–23. https://doi.org/10.1016/j.learninstruc.2015.02.002.

Tabors, P. O. (2008). *One child, two languages: A guide for early childhood educators of children learning English as a second language* (2nd ed.). Paul H. Brookes Publishing. Baltimore, MD.

Vasilyeva, M., & Waterfall, H. (2011). Variability in language development: Relation to socioeconomic status and environmental input in. In S. B. Neuman, & D. K. Dickinson (Eds.), *Handbook of early literacy research* (3rd ed., pp. 36–48). Guilford Press.

Vukelich, C., Enz, B., Roskos, K., & Christie, J. (2020) Helping young children learn language and literacy; Birth through kindergarten. Pearson.Hoboken, N.J.

Westberg, L. (2013). The National Early Literacy Panel (NELP), 2002–2006. *ICPSR Data Holdings.* https://doi.org/10.3886/icpsr27421.v1

WIDA: World-class instructional design and assessment: An educational consortium of state departments of education. (2014) https://wida.wisc.edu/sites/default/files/resource/Early-ELD-Standards-Guide-2014-Edition.pdf

-oral lang. is key to all literacy

- b.k. is how a child is understanding, it's growing (cummulative & exponential) list. comp. & reading comp.

- 3 tiers of vocab

-programs for Multi-Lang. Learners

9 Play, Cognition, and Early Literacy

Focus and Big Ideas

- Play supports learning
- Categories of play
- The quality of play matters
- Embedding the Foundational Anchors of literacy
- Supporting multi-language learners through socio-dramatic play

How Can Play Support Learning?

Children love to play. They find opportunities to play even without toys or safe, supportive surroundings, even when their daily lives are impacted by violence and war (White, 2012). Growing up in poverty in Apartheid South Africa, Daily Show host Trevor Noah fondly remembers his favorite toy being a brick—strategically chosen and proudly used as a fast, crash-seeking car (Daily Show, 9/17/18). The United Nations High Commission on Human Rights (1989) states that play is a right of childhood. Despite that pronouncement and evidence that play supports accelerated development (Landscape Structures, Inc., 2021), there is intense national pressure to increase academic standards in early childhood classrooms and to decrease the amount of time children have to play. Play is rarely seen today in kindergarten classrooms. Many administrators and early childhood teachers are unclear about or unaware of the relationship of play to children's future school success. "Our society has created a false dichotomy between play and learning" (White, 2012).

All social animals in the natural world, from wolf pups to human children, play. Play is the way in which they develop many of the behaviors and cognitive processes needed for survival, socialization, and learning about the world around them. Their play and learning are one and the same. Through physical play, children develop coordination, balance, and a sense of their body in relationship to their environment. They learn to use tools, a pail and shovel, or a stick to poke in the dirt. They practice and repeat playground activities or tree climbing. They learn how to negotiate roles, analyze risk, solve problems, and experience winning and losing. Learning through play continues

DOI: 10.4324/9780429284021-9

as children develop literacy. Due to misunderstandings or insufficient knowledge about how children become literate, play is frequently overlooked or dismissed and is lost as a meaningful tool for literacy learning.

Standing on the shoulders of Montessori, Froebel, Vygotsky, and Piaget, renowned researchers Bodrova and Leong (2007, 2015)would refute the separation of play and learning, saying that *play is the work of the child*; that serious cognitive and social-emotional work **can** be accomplished during play. The U.S. Association for Play Therapy has demonstrated the statistically significant effectiveness of play therapy as a mental health intervention for children from 3 to 13 (Bratton, Ray, Rhine, & Jones, 2005). Educators and researchers have found that assessing children, as they engage in a guided play situation, provides more valid and useful information than some of the more traditional assessment tools (Linder, 1993). Classroom observation reveals children playing out many life situations over which they have little control and controlling them in their own way.

How Does Play Support Brain Development?

Research continues to support the positive social, emotional, and cognitive benefits of providing classroom opportunities for young children to play (Banerjee, Alsalman, & Alqafari, 2016; Leong & Bodrova, 20212; Hirsh-Pasek, Golinkoff, Berk, & Singer, 2009) Long sustained periods of play engagement are directly related to the rate of growth and the size of parts of the brain, the **cerebellum** and **prefrontal cortex** (Pellis, Pellis, & Bell, 2010). The cerebellum contains more neurons than the rest of the entire brain and is responsible for key cognitive functioning such as attention, language processing, sensing musical rhythm, and movement. The prefrontal cortex is responsible for executive function such as planning and organization, self-regulation, managing frustration, modulating emotions, and working memory; all critically important to the Foundational Anchors of literacy. Young children in classrooms that include time for play with literacy have been shown to outperform those in classrooms that provide only direct instruction of literacy (Van Oers & Duijkers, 2013). So, how can we plan for effective play opportunities that will support literacy learning in young children?

Categories of Play

What do we mean by play? The term play can be confusing. It refers to a wide continuum of activities in the same way that the term food can mean anything from a candy bar to a balanced meal.

1. **Active play:** *Active play* requires children to use physical movements such as running, jumping, and playing games like chase, hide-and-seek, tag, and rough and tumble play. It helps support children's physical

development of coordination, strength, balance, and motor skills, problem-solving and negotiation. Active play also relates positively with children's self-confidence and positive self-esteem (IPEMA, 2021).

2. **Creative expression play**: By engaging in *creative expression play*, children articulate their feelings, thoughts, and creativity by painting, drawing, sketching, coloring, writing, making music and noise, creating sculptures and pottery, constructing crafts, and other forms of artistic expression. Children use materials in unique or unusual ways, stimulating new ways of thinking and problem-solving. This can occur at choice or center's time if the resources and time for use are available.

3. **Games with rules:** Games with rules require children to both learn and follow the specific requirements of play. Board games, such as candy land, picture dominoes, and memory games, help children develop self-regulation and reasoning skills. In strategy games, they must consider both offensive and defensive moves at the same time, a complex cognitive skill. They must also learn the social norms of both winning and losing.

4. **Language play:** Children manipulate the forms and functions of language as a source of fun for themselves and/or for the people they are with. Most hearing able children, regardless of cognitive level, play with language or respond to language play. Like other types of play, it is a source of fun. Language play is developmental, increasing in complexity as children play with and manipulate their native language. Typical three-to-five-year-old children love to produce singsongy nonsensical speech, manipulate words and syllables of words (November-Yesvember), rhyming of real and nonsense words (fishy, dishy, twishy, kishy), rhyme play (I'm a bear, look at my underwear), nonsense names (Mrs. Pumpy-Dumpy), and misnaming for fun and giggles (calling pants a shirt and vice versa) (Crystal, 1996).

5. **Pretend or imaginative play:** Children engaged in pretend play are playing "as if" something or someone is real or different than it actually is. They are symbolically creating something beyond what is literally there. A child playing alone says aloud that her stuffed puppy is sick. She quietly tells herself that the puppy needs a cup of Sweet Dreams tea with a teaspoon of honey and then be put to bed. The child takes a cup from her play kitchen and pretends to fill it with water from her sink. She runs to tell her family not to make any noise because the puppy is sleeping. To the child, the puppy is alive and really sleeping, although she knows the difference between real and pretend. Pretend play is a cognitive skill and the beginning of symbolic and abstract thought, the thinking necessary for reading and writing.

6. **Socio-dramatic play** includes both pretending and social-interaction. When played at a high level, it is a type of cooperative imaginative play in which children work together to take complementary roles in an agreed upon imaginary scenario such as a doctor's office or a pizza restaurant. Roles for a pizza restaurant might include a cook, a waitperson, and a

customer. Socio-dramatic play generally peaks between the ages of four and six (Johnson, Christie, & Wardle, 2005) when children reach the level of symbolic thinking where they can easily represent objects and actions in a nonliteral way. For example, they might use a frisbee as a steering wheel of a firetruck and a pool noodle as a hose to put out a fire. When they play, children use the language and behaviors they perceive their role, the person they are portraying (e.g., a firefighter, doctor, chef, mother, or receptionist) would use to act out their role and converse with other children involved in the scenario. They enforce roles with play peers, "No, I'm the mom. I put the baby to bed. You're the auntie so you get us a Coke."

By classifying the kinds of play in which children engage, adults are better able to analyze the cognitive behaviors in which children are engaged. Have the children invented their own scenario with superheroes who fight villains? Or is this strictly physical play, without a scenario, as they chase one another? Perhaps there is some element of creative play as they use their jackets for capes. Only careful observation can assist the teacher in understanding what the children are thinking, doing, or trying to do. Adults can only see what is happening on the outside, while all the cognitive action is happening on the inside.

The Quality of Play Matters

All types of play are important to child development and should be offered in the classroom. Socio-dramatic play can be planned to support children's learning across domains, including the development of the Foundational Anchors of literacy. Most early childhood classrooms incorporate socio-dramatic play into their curriculum. It is sometimes referred to as "free play" or "dress-up." Not all socio-dramatic play observed in classrooms, however, supports higher thinking and significant literacy learning.

Socio-dramatic play can only be an effective indirect literacy learning context when children play at a mature, **high level**. In high-level play, children "create an imaginary situation, take on and act out roles, and follow a set of rules determined by those specific roles (Bodrova & Leong 2015). Each of these features plays an important function in the development of higher mental functions." It must be stated that facilitating high-level play requires much more than setting out dress-up clothes and adding paper and pencil. As you read the following scenarios, consider the features of teacher planning and interactions that will contribute or distract from taking play to a high level.

Low-Level Play

In Scenario 1 (Figure 9.1), the children are engaged, enjoying themselves, intrinsically motivated, process oriented, and free to make choices. The play described would be considered **low-level play,** however. It will add very

---

Scenario 1: No theme or Narrative to the Play

Imagine a dramatic play area set up with wooden kitchen appliances, a sink, a table and four chairs. On the table is a tablecloth and flowers in a vase. Plastic plates, bowls, flatware, plastic food, oven mitts, and muffin tins are set on low shelves. Also in the center are a cash register, play money, doctor's instruments, and an assortment of hats for community helpers. Various unrelated dress-up costumes are hung from hooks on the wall.

Helena, age four, put a purple tutu over her clothes and announced she was a princess. She noticed and retrieved some kitchen props, pretended to stir batter in a bowl and poured it into a muffin tin. She opened the oven and put in the tin. "I'm making cookies!" she announced to no one in particular.... "They are done in 10 hours!"

Another child, Martin, a young five-year-old dressed in a construction worker's hat, asked if he could have a cookie. Helena answered that they weren't done yet. Martin noticed a box of props for playing doctor or hospital, found a stethoscope and blood pressure toy, and sat down to figure out how they worked. He pretended to listen to his own heartbeat. Helena took the muffin tin and left the center, going from child to child in the block, writing, and art centers, asking, "Who wants a cookie?"

Figure 9.1 Play Scenario 1: Low-Level Play

little to children's development of cognition or the Foundational Anchors of literacy. This low-level type of play will most likely continue throughout the year if the teacher does not assist the children in creating high-level play.

Low-level play is typically found in dramatic play centers that **do not** have a **theme** (Morrow & Rand, 1991). The **theme** of a socio-dramatic play center is a **place**, such as a doctor's office, a birthday party, or an airport, with which children are familiar. Children act out the roles of people who work, visit, attend, or live there. When centers are a repository of a variety of unrelated costumes and props, the center does not reflect a specific place. When participating in low-level play, children *react* to the props at hand and do not plan a "what- if...." scenario to their play. Their attention is determined by the props within their direct line of vision. Children might focus their entire attention on how objects feel and work, using their time to move from prop to prop. Perhaps they are unfamiliar with an object, its purpose, its name, the actions it performs, and who might use it. Therefore, children examine the props with little or no context, do not extend their vocabulary or background knowledge, and have no need for any interaction with other children.

During low-level play, children use little or no role-based language, Tier 2 or Tier 3 vocabulary. They may describe their own actions as they play or interact briefly with a peer, sometimes competing for props. Their reactions to props sometimes encourage them to take on simplistic roles like a baker, a princess, or a doctor. Any scenario that develops usually lasts for a few seconds or minutes, but rarely longer. Children do not collaboratively think forward, missing valuable opportunities to develop and practice executive function (Leong and Bodrova, 2007). During low-level play, children frequently violate the implied rules of a role, such as when Helena used baker's language while dressed as a princess and Martin, wearing a construction worker's hat, explored the doctor's tools (Bodrova & Leong, 2007).

Despite the fact that a theme was chosen, the play described in Figure 9.2 also remains at a low level. Each child in this class of 16 may get several 20 minute opportunities during the week to go to the Space Center. Next week, the theme will be Camping. Chris works very hard to produce different themes every week, decorating the center, attempting to find songs, books, and new props to entertain and interest the children. He reorganizes the center daily as clean-up only involve children putting the costumes, scientific tools, and the control panel on random shelves without sorting tools and clothing into different categories. While very demanding of teacher preparation time, this play did not facilitate children taking roles such as astronauts or scientists and using props to play a complex theme-related scenario. The children did not integrate background knowledge or use space related Tier 3 vocabulary. They did not use literacy to accomplish any tasks. This limited the children's social and cognitive development, including the development of their Foundational Anchors of literacy.

Scenario 2: Using Themes but Changing them Every Week

This week's theme in the dramatic play area is Space. Chris has worked very hard and focused on decorating the center to look like a specific place. He has hung a dark blue background with peel and stick stars on the wall behind it. From his prop box on Space, Chris took out helmets from StarWars costumes, two pairs of snow pants, moon boots, posters of the planets, a large stone to represent a moon rock, various scientific tools such as a balance scale and a pretend telescope, and a rocket control panel he made of cardboard and covered with foil. Throughout the week, he read aloud from several books about outer space, taught the children a song about the planets and a finger play about a rocket blasting off. They watched a video about the solar system.

The children began to play in the center on Monday. The first four students were excited to go to the dramatic play center and rushed in to grab helmets and pants. They fussed for several minutes over who got to wear the boots. Chris approached the center and suggested they take turns, to which they reluctantly agreed. He pointed out the control panel and one child played with the stickers that represented knobs. The other three children began to examine the telescope, the moon rock, magnifying glasses, the balance scale, and then looked around for any other props. The conversation was mostly about who got to wear what. Randy announced that he was the dad and that Camille had to be the mom "because she's a girl." The other two boys left the center to find two long blocks to use as guns to kill aliens.

After 15 minutes, the children were bored and asked Chris, "How long till the bell rings?" "Five more minutes", he told them. "You can start your clean up." Michael burst into tears because he hadn't had a turn to wear the boots.

Figure 9.2 Play Scenario 2: Low-Level Play

Low-level play is often observed when the socio-dramatic play center has a theme, but the theme changes too frequently. The play feels scattered and random to the children as well as to the adult observer. Challenging disruptive behaviors frequently emerge. This represents an *awareness* rather than an *investigative* curriculum. Children have not had the opportunity or time to learn enough information or vocabulary to understand the role of an astronaut and the purpose of the materials. The read-alouds and videos Chris used were not directly connected to the work of astronauts so children did not apply that information to their play. Chris did not model a scenario or the roles the children could take. Children did not know or did not remember that astronauts are scientists who conduct experiments in space. They used what they knew... mom and dad and alien killers... to create what little story they could. There was limited oral language and no emergent reading or writing. The posters, like wallpaper, were ignored. Next week's play is unlikely to build on anything that happened this week. The children had learned to rush in and be the first to grab props. With continued use of weekly themes, these are the behaviors that will be repeated all the while overwhelming the teacher with setting out new decorations and toys.

High-Level Play

The scenario in Figure 9.3 illustrates **high-level play**. The teacher has designed it carefully so that it functions as an effective Indirect Literacy Learning context. In high-level play (also called well-developed, high-quality, complex, or mature play), children work together to take roles and plan at least the beginning scenario of the play. They use language and theme-related vocabulary to describe their roles and actions to each other using future-oriented phrases such as, "Let's pretend your car has a broken engine and you need to get it fixed. Julia and I will be the mechanics and tell you what's wrong and how much it will cost. You wait in the waiting room while we are working. You can read magazines or watch TV. I'll put the car on the lift and we'll see what's wrong."

Sometimes children spend more time planning the scenario than actually playing it because it feels like important work and stimulates their creativity and imaginations. Children may take multiple roles over the course of the scenario. They "become" the role and their actions follow the "rules" for which they have become. They will accept new ideas and build on ones they have already played, expanding the scenario. (Bodrova & Leong, 2007). High-level play rarely occurs in an early childhood setting **without** thoughtful, intentional, and purposeful planning by the teacher.

In high-level play, children demonstrate their content knowledge of the mechanic's shop by negotiating interactions between the mechanics and the customers. They do not, however, rely on props to remain focused in the scenario. In well-developed play, children can remain in the play for an hour or longer. They use Tier 3, vocabulary of the theme such as appointment, maintenance, transmission, engine, lift, bay, jack, and repair.

Scenario 3: A Well Planned Socio-dramatic Play Center Aligned with A Four to Six Weeks Investigation

The children had been playing in the socio-dramatic play center each day for two weeks. The theme of the center was an auto mechanic shop within a gas station and four children were deeply engaged in playing the scenario. The teacher had read several informational books about the theme. She spent time on the pictures helping children speculate what the people were saying and doing. The children had recently taken a walk to a mechanic shop/gas station several blocks away. The teacher planned the field trip carefully so that the owner expected them and the mechanic knew the types of questions the children would have. The owner could show them his appointment book, repair orders, parts orders, and work log. When they returned to the classroom, the children talked about what they had learned and then added information to an ongoing chart about the Mechanic Shop. The following week, the children watched a video of a mechanic working on the engine of a car and with teacher guidance, they easily connected what they saw in the video with what they had seen on their field trip. On another day, the teacher's friend demonstrated how to change a tire on the teacher's car, naming the tire iron, lug nuts, wheel, and spare tire, Tier 3 vocabulary.

At the beginning of the investigation, the teacher had thoughtfully planned the center and selected props. Because she had sent a letter home to families about their upcoming study of the mechanic shop, donations of materials arrived regularly. They included a discarded refrigerator box the children made into a car during several small group times, an old steering wheel, metal and plastic tools, and an old vacuum hose that the children could use to fill the car with gas. In addition, the children suggested props they should add based on what they had learned across their experiences.

As a mechanic shop, the socio-dramatic play area had a reception area for customers to read the list of services offered, chairs for them to sit and wait, a counter across which a mechanic could talk to the customer, write down exactly what the vehicle would need, and accept payment for gas and other services, a bay for a mechanic to work on the cardboard vehicle, and an area to the side that customers could use to fill their cars with gas.

The children who chose that center eagerly talked about who they wanted to be and negotiated so that roles were filled. The customer had to describe the problem with their car. The counter mechanic wrote down the services the customer requested and showed them the waiting area and the magazines they could look at while they waited. The mechanics talked about which tools they needed and then began to work. The children stayed engaged in this complex theme for 45 minutes, until they were required to prepare for a transition to lunch.

Figure 9.3 Play Scenario 3: High-Level Play

Teachers plan for children to develop many cognitive strategies during high-level socio-dramatic play. These include executive function, cooperative planning, negotiation, problem-solving, self-regulation, leadership, decision-making, critical thinking, adaptability, persistence, and awareness of their own emotions as well as those of others. If the teacher has planned appropriately, children will play at their scenarios for a sustained period of time, providing multiple opportunities for cognitive development, including habits of thinking and appropriate interactions with peers, constructing

Differences between High-Level and Low-Level Play	
Low-level	**High-level**
Engage in simple, repeated roles Limited interactions with peers	Take on differentiated roles Roles have rules Rules require executive function, including self-regulation and working memory
Dependence on props	Pretend situations are not prop dependent
Reactive: driven by materials Use of materials for literal purpose	Driven by knowledge of the theme Symbolic use of materials
No unified theme	Complex interwoven theme
Isolated episodes that frequently change	Sustained focused engagement
Language used only to comment on action as it happens	Conversational oral language Use of advanced theme-related vocabulary.
Reactive: driven by props and current situations	Future oriented: make-believe, beyond the present

Figure 9.4 Differences between High-Level and Low-Level Play
Source: Adapted from Bodrova and Leong (2015).

emerging cognitive and social skills (See Figure 9.4). Quite the significant learning for an activity that is so much fun!

High-Level Play Supports Literacy Development

Socio-dramatic play has the opportunity to be a very powerful **Indirect Learning Context**. The literacy learning potential of a socio-dramatic play center is significantly increased when it is related to classroom curriculum by being aligned with a **topic** of investigation with a designated **theme** (Roskos & Christie, 2017). An example would be if the theme of the doctor's office socio-dramatic play center was part of a classroom investigation such as the Human Body or All About Me. When intentionally planned, it provides opportunities for children to playfully engage with and learn about literacy; hypothesizing about, applying, reinforcing, and practicing what they already know about the forms and function of print. This chapter will provide teachers with understanding and guidance to plan indirect learning contexts in which children can construct critical cognitive processes and Foundational Anchors of literacy within the context of **high-level play.**

Foundational Anchors of literacy develop during high-level play when children use oral and written language within the context of the play scenario. While playing a role, children use literacy in functional or purposeful ways, attributing meaning to their emergent writing and reading when it is important to the play situation (Burns, Griffin, & Snow, 1998). The firefighter, for example, needs to answer an urgent phone call and write down the name and address of the person whose house is on fire. She might also refer to a map on the wall where the teacher has marked children's addresses. An excited conversation will likely ensue as the firefighters get ready to drive to the house and put out the fire. As children use literacy to accomplish tasks, they are learning about *the function* of print. As they purposefully use literacy, children also begin to notice the *forms* of print and the way it is organized. For example, while reading a menu, they begin to notice the headings, illustrations, or photographs, the way print has been arranged in a list. They recognize familiar letters and notice new ones; they independently hypothesize about and practice print concepts such as directionality, wordness, and use of punctuation. This is important cognitive work that is reinforced and nudged forward each time children return to the play. Well-planned high-level socio-dramatic play that includes the intentional use of literacy is called **literacy-enriched play, or play in which children use literacy for functional purposes.**

Literacy Props

Materials used to support literacy development in socio-dramatic play are called **literacy props.** Literacy props include such things as receipt books, recipes, restaurant order pads, price lists, signs, magazines, menus, blueprints, prescription pads, medical charts, invitations, thank you notes, and appointment books. They represent the reading and writing that adults use in their work and daily life experiences. Literacy props, therefore, allow children to carry out their roles with authenticity. Research indicates that including literacy props in socio-dramatic play is critically important and results in significant increases in the amount of time children spend engaged in literacy activities (Roskos, Christie, Widman, & Holding, 2010). Teachers modeling the ways in which the literacy props are used, highly impacts the degree to which children actually use them. The more time children use literacy props in socio-dramatic play, the more opportunities they have to think about, reinforce and construct important concepts about print (Vukelich, Enz, Roskos & Christie 2020).

If a child is playing a customer in a grocery store, they would use reading and writing to "get things done." This could be writing a grocery list, reading labels and signs, using coupons, writing a check, using a credit card, and comparing or locating items on a shelf. For a hair and nail salon, literacy props might include an appointment book, a list for patrons to select services and purchase items, price lists, receipt books, signs for various areas of the salon such as the nail station, magazines for waiting patrons, and signs with the name of the store as well as Open and Closed. The teacher demonstrates the use and purpose of these reading and writing activities during whole group time, when providing ongoing information about the topic and theme.

Building Language Comprehension during Play

High-quality socio-dramatic play in which children use literacy for functional purposes grows children's **language comprehension**, a critical aspect of skilled reading and reading instruction. In addition to word identification skills, readers require language comprehension in order to understand (comprehend) text. Using language contextually in play adds to the child's knowledge base and vocabulary. Language comprehension includes:

- background knowledge,
- vocabulary,
- verbal reasoning,
- complex language structures,
- literacy knowledge (print concepts, etc.)

Language comprehension can be significantly developed during high-quality socio-dramatic play aligned with a topic of study. New learning about the topic must be continually provided by the teacher through read-alouds, videos, field trips, topic-related experiences and activities, artifacts, props, and guest speakers. In this way, children's interest, motivation, and learning are nurtured and integrated into their play. When a variety of topics are explored and played throughout the year, opportunities for developing language comprehension abound. Children engaging in high-level play will use literacy to complete tasks their roles require. Children will only use literacy to the extent they have sufficient background knowledge about the person they are playing and how that person uses literacy. It cannot be overstated that children cannot play at a high level **what they have not learned or experienced**. Experience can either be **direct** such as baking as a class before opening the Play Bakery, or **vicarious** through read-alouds, websites, videos, and/or classroom visitors. The deepest understanding always results from a combination of both direct and vicarious experiences.

Planning Is Key

Intentional, thoughtful planning is necessary to ensure all children engage in the high-level play required to develop children's Foundational Anchors of literacy. Research indicates that "teachers believe play is an important part of the curriculum, yet they often fail to **plan** for play experiences and rely on their instincts in lieu of specific goals and objectives for play" (Bodrova & Leong, 2007; Rice, 2014). Certainly, collecting materials and props for any play scenario is demanding for a teacher. But, children need more than entertaining materials for learning, specifically literacy learning, to occur.

Incidental literacy learning frequently occurs when children scaffold each other's use of literacy in a pretend scenario. It also occurs when an insightful teacher notices and capitalizes on a teachable moment during children's play. "Incidental learning can be powerful but it can also be haphazard,"(Touhill, 2013)For every child who develops a clear understanding of a particular literacy concept, there are potentially many others who do not. "Such learning is too important to be left to chance. If we want children to make important connections and to transfer knowledge and understanding between experiences, then we need to **think beyond** a purely incidental approach" (Touhill, 2013).

Intentional planning for children's high-level socio-dramatic play that effectively supports literacy development begins with teachers:

- identifying and beginning the study of a class investigation;
- identifying an appropriate theme for the socio-dramatic play center, and the roles children can play;
- providing sufficient and ongoing opportunities for children to build background knowledge about the topic of investigation and the theme;
- adding, explaining, and modeling the use of appropriate literacy props;
- allocating an adequate amount of time for children to engage in socio-dramatic play; and
- using the appropriate level of teacher involvement with the children before, during, and after play (Christie, 1990).

Why Should Socio-Dramatic Play Centers Have a Theme?

The beginning of the school year should start with a topic of investigation and a socio-dramatic play theme that is very familiar to children. This might be the home or the grocery store. For many children, this may be their first opportunity to experience high-level play. Teacher support, encouragement, and participation can lead children to develop their play *beyond* reacting to materials. As they play in the first themed dramatic play center of the school year, the teacher's goals are for children to

- identify, take, and remain in roles for a gradually increasing period of time;
- invite and include children who are multi-language learners (MLLs), shy, low language, or otherwise unfamiliar with socio-dramatic play.
- collaborate with other children to create and play an agreed upon scenario;
- converse appropriately while playing roles;
- use appropriate theme-related props;
- use literacy props in authentic ways to accomplish role-specific goals such as reading a bedtime story to a baby or making a grocery list; and
- learn and practice clean-up routines.

This first topic and socio-dramatic play theme of the year should last three to four weeks. During those weeks, ongoing learning is crucial, even for those topics with which children have some background knowledge. For example, some children have had many experiences with airports; visiting family and taking vacations. Others have never been to an airport. Therefore, when planning an airport investigation and theme, it is important to assess what all children already know about the airport and create opportunities to ensure **all children,** even those who seem to know a lot about the topic, build new content knowledge. This becomes the language comprehension children will need to successfully comprehend future text.

Changing topics and themes every week or biweekly is strongly discouraged. As demonstrated in the space scenario, this short-time frame does not allow children to develop concepts, or to use language and vocabulary about the topic. It does encourage children to enter a center and just react to the materials, without establishing character roles or how they might use the materials for a specific purpose. The children are enamored of the "new stuff," which may appear to be engagement, but competing for possession and getting everything out is superficial and does not promote cognitive and language development. It takes time and background knowledge to move beyond that into a scenario.

A four-to-six-week exploration of a topic and theme is preferred as new props, information, and experiences are shared with the children during the weeks they are playing the theme. New information is provided through read-alouds, field trips, videos, artifacts, props, visiting experts, etc. These develop and expand background knowledge about the topic and theme, maintain curiosity and engagement, further the narrative or scenario, and offer additional opportunities for emergent reading and writing.

What Kind of Topics and Themes Support High-Level Play?

Additional choices for topic-related and themed play include familiar neighborhood businesses such as a local restaurant or drive-thru, a bakery, a hair and nail salon, a doctor's office or a hospital, a fire station, a veterinarian's office, big-box stores or Dollar-type stores, or a mechanic's shop. The teacher's decisions on a theme must value the culture of the children's community for several reasons. First, children play at the highest level when they can tap into their funds of knowledge, and second, the play center must not be anglo-centric, or reflect bias. This is an opportunity to practice culturally responsive teaching by developing your own understanding of the children's culture and daily lives. Paying attention to the resources available to children in their neighborhood can lead to themes such as after-school care at the military base, a farmer's market that sells food common to local cuisine, a salmon cannery on the coast of Alaska, or an Urban Farm; places unique to their daily lives and location. For instance, recreating a Pho Bowl Shop affirms the children's familiarity with the topic and theme and makes the play highly personal and engaging, facilitating clear connections, and understandings of the oral and written language observed and used in that setting. This provides children with concrete experiences on which to build new understandings.

How Much Time Should Children Spend in Play?

Children should have opportunities to engage in socio-dramatic play for **at least 30 minutes per day**. Forty-five minutes to an hour of sustained play is preferred. This allows children's socio-dramatic play to become complex and well-developed; high level. Two 15-minute time frames do not meet this criterion (Christie, Johnsen, and Peckover, 1988). If children are allowed to remain in the play for **at least** 30 minutes, they are more likely to add to their previous play, increase the complexity of the scenario, add and appropriately use literacy props, integrate new background knowledge, and use more topic and theme-related (Tier 3) vocabulary each time they play (see Figure 9.5).

Teachers must work toward building up the children's stamina for play. If the theme fails to maintain children's engagement, teachers must carefully analyze their own preparation of children's background knowledge about the theme, the design of the center, the props and literacy props provided and modeled, and the children's involvement in ongoing changes to the center. As with all learning opportunities, the level of experience children have had with socio-dramatic play will affect their understanding of how to play.

Why Does Center Design and Choice of Props Matter?

To encourage high-level socio-dramatic play, the center should feel welcoming and organized, it should authentically reflect what children have learned about the topic and the theme and provide enough space for up to four children to play at one time. If it is too large or too open, interaction between children, cooperation, and conversational oral language opportunities may be negatively impacted. If it is too small, children cannot move

Anchor Under Construction

Four-year-old Eric's favorite place was the local Starbucks. He watched his mother order and she pointed out how the barista put her name on her cup and his name on his cup. In the backyard, Eric began to play Starbucks. He began with a few cups and his mother began to add the other things he would need; a marker for the names, a pitcher, spoons, and a green t-shirt to wear as an apron. She ordered coffee, and Eric wrote her name on the cup, MOM, pretended to make coffee by stirring the pitcher and pouring it into her cup. This role play went on for many weeks and grew in its complexity as Eric noticed new things on every trip to Starbucks. When Eric got to kindergarten, high-level, socio-dramatic play in which he used literacy for purposeful purposes was familiar to him.

Figure 9.5 Early High-Level Play Experience: Starbucks

around comfortably to act out their roles, locate props, and complete their role-specific tasks. Frustration may ensue. Tempers can flare.

The center should be placed in an area where children will not be interrupted and where their conversations will not interrupt the play of others. The socio-dramatic play center is considered a noisy area and, therefore, should be placed away from quieter areas such as the library or manipulative centers. Socio-dramatic play centers are often placed strategically close to the block area so that children can engage in "small world" play of the same topic with blocks, people, cars, trucks, animals, etc. It is also sometimes placed near the writing center that can provide additional writing resources.

The socio-dramatic play center should reflect the theme in its construction, design, and materials (props). A combination of real (authentic) props, pretend purchased props, and teacher/child created props should be intentionally considered for optimal use and learning. Props can be added as children learn more about the topic and theme rather than presented all at once. Children four--to-six-years-old require fewer real or actual props than toddlers and young preschoolers. They can easily use symbolic props of their own or the teacher's creations to engage in complex imaginary play. For example, children can use a pool noodle as a hose in the fire station and a unit block as a phone. Theme-related props, both actual and created, should be placed in the area so that children can authentically take roles and act out scenarios. For example, authentic, real props for a hair and nail salon might include wig holders, wigs, brushes, combs, hair dryers and straighteners (with cut cords), hair rollers, tables and chairs, hair caps, empty nail polish bottles and brushes, curlers and bobby pins, hair clips, and empty bottles of hair products. Accumulated pretend props, purchased, or donated might include a small cash register, pretend money, and capes. Teacher/child created props could include signs, a check-in and appointment book, credit cards, a list of services and price lists, etc. The list is only limited by imaginations of the teacher and children, but each prop should be safe and considered carefully for its purpose and contribution to the play.

In addition, the props should reflect items authentically used by the ethnicities and cultures of children in the class. In the example of a hair and nail salon, it must include the specific cultural norms for haircare of members of the classroom community. Teachers should learn about the norms represented by the children and support their use with clear language and modeling. Opportunities for parents or experts to visit the class and demonstrate/talk about haircare requirements, as well as children's books that engagingly explain these concepts should be considered. Participating in the cultural norms of the adults around them is authentic for children. Expanding their understanding of cultural norms beyond their own must be planned for children to see the value and affirm that every culture is "normal," valid, and important.

Teacher Scenario: The Doctor's Office

Goals and Outcomes

Noemi's preschool class had started an investigation into children's health. Consider the process in which Noemi purposefully planned to facilitate high-level play in which children use literacy for purposeful reasons within the theme of a Doctor's Office.

Background Knowledge and Vocabulary

Noemi considered what she specifically wanted the children in her class to learn about the doctor's office. She began a list, knowing that it would expand as she previewed materials, developed her own additional background knowledge, and assessed the children's current background knowledge. This would include what children need to know in order to play each role in the scenario. For example, the needs of the sick people who visited the Doctor's Office, the people who worked there, the various jobs in which they engaged, the equipment and props they used, and how they used literacy to help them organize and complete tasks. In addition, she started a list of topic-related Tier 2 and Tier 3 vocabulary that she wanted the children to become knowledgeable of and able to use in conversation. This list, too, would expand as she dived into her preparation and organization of the investigation.

Assessing Background Knowledge

Prior to setting up the socio-dramatic play center, Noemi guided the children to discuss their own experiences at the doctor's office. She recorded the children's thoughts, ideas, and questions on a large piece of chart paper. They reread it back together as she used a pointer, demonstrating the direction readers read and writers write. During a future Center's Time, Noemi knew she would observe children at the chart, using the pointer to "be the teacher" and reread the familiar text, an effective talk-to-text strategy for developing children's Foundational Anchors of literacy.

Later, Noemi analyzed what the children knew, what they "thought" they knew (and about which they might need clarification), and things they wondered about the doctor's office. She thoughtfully considered the type of themed socio-dramatic play center she would set up, the content knowledge and vocabulary she wanted the children to develop, and the potential field trips, guest speakers, video snippets, and read-alouds she could use to facilitate rich play with abundant opportunities for the children to construct Foundational Anchors of literacy. This was going to be a fun investigation for both the children and Noemi!

Prior to the Doctor's office, children had been playing the Fire Station theme for four weeks and would bring some of their learning forward to the new theme. They had practiced assuming and staying in roles, planning scenarios, and creating props with others. They knew that some previously used props would be in the new scenario but that props are not limited to what is already made and available. They could use other materials from the classroom to create new props for the Doctor's Office, suggest props during lessons to expand content knowledge, and bring others in from home. They know that doctors, like firefighters, are all genders, colors and come from any cultural background. They are curious about how it will feel to play the role of an adult in this new scenario.

Identifying Children's Roles and Literacy Props

As Noemi prepared to change her socio-dramatic play center from a Fire Station to a Doctor's Office, she considered the roles children could play. She knew that three roles were probably adequate to start: the receptionist, the doctor, and the patient. She could add more when the children had more information and experiences with the topic, children's health, and theme, the doctor's office. Noemi would make enough lanyards with pictures and text so that two children could be patients and eventually they could add another doctor.

Props and decor would make the center easily identifiable as a doctor's office, stimulating children's imagination and theme appropriate play. Copies of the read-aloud books about children's health and the doctor's office would be placed in the library area. Noemi knew from her experience that children are more likely to choose and reread books that she has read aloud to them. She would show the children other topic-related books as she placed them in the block area to support their "small world" doctor's office play. She then put her mind to how she would introduce the theme on the first day. She wanted to engender excitement and curiosity.

Ensuring High-Level Socio-Dramatic Play Includes Children's Functional Use of Print

Noemi imagined how the children could engage in high-level play and use literacy authentically in each of their roles. Visualize with her and think about how much the children would enjoy this play while constructing Foundational Anchors of literacy.

- At the doctor's office, children can read signs such as Doctor's Office and Please Check in HERE. The child playing the **receptionist** can use literacy to carry out various tasks, e.g. answering the office phone, writing the names of children requesting visits in an appointment book, reading the sign-in sheet, calling the next patient, taking an insurance card and copay, and letting the doctor know the patient is ready to be seen. The child can use the words he has heard or has learned that a receptionist uses and stays within the role-related behaviors. You will not hear "the receptionist" suddenly announce he has a fever unless he intentionally changes roles.

- The **patients** will stay in their roles as patients, not allowing themselves to answer phones or take temperatures, no matter the temptation. When children maintain their roles, they are practicing self-regulation, a type of executive function and a Foundational Anchors of literacy. Noemi prepared physical reminders to help children remain in and play their roles. These included a lanyard or a name tag with the role printed on it and clothing specific to the role. When **patients** arrive to see the doctor, a numbered clip board is provided for them to write their names. They may choose to write as much of their names as they can, copy them from a list Noemi has provided, or use emergent writing. They can fill out a form that requires them to write their name, age, and draw or write a description of their symptoms. Noemi thought a medical history check-list would be fun too. For example, "Have you ever had a fever? Have you ever broken a bone," etc.
- The **receptionist** will refer to the list to call patients and cross off the names one at a time as they go in to see the doctor. When he takes appointments, he can write in the appointment notebook Noemi created. It has lines and spaces for names and arrival times. He might copy children's names from Noemi's list, ask the patient to spell her name, or use emergent writing.
- When the **doctor** welcomes the patient into her office, she can review the patient's medical history and take notes on a chart as they engage in a detailed question/response discussion about current symptoms. This interaction has been modeled several times during large group times. On the chart, Noemi made several different boxes with easy to differentiate icons. For example, one box is used to record the patient's temperature, one for blood pressure, and one to write down the patient's symptoms. There is an additional small pad of papers marked "prescription" on the top so that the doctor can write one for the patient if necessary.

Embedding the Foundational Anchors of Literacy

Noemi knew that each of the ten Foundational Anchors of literacy could be developed and practiced during this investigation and intentionally planned for children to do so. See her list below where she considered each anchor and how children could develop them.

1. **Oral language**
   - Children use language to negotiate role-taking, scenario actions, and problem-solving.
   - The receptionist talks to patients on the phone and in the office.
   - The doctor and patient engage in reciprocal conversation about the patient's symptoms.

2. **Background knowledge and vocabulary**
   • After intentional introduction of related concepts and vocabulary, all players use the theme-related language and vocabulary of the roles they are playing. This is further developed by additional experiences such as read-alouds, guided discussions, field trips, videos, and guest speakers. Posters label the skeleton, the ear, and the eye.

3. **Book awareness**
   • Patients look at magazines. Doctors look at informational books about the human body.

4. **Alphabet knowledge and phonics**
   • Environmental print such as signs, health brochures, and posters encourage children to examine letters and construct meaning of new vocabulary.
   • Children examine print and use what they know about letters and sounds to read and write names, write prescriptions, and take notes.

5. **Phonological awareness and phonemic awareness**
   • Children will try out and practice the pronunciation of Tier 2 and Tier 3 words that may be unfamiliar with them.
   • Depending on the children's degree of understanding that letters represent specific sounds, children will emergently spell names and words they need to write. The teacher has intentionally modeled this process throughout the day for a variety of purposes.

6. **Print concepts**
   • Children will notice and use the various forms print takes depending on its purposes. Names are written in a list to be checked off, doctor's notes are written in a chart and contain limited but important information.
   • Directionality of print will be modeled when the teacher introduces the various literacy props at whole or small group time.

7. **Emergent writing**
   • The receptionist, patients, and doctor all use writing to gather and communicate information.
   • The patient writes her name when she signs in.
   • Children refer to a list of theme-related words Noemi made in large group time with the children and placed in the center. These words were rewritten and put on a poster in the writing center.

8. **Emergent reading**
   • Patients read magazines in the waiting room and examine their prescriptions.
   • Environmental print such as signs, brochures, and posters encourage children to pretend read and construct meaning using various sources of information.
   • Class produced books about the topic.

9. **Positive dispositions toward literacy and literacy learning**
   - Literacy is used in a fun, risk-free environment that encourages them to feel and think like readers and writers.
   - Children's confidence in their mastery of literacy usage will motivate them to approximate reading and writing tasks in other situations.
10. **Executive function**
   - All children practice self-regulation and perseverance when they remain in their roles and use the language aligned with their role.
   - Children set goals for the scenario and negotiate role taking and problem-solving.
   - Children persevere when they attempt the challenges of Emergent Reading and Writing.

Proficient readers and writers engage in self-monitoring and self-advocating behaviors to make sure they comprehend what they read and effectively communicate their thoughts through their writing. Children practice these emerging skills while playing the doctor's office when they:

- **seek information** from a play peer about the identity of a word on the patient's Medical History.
- **check to see if their hypothesis is correct** about the spelling of a word when a child asks a teacher or a play peer, "Is this how you write 'shot'?"
- **self-monitor and revise** what the child perceives as a mistake when she declares, "Oops, Dr. has a dot after it." (Vukelich, Enz, Roskos &Christie 2020).
- **produce class books** such as "Cover your Cough" or "Hand Washing like a Doctor," and reread them.

Supporting Multi-Language Learners (MLLs) through Socio-Dramatic Play

In her master's thesis, preschool teacher, Janaki Niranjanan, described how her socio-dramatic play center offered a safe environment for a new student, a MLL, to make connections between his own culture and his new one, to try out English language and literacy, and to build relationships with other children. The child, anonymously referred to as "John," was from India. His native language was Punjabi and he spoke only a few words of English when he arrived.

Dual language learners typically go through an initial stage of silent observation, and John was no exception. But while initially shy and reticent to involve himself in other children's play, he gradually participated in the socio-dramatic play kitchen center. He initiated imaginative play by using cups and containers to create a tea party scenario similar to those he experienced in India. The teacher "encouraged John to use tumblers (teacups) from his native country, India, to play the pretend tea-party game. He called himself 'Tea Wala' (an Indian name for a tea-seller) and pretended to pour tea for his friends. This culturally influenced make-believe play encouraged him to incorporate his personal experiences into his play, allowing him to feel more comfortable in a new environment" (Niranjanan, 2016).

Research indicates that all children benefit when their learning environment includes culturally relevant and culturally familiar objects (Kirova, 2010). Play is influenced by culture and culture includes language (Niranjanan, 2016). Therefore, culture should not be considered an "add-on" to a generic play theme. It must be considered an important component of the curriculum. Socio-dramatic play centers that reflect children's culture provide them with opportunities to validate their own knowledge and ways of being in the world and to connect them with a new culture. Opportunities should be intentionally planned for all children to develop knowledge and appreciation for other children's culture and language. The socio-dramatic play center offers opportunities for children to use and value their own funds of knowledge and connect them to the culture and language of others. "Play is a vehicle for preserving cultural group identities while creating a common culture" (Kirova, 2010). In JN's preschool classroom, other children became curious about John's pretend Tea Wala play. One child approached John and asked whether she could join his play. As a result, John slowly started to pick up English words and communicate with the other child and the teacher. "Both children shared their own cultural knowledge and created a common ground for communication and interaction" JN 2016.

A child's ability to use their first language influences the development of their second language..The home environments of all children influence their primary language and so authentic home-school partnerships with families of MLLs are essential. Enlisting families of MLLs to bring representations of the child's culture into the classroom can be extremely valuable. Books written in Punjabi and contributed by John's family were included in the play center and John emergently read them aloud to other children in his native language. John gradually became comfortable in the classroom and over time his group of friends expanded, and his language proficiency grew. When MLL children's own language and culture are recognized and affirmed in the classroom, they are more likely motivated to engage in language and literacy opportunities with other children (Kirova, 2010).

Children use language more freely (both quantitatively and qualitatively) when they are engaged in socio-dramatic play as opposed to talking directly with the teacher. Multiple language learners greatly benefit from peer play rich in social interactions. Socio-dramatic play offers opportunities for them to observe and listen to varied linguistic exchanges in a more authentic setting. Academic language that was used by the teacher in preparation for the theme is more likely to be used by children in the risk-free context of play. Children's use of explanatory talk (explaining in child-talk) and narrative talk (creating the story to guide the play) provides the opportunity for them to further their understanding of the theme by offering clarification from their own perspective. The objective of the play experience becomes apparent to all children involved as they use verbal and non-verbal cuing to reach a general understanding of the experience (Banerjee, Alsalman, & Alqafari, 2016). These interactions provide the perfect opportunity to expose MLLs to vocabulary and language skills needed in acquiring a second or third language (Aukrust, 2004).

Spotlight

High-level play in an indirect learning context that offers effective and authentic opportunities for children to try out, practice, and apply the ten Foundational Anchors of literacy. Planning an effective dramatic play theme requires that teachers make themselves aware of children's background knowledge of and experiences with the topic. Providing initial and ongoing learning about the topic is crucial to supporting the background knowledge and vocabulary required for children to engage in play that is at a high level. Teachers must be cognizant of helping children understand the reason each player would use literacy in the play, the construction of the props and the appearance of the print, and the requisite explaining, demonstrating and modeling of the use of each literacy prop. In this way, literacy development can be embedded authentically, enjoyably, and effectively into children's socio-dramatic play.

Teachers are pressured to limit the time for children to remain engaged in play when understanding the cognitive value of play is lacking. Teachers must understand the whys, the whats, and the hows of facilitating high-level play in which children use literacy for purposeful reasons. They must articulate its importance in the curriculum to families, other teachers (especially teachers in the older grades), and administrators.

References

Aukrust, V. (2004). Explanatory discourse in second language learners' peer play. *Discourse Studies, 6*(3), 393–412.

Banerjee, R., Alsalman, A., & Alqafari, S. (2016). Supporting sociodramatic play in preschools to promote language and literacy skills of English language learners. *Early Childhood Education Journal, 44*(4), 299–305.

Bodrova, E., & Leong, D. J. (2007). *Tools of the mind: The Vygotskian approach to early childhood education*. Pearson.

Bodrova, E., & Leong, D. (2015). Vygotskian and post-Vygotskian views on Children's play. *American Journal of Play, 7*(3), 371–388.

Bratton, S. C., Ray, D., Rhine, T., & Jones, L. (2005). The efficacy of play therapy with children: A meta-analytic review of treatment outcomes. *Professional Psychology: Research and Practice, 36*(4), 376–390. https://doi.org/10.1037/0735-7028.36.4.376

Burns, M. S., Griffin, P., & Snow, C. E. (1998). *Preventing reading difficulties in young children: Intellectual property in the information age.* National Academy Press.

Christie, J., Enz, B., & Vukelich, C. (1997). *Teaching language and literacy: Preschool through the elementary grades.* Addison-Wesley-Longman, Inc.

Christie, J. F. E., Johnsen, P., & Peckover, R. B. (1988). The effects of play period duration on Children's play patterns. *Journal of Research in Childhood Education, 3*(2), 123–131. doi: 10.1080/02568548809594934

Crystal, D. (1996). Language play and linguistic intervention. *Child Language Teaching and Therapy, 12*(3), 328–344.

Hirsh-Pasek, K., Golinkoff, R. M., Berk, L. E., & Singer, D. (2009). *A mandate for playful learning in preschool: Applying the scientific evidence.* Oxford University Press.

IPEMA. (2021, October 15). *Home Page.* Retrieved November 12, 2021, from https://ipema.org/

Johnson, J. E., Christie, J. E., & Wardle, F. (2005). *Play, development, and early education.* University of Guelph Humber.

Kirova, A. (2010). Children's representations of cultural scripts in play: Facilitating transition from home to preschool in an intercultural early learning program for refugee children. *Diaspora, Indigenous, and Minority Education: Studies of Migration, Integration, Equity, and Cultural Survival, 4*(2), 74–91.

Landscape Structures, Inc. (2021). *Developmental benefits of play.* Retrieved December 1, 2021, from https://www.playlsi.com/en/playground-planning-tools/education/development-benefits-of-play/

Leong, D., & Bodrova, E. (2012). Assessing and scaffolding: Make-believe play. *Young Children, 67*(1), 28–34.

Linder, T. W. (1993). *Transdisciplinary play-based assessment: A functional approach to working with young children* (Rev. ed.). Paul H Brookes Publishing. Minneapolis, MN.

Morrow, L. M., & Rand, M. K. (1991). Promoting literacy during play by designing early childhood classroom environments. *The Reading Teacher, 44*(6), 396–402.

Neuman, S., & Roskos, K. (1990). Play, print and purpose: Enriching play environments for literacy development. *The Reading Teacher, 44*(3), 214–221.

Niranjanan, J. (2016). Enhancing preschool ELL's early literacy skills through socio-dramatic play. University of Victoria. Project submitted in partial fulfillment of the requirements for the MA in early childhood education, Department of Curriculum and Instruction. http://hdl.handle.net/1828/7127

Pellis, S. M., Pellis, V. C., & Bell, H. C. (2010). The function of play in the development of the social brain. *American Journal of Play, 2*(3), 278–296.

Rice, M. R. (2014). What can we learn from children's play? Using authentic assessment in the early childhood classroom. *Innovations and perspectives.* Virginia Department of Education's Training and Technical Assistance Center. VCU.

Roskos, K., & Christie, J. F. (2017). *Play and literacy in early childhood: Research from multiple perspectives.* Routledge.

Roskos, K. A., Christie, J. F., Widman, S., & Holding, A. (2010). Three decades in: Priming for meta-analysis in play-literacy research. *Journal of Early Childhood Literacy, 10*(1), 55–96. https://doi.org/10.1177/1468798409357580

Touhill, L. (2013). Play-based approaches to literacy and numeracy. NQS PLP e-Newsletter. https://pdf4pro.com/view/play-based-approaches-to-literacy-and-numeracy-5b1760.html

United Nations Convention on the Rights of the Child. (1989). Article 31. https://www.unhcr.org/uk/4aa76b319.pdf

Van Oers, B., & Duijkers, D. (2013). Teaching in a play-based curriculum: Theory, practice and evidence of developmental education for young children. *Journal of Curriculum Studies, 45*(4), 511–534.

Vukelich, C., Enz, B., Roskos, K., & Christie, J. (2020). Helping young children learn language and literacy: Birth through kindergarten. Pearson.

White, R. E. (2012). *The power of play: A research summary on play and learning.* Minnesota Children's Museum.

10 Socio-Dramatic Play

The Teacher's Role

Focus and Big Ideas

- Guided play = free play + teacher guidance
- Responding to trauma with informed practice
- Planning for guided play
- Lesson plan template
- Effective strategies for multi-language learners during play

Guided Play = Free Play + Teacher Guidance

Free play offers children active engagement and complete autonomy to play in whatever way they want. They can choose everything—their play materials, interest area, and actions. "Children thrive when they engage in free play. If we expect children to meet certain specific learning goals, however, some adult support is necessary" (Weisberg, Hirsh-Pasek, Golinkoff, Kittredge, & Klahr, 2016). **Guided play** refers to learning events that intermingle the child-led nature of free play with a focus on learning outcomes and related teacher guidance. For meeting the outcomes of an effective literacy curriculum, the goal is for the children to engage in **high-level socio-dramatic play in which children incorporate functional literacy**. No matter how well-designed and literacy-rich a play environment is, teacher involvement is also necessary to help ensure that children use literacy for specific purposes and specific literacy learning occurs (Pyle, Prioletta, & Poliszczuk, 2018).

Teacher guidance includes teacher pre-planning of the **environment** and active **teacher involvement** (Christensen and Kelly, 2003). Setting up the environment of the dramatic play area to facilitate high-level socio-dramatic play in which children incorporate functional literacy was discussed in Chapter 9. This chapter will focus on the teacher's guidance and involvement directly with the children in order to ensure that specific literacy goals and outcomes are reached.

Teacher Guidance

Observations across early childhood settings reflect a range of teachers' perceptions regarding their own role during children's socio-dramatic play.

DOI: 10.4324/9780429284021-10

In play-based classrooms teachers often leave children on their own to figure things out. This practice is challenged by an increasing body of research
(Christie, 1990). In contrast, some teachers involve themselves in children's
play to the extent that they regularly become co-players. This can result in
children's inability to sustain play without adult participation.

Children's quality of socio-dramatic play and literacy development can be
greatly enriched through various types of teacher interactions during their
play (Christie, 1990; Morrow & Rand, 1991). For example, teachers can assist
non-players to engage in role-playing, help more proficient players enrich
their roles and the complexity of the scenario, and encourage all children to
incorporate literacy use into their roles. With adult guidance, children have
been shown to increase their level of literacy learning in the socio-dramatic
play center than if they are engaging in free play (Morrow, 1990).

Teacher Guidance during Play

Teacher explanations and modeling of the purpose and use of the literacy
materials in the center are the keys to children actually taking advantage of
the literate environment that the teacher has set up (Cutter-Mackenzie &
Edwards, 2013). Using the I Do, We Do, You Do steps of explicit instruction
(see Chapter 6) is highly effective for this purpose. The I Do and We Do
occur prior to children's start of play to help them understand how and why
each player uses literacy. This continues throughout the weeks of play as new
learning and literacy props are introduced.

Demonstration and modeling of the literacy props can be provided in both
large and small groups, depending on the needs of the children and the familiarity and complexity of the prop. Research indicates that children are more
likely to use literacy and stay engaged in complex scenarios over a lengthy
period of time if teachers intentionally take time to explain why and how
people in the theme use literacy (Morrow & Rand, 1991). Just placing literacy props in the center rarely results in children using them appropriately or
even using them at all. The more children learn about the roles of people, the
jobs they do, and how they use literacy in the scenario, the higher the quality
and level of play.

If a child does not stay engaged in a socio-dramatic play center or does
not create high-level play, which incorporates the functional use of literacy,
there may be several reasons. It may be that they are not familiar enough
with the investigation topic and theme. They may need additional modeling
and demonstration to learn to use literacy props. They may not know how
to play cooperatively in a make-believe world. The environment itself may
need redesign. It may be something else. Sometimes lower level play is an
initial response to new props as children take time to explore them, learning
how they work and feel. They may explore the literacy props until they are
satisfied they understand them and then move into high-level play in which
they incorporate functional literacy. This low level, initial exploratory play

can be purposeful for children. However, as explained earlier, if the theme changes every week, the children do not get much beyond reaction to and exploration of props.

The Teacher as Observer

A teacher intentionally observing children's play is called the **Observer** or **On-looker** (Roskos & Neuman, 1993). Observation of children during their socio-dramatic play is the least intrusive type of teacher involvement but critical to making decisions that will support high-level play and children's literacy development. The Observer supports literacy-related play by giving positive reinforcement to the children as they use reading and writing in their play (Roskos & Neuman, 1993). Pragmatically speaking, teachers cannot be Observers for the entire time children are playing. However, as children begin their play and throughout their play, teachers should make time to purposely observe.

With purpose and intent, the Observer watches children at play. The Observer notices whether or not a child is:

- engaging in co-operative, pretend play aligned with the theme;
- taking, playing, and remaining in designated roles;
- exploring or using props appropriately in their play;
- using literacy props;
- using the language of the person (role) they are playing;
- creating increasingly complex scenarios;
- demonstrating an understanding of theme-related content knowledge;
- using advanced vocabulary (investigation and theme specific);
- using increasingly more complex oral language;
- demonstrating understandings about concepts and conventions of print;
- using emergent reading and writing with ease and familiarity;
- interacting positively with other children;
- using language to problem-solve appropriately when issues arise.

Once the environment is determined to be effectively designed, purposeful observation helps the teacher determine the type of guidance or intervention, if any, required to help children engage and remain engaged in high-level play that incorporates functional literacy.

Purposes for teacher intervention in children's play include:

- encouraging children who are not taking a role to engage in the play. Children may be standing back or exploring materials in a literal, non-pretend way;
- encouraging children to increase the complexity of their play;
- encouraging children to include literacy in their play;
- clarifying or untangling confusions;
- scaffolding children's knowledge of literacy as they use literacy props.

Outside and Inside Intervention

If the teacher determines that intervention is required to encourage any of the above player behaviors, they determine the amount and type of support with which to start. Support is organized into **outside and inside intervention** (Christie, 1990; Smilansky, 1968). With **outside intervention**, a teacher makes comments or suggestions to children while they are playing but remains outside of the play. **Inside intervention** can be used if outside intervention is not appropriate to the situation or successful. It requires the teacher to take a role or briefly step into the play as a co-player. It is the most supportive form of intervention and should be limited to a specific goal and then discontinued.

Outside intervention is used, for example, when a child is playing with the controls of the pretend airplane, spinning them around and around in a non-pretend way, while the other three children are engaged in an airport scenario. A teacher, kneeling at the child's level, can say, "Excuse me, sir. These friends want to fly to Arizona, and they need a pilot to take them. Here's a pilot's hat. Can you be the pilot and fly them there?" This type of interaction, while brief, is typically successful for engaging a "nonplayer" in the play scenario.

Another form of **outside intervention** is where the teacher is not in the scenario but shares ideas, reinforces language and actions, asks probing questions, or observes and notes what is supporting the play to keep it at a high level. This type of outside intervention can also be used to scaffold children's understanding of literacy; showing how to use the name chart to write another player's name, helping a child use what they know to write a prescription, or helping the child understand how to choose an item from the bakery, etc.

Inside intervention is used, for example, if children are playing in the restaurant center but all of the players are in the kitchen. The teacher can step into the play, as a **co-player**, take a seat at the table, and say, "Excuse me. I would like to order lunch. Is there someone who can bring me a menu and take my order?" Usually, that is all that is required to promote a scurry of children taking differentiated roles and using literacy props such as the menu and order pad. The teacher can invite another child to sit and order with them so that when they step out of the play, that role will easily be replaced. Children typically respond positively to teachers' inside intervention and imitate the behaviors the teacher models (Christie, 1990; Smilansky, 1968). "Once the imitated behavior becomes part of children's play repertoire, they quickly generalize and modify it to fit new situations" (Christie, 1990). For example, they will transfer the modeled use of an appointment book in a doctor's office to an appointment book in a hair salon. Children also learn from each other as they play. Children will model for others what has been modeled for them. They watch and contribute to each other's attempts to read and write, solidifying understandings the more they engage with print in meaningful and risk-free contexts.

Not all children feel capable of participating in high-level socio-dramatic play. In this case, the teacher must become the **play leader** by modeling, participating or coaching these children as they play, and reinforcing their attempts to try out new language and new actions. This is called **leading the play**. Children who have experienced trauma, children who are shy, withdrawn, or anxious, children with speech and/or language challenges, and children who have not had prior opportunities to participate in high-level, socio-dramatic play may be unable or unwilling to try this out. In these cases, the teacher can become a play leader and gently guide the child. There are many reasons why a child may be reluctant to participate and there are many ways the teacher can help. It is only through active participation that children get the cognitive and literacy benefits from this play, so it is important not to let a pattern of resistance continue.

The most supportive way to lead the play of a reluctant child is to enter the scenario and model the role for the child. "First, I'll be the receptionist and then you be the receptionist." The teacher slips into the role, "I hear the phone ringing. Hello, this is the doctor's office. Are you sick?" The teacher hands the phone to the reluctant child and says, "Let's answer the phone together." Teachers should support the child as needed, reinforcing language and actions that fit the receptionist. The teacher switches back and forth with the reluctant child, drawing in other children playing their roles. As the teacher withdraws support, they need to record their observations and next steps for the child. Modeling as a play leader may be needed several times for a child. It may be needed again when the investigation and theme change.

For the child who becomes confused, loses the thread of the scenario, changes roles, or continues to primarily react to props, the teacher may enter the play as a type of co-player and engage the child in the scenario. The teacher is not expecting the child to know what to do but uses actions and language to guide them. For example, the teacher can arrive at the doctor's office and say, "Hello. I am a new patient. Can you help me get a turn to see the doctor? Are you going to ask me to sign-in?" Reminding the child of his role as receptionist by playing with him and offering suggestions for appropriate actions (in character) can draw the child into the imaginary world. Reinforcing the language and actions is an essential step. Reinforcement gives the child information about what led to their success. "You said, 'Here's the waiting area,' because that's what the receptionist is supposed to say. Now everyone knows you are a good receptionist." Specific reinforcement of the child's actions and words increases the likelihood that the successful behavior will be repeated. Again, this is not a one-time support. The goal is for the child to become a full and independent playmate, acting out ideas.

Responding to Trauma with Informed Practice

Many young children have experienced or witnessed some form of trauma in their short lives and the effects can be far-reaching. Their response behaviors may perplex and overwhelm them as well as their peers and their teachers. All teachers must develop a foundational awareness of current research, best practices, and appropriate identification and responses to trauma-impacted children. Socio-dramatic play provides a valuable context for teachers to observe children engaging in their regular manner of functioning in order to analyze, respond, and intervene appropriately. Seeing a child's activities as misbehavior, rather than a meaningful attempt to understand their world, can deepen their hurt.

Trauma occurs across all races, ethnicities, cultures, and socio-economic households. It can include, among many other things, experiencing parents' divorce, mental or physical illness of a family member, food insecurity, job loss, witnessing or being a victim of violence, homelessness, a car accident, bullying, or moving and changing schools.

- Dean did not participate appropriately in cleaning up the center. He was currently living in a hotel for homeless families and experienced disorganization as a feature of home.
- Anita was now in a stable home with her aunt but had lost her mother to domestic violence and her father to prison. She did not cooperate and became disruptive with play peers in "mom and dad" scenarios.
- Some trauma is not immediately obvious to the teacher. Matt came from a professional home with economic advantage. His father's alcoholism and repeated frightening drunken incidents and rages were a family secret.
- Children provide hints for us when we least expect them. At cleanup time in the play center, Deena yelled to her play peers, "Clean up quick! The cops are coming!"

Children who have been impacted by trauma may have difficulty initiating and sustaining play with children of their own age. They may prefer to engage with younger children because their play skills, reflective of their general interpersonal skills, may be below the level typical for a child of their own age (Ginsburg, 2007; Stubenbort, Cohen, & Trybalski, 2010). Children's capacities for imaginative and creative play can be negatively impacted by trauma (Ginsburg, 2007). Children who have experienced trauma may acquiesce to commands by other children or initiate play scenarios that they do not actually want to play, replaying the helplessness felt during or as a result of a traumatic circumstance. Children who have experienced trauma may not persist in play or develop crucial cognitive and social skills because the feelings that arise during play may overwhelm them (Statman-Weil, 2015). Rather than provide relief, play may actually activate a stress response and the re-living of a traumatic experience.

Children who have experienced trauma may remain playing at a low level. This precludes them from developing healthy relationships with classroom peers and constructing the cognitive strategies and executive function skills typically developed during high-level socio-dramatic play. These skills include self-regulation and the confidence and competence to negotiate and problem-solve with others (Streeck-Fischer & van der Kolk, 2000). These are critical skills for social-emotional as well as cognitive development, including the construction of Foundational Anchors of literacy. When children remain at a low level of play, there is reason for concern. Inside intervention strategies should be initially tried. Additional outside resources may also need to be accessed by the teacher such as the school social worker or psychologist. If child abuse is suspected, the teacher and other school professionals have a legal responsibility to notify Child Protective Services. The end goal of including the child in play and with play peers is important and worth working for.

Sometimes children show us signs of their trauma in obvious ways by acting out, becoming easily frustrated, or breaking rules. While with others, the signs are much more subtle or nonexistent. Aware that many young children experience trauma, some teachers create a housekeeping or home center *as well as* a themed socio-dramatic play center in their classrooms. Providing a specific center **or** a place in another center that feels safe and is conducive to children taking a familiar familial role is very important. A familiar home center and props may provide comfort. If your classroom cannot support two separate centers, consider including a small rocking chair, baby blankets, and multiracial baby dolls in either the themed center or another center such as the library area. Small world play, dollhouse, firehouse, or auto center, which allows the child to play alone or with another child, can also create a safe means for the child to play at the theme and maintain a sense of control and safety. This may be an opportunity for intervention. Like the lifeguard at the pool, the teacher is often the first, and perhaps the only adult, to notice when children are behaving in non-typical ways. The teacher must take the necessary time and action to get to know and understand the child. Spending time with the child one-to-one may provide them with the opportunity to disclose concerns, share grief, or just have someone with whom to talk.

Planning for Guided Play

Guided play is an indirect literacy learning context. Teacher indirect literacy learning events are as carefully planned as teacher direct instructional events. They are defined as carefully planned opportunities in which children can choose to engage purposefully with literacy, to accomplish a goal, and use it either independently or with peers. If you have never planned or are unsure about planning for high-level socio-dramatic play in which children use literacy for functional purposes, it may, at first, seem overwhelming. We have found that thinking about it in terms of what we should consider before, during, and after the children play the theme simplifies the process.

Using an Assigned Curriculum

Teachers are sometimes required to use specific curricula. A curriculum selected by school districts, corporate childcare facilities, or non-profit agencies, however, may not include themes for the dramatic play center that are easily "playable." It is therefore often difficult to identify and plan a robust socio-dramatic play center in which children can take roles, create complex scenarios, engage in high-level play, and use literacy for functional purposes related to the theme. Listed in Figure 10.1 are themes from various popular curricula that do not initially lend themselves to robust socio-dramatic centers and ideas for the individual teacher to expand on them.

Required curriculum theme	Expanded socio-dramatic play center
Clothes	• A dry cleaner and/or laundromat • A clothing store
Community helpers Helpers should not initially be combined. Children should learn about and play with each one separately. This enables them to develop deep background knowledge and well-developed scenarios	• A fire station • A police station • A hospital • A doctor's office or health clinic • A recycling center
Fall	• A farmer's market; it can be connected to an apple orchard or farm
Dinosaurs	• A fossil dig (children play as paleontologists). • A Nature and Science Museum
Space	• A space shuttle or rocket ship includes a space area to explore with "moon rocks" for astronauts (scientists) to gather and study
Tubes and tunnels	• A post office (mailing tubes can be included in the props) • A train station (create a tunnel and tracks)
All about me (Typically, the first theme of the school year)	• Begin the school year with a home theme. Include props suggested by the children that reflect their own homes. Change after three to four weeks • Restaurants or markets that reflect the culture and community of the children
Construction	• A construction site; possibly connected to an architect's office in which children can create blueprints • Authentically aligning the socio-dramatic play center with the block area

Figure 10.1 Overcoming the Limits of Assigned Curriculum

Field Trips that Support the Foundational Anchors of Literacy

Field trips can provide children with meaningful and memorable opportunities to learn about a particular topic of investigation. Thoughtful planning is required for a field trip to be successful, enjoyable, meet the identified literacy outcomes, and truly support the development of the Foundational Anchors of literacy.

Field trips are frequently used as a culminating experience, a celebration of learning. They are, however, a significant way to build children's background knowledge, vocabulary, and general understanding about a topic early in the investigation. Teachers should consider scheduling a field trip closer to the beginning. Children tend to play at a higher level *after* they have actually visited a fire station, an ice cream parlor, a pizza restaurant, the aquarium, a science and nature museum, or a pet store. Children see adults using literacy for functional purposes and understand where literacy fits into their play.

Field trips level the playing field for children's content knowledge and vocabulary, narrowing the gap between those children who seem to know every fact and detail about dinosaurs and those who know almost nothing and are perplexed by their strange sounding names. Field trips provide a common language and experience for a class, encouraging children to perceive themselves as a community of learners. Teachers who have the opportunity should take children on multiple field trips for as many of their investigations as possible. Field trips do not have to be elaborate, expensive, or require school or district transportation. Children may walk to a local business or take advantage of public transportation or transportation provided by parents and other volunteers.

Planning a Field Trip

Teachers should plan for a field trip in much the same way that they plan for socio-dramatic play. They thoughtfully consider what they can do before, during, and after the adventure to ensure it goes smoothly and helps children build critical content knowledge, vocabulary, and Foundational Anchors of literacy.

Before the field trip:

- Field trips should take place after children have done some initial investigation of the topic, e.g., listening to read-alouds about the topic, learning about and exploring artifacts and props, talking with guests who have experience on the topic, and playing the theme. After two to three weeks of an investigation, children should be prepared to learn about the topic outside of the classroom.
- It is **highly** recommended that the teacher visits the location before the day the children arrive. Meeting and developing relationships with the manager and other people who will be working there during the field trip is extremely helpful for everyone. Sharing what you want the children to focus on and learn goes a long way in preparing the adults for

your visit. It often encourages them to go the extra mile and plan special things for the children because they know what you want the children to get out of it.

- The day before the field trip, the teacher should use a teacher-directed literacy activity and guide the children to create a chart and dictate a list of what and who they think they are going to see when they visit. Children should be urged to hypothesize how the adults will use literacy at the location. This focuses the children's thinking about the actual trip and builds anticipation for their visit.

The day of the field trip:

- On the day of the field trip, revisit the chart with the children, reading aloud each item and person they expect to see. This further prepares the children's thinking and focuses their attention on specific materials and adult behaviors they expect to see. Helping children plan ahead like this encourages them to practice executive function and discourages them from reacting to everything within their sight. Including the volunteers in this activity helps the adults to focus and talk with the children during the field trip about the things they see.
- If possible, there should be enough volunteers so that each adult can be responsible for no more than four children. Each child should have a partner because it encourages oral language use and cooperative learning to construct and solidify understandings about what they see.
- Talking with the volunteers and providing them with a list of specific things to look for and discuss helps them to use the advanced, Tier 3 vocabulary of the topic and engage the children in topic-related conversations. Everyone should be looking for how the adults at the location are using reading and writing in their jobs.
- Bring the children's attention to signs and labels, encouraging them to use cues to hypothesize about their meaning. Adults should respond to their attempts, coaching and solidifying what they know about print.

After returning from the field trip:

- As a follow-up to the field trip, bring the children's attention back to their dictated list. Read through each item, discussing whether or not they saw what they thought they would see and why. Encourage children to converse rather than simply providing a yes or no. This is a great opportunity to further develop their oral language, clarify content knowledge, and use the advanced vocabulary of the theme. Ask the children if anything surprised them. Cross out the things they did not see. Add the new things they saw.
- Refer to the visit and discuss with the children whether or not they should add any theme-related or literacy props to the socio-dramatic play center. Follow up with these.

- Keep the chart in the classroom throughout the time the children are investigating the topic. Ensure the children know where it is located and that it is at their eye level. Remind them that they can read the chart during independent Choice Time. Opportunities to revisit this list are a talk-to-text strategy to support children's emerging understandings about print.

Lesson Plan Template

Planning for high-quality socio-dramatic play in which literacy is used for functional purposes can initially feel overwhelming. Figure 10.2 offers a template to support both the planning of an investigation and the related theme of the dramatic play center.

Planning the investigation and the theme of the dramatic play center	Notes and reflection
1. Topic:_____ 2. Theme: (dramatic play center)_____	
3. List five to eight concepts you want the children to **learn about this topic** (content knowledge)	
4. **Background knowledge** How will you determine what the children already know about the theme of the dramatic play center? (schema) What type of knowledge about the theme of the dramatic play center will you help them build **before** they play? What key vocabulary (Tier 3) do you want them to learn and use?	
5. **List the roles of people who participate in the theme:** (who works, visits, lives there?)	
6. **Design the dramatic play center**	
7. **List and describe the props**	
8. **How does each person (role) use literacy?**	
9. **List and describe each literacy prop. Explain how each prop is used and why?** 10. **Introduction/demonstration/modeling use of literacy props:** (whole group, small group)	
11. **Identify and describe each of the Foundational Anchors of literacy that you plan for children to develop through engagement in high-level play on this topic and theme?**	

Figure 10.2 Lesson Plan Template. Supporting High-Level Play in Which Children Use Literacy for Functional Purposes (see Appendix) *(Continued)*

1. Oral language
2. Background knowledge and vocabulary
3. Book awareness
4. Alphabet knowledge and phonics
5. Phonological and phonemic awareness
6. Print concepts
7. Emerging reading
8. Emerging writing
9. Positive dispositions toward literacy and literacy learning
10. Executive function

12. Resources:
    Read-aloud books: (informational and fiction)
    Resource books on the topic (for adults):
    Resource and emerging reading books (informational and
    fiction for children):
    Videos:
    Guest speakers:
    Field trip(s):
    Additional resources:	

Topic-related materials in other centers: Ensure that these materials are introduced to children so that they understand how they can be used and authentically connected to the theme.	**Related resource materials in the writing center** (Theme related: e.g., extra prescription pads, clipboards, blank books, list of children's names, printed words that children can copy and might use in their play)	
Introduction of the dramatic play center theme		
To the children: (i.e., read aloud, video, special guest, guided small group rotations)	**To the parents**: (i.e., letter, bulletin board)	
Small groups: (e.g., creating literacy props, language experience stories, class and individual book making)		
Share the learning		
How will children personally respond to their learning about the theme and the play? (substantive conversation, revisit their work products created along the way, language experience charts, art, book-making, Assisted Writing, and drawing)		
Celebrate the learning		
How will children share their learning? (with each other, with families, with the larger community if appropriate?)		

Figure 10.2 (Continued)

Reflect on the children's literacy learning	
Analyze and reflect on the children's use and understanding of each Foundational Anchor of literacy as it relates to the goals and outcomes set.	

1. Oral language
2. Background knowledge and vocabulary
3. Book awareness
4. Alphabet knowledge and phonics
5. Phonological and phonemic awareness
6. Print concepts
7. Emergent reading
8. Emergent writing
9. Positive dispositions toward literacy
10. Executive function

Analysis and self-reflection
Consider:

1. What worked well?
2. What was challenging? What would you do differently next time?
3. Describe the children's use of literacy?
4. What supported their use of literacy?
5. What outside and inside interventions were effective?
6. What would you do differently next time to support literacy learning?

Figure 10.2 (Continued)

Effective Strategies for Multi-Language Learners during Play

Research indicates that high-level dramatic play is a very effective strategy for constructing and extending oral language in children whose first language is not English (Dupree & Iverson, 1994). Remember that children will play what they know and **authentic socio-dramatic play leads to meaningful learning in language and vocabulary** (Salinas-Gonzalez, Arreguín-Anderson, & Alanís, 2018). Therefore, teachers should create socio-dramatic play themes that are culturally relevant to children. This ensures that they can engage in and contribute to high-level play. Determining the actual theme for this type of play can be aided by listening to children's everyday conversations, particularly as they discuss their family activities (Salinas-Gonzalez et al., 2018) Intentionally make time for children to discuss their home lives and family outings, for example, during whole group morning meetings, read-alouds, and sharing times. In addition, listen to conversations *between* children as they communicate and describe their interests to each other. Grocery stores, restaurants, and family-living themes should include examples of food from all children's cultures. Signs, menus, and other literacy props can be printed in dual languages. Observe the children's play frequently to add additional props necessary to expand the theme, support their language use, and hold their attention. Add props gradually, in phases, to build on children's knowledge, moving from basic items and use of print to secondary (Salinas-Gonzalez et al., 2018). Encourage parents to contribute props to the theme. Not only does this lend authenticity to the play but opens the door for parents to be comfortably involved in their children's education.

Play during Second-Language Acquisition

During play, children who are learning English as another language can try out their understanding of the new language in a risk-free, supportive environment. Children's current stage of second-language acquisition (or third, etc.) (Krashen & Terrell, 1998) will determine the extent to which they actually engage in conversation. In the **first** stage, called the **preproduction,** silent, or receptive stage, children may not speak in the classroom language at all but focus on watching the actions of play peers, trying to make sense of vocabulary. Multi-language learners (MLLs) may repeat the language of the other children, practicing what it feels like to talk in the classroom language. Children in the **second stage** of second-language acquisition, the **early production** stage, may try to engage in the play by using the vocabulary and even short phrases that they have learned. They may use two-word sentences. They are collecting new words rapidly in this phase and benefit from explicit teaching of the vocabulary that will be used in the play. Children in the **third** stage, the **speech emergence** stage, combine or connect words into phrases and produce simple sentences. During the **fourth** stage of second-language acquisition, the **intermediate fluency** stage, true conversations emerge. They begin to think in a second language. MLLs need time to talk without being corrected. Remember to encourage families to continue to talk and read aloud to their children in their native language. Proficiency in a first language will make learning a second language easier (Krashen & Terrell, 1998).

Providing children with this time to listen and observe without teacher intervention during play is important. Effective planning for play for MMLs requires that teachers identify important and useful vocabulary. Explicitly teaching one or two theme-related words a day at group time is crucial. Teachers should also intentionally observe vocabulary that an individual child might benefit from learning. This can be introduced or reinforced during children's play and repeated at different times during the day.

Spotlight

Free play is an important type of play from which children can learn and grow. It has a place in every early learning environment. Our focus is on how play can significantly contribute to literacy learning, specifically how to plan for and develop high-level socio-dramatic play that includes children's use of functional literacy. Socio-dramatic play can provide an opportunity for children to notice how and why literacy is used in the world of adults and use reading and writing for their own purposes during play. In order for children to maximize the impact on their Foundational Anchors of literacy, the play must be at a high level. For example:

- children play together in a pretend setting, e.g., shoe store;
- children assume roles determined by who would actually be in the setting, e.g., shoe salesperson, customer, and shelf stockperson;
- children use literacy, reading and writing, to accomplish the tasks their role would have to accomplish, e.g., salesperson writes receipts, customer fills in the "Return or Exchange" form, and the shelf stockperson reads signs to put shoes on the correct shelf;
- the teacher provides means for children to build cumulative background knowledge and vocabulary about the topic, e.g., books, videos, field trip to a shoe store, and a visit from a shoe salesperson;
- The teacher observes and intervenes if needed, in order to support high-level play.

MLLs benefit from the opportunities for language acquisition when playing pretend and using as much language as they can during their current stage of acquisition. Parents can help build background knowledge about the current topic and the world, in general, by maintaining their use of their native or primary language. Planning for play takes time and energy, resources, and effort. The pay-off is literacy learning.

References

Christensen, A., & Kelly, K. (2003). No time for play: Throwing the baby out with the bath water. *The Reading Teacher, 56*(6) 528–530.

Christie. J. F. (1990). Dramatic play: A context for meaningful engagements. *The Reading Teacher, 43*(8), 542–545.

Cutter-Mackenzie, A., & Edwards, S. (2013). Pedagogical play types: What do they suggest for learning about sustainability in early childhood education? *International Journal of Early Childhood, 45*(3), 327–346. doi:10.1007/s13158-013-0082-5.

Dupree H. & Iverson, S. (1994). Early literacy in the classroom: A new standard for young children. Bothell, WA: The Wright Group.

Ginsburg, K. R. 2007. The importance of play in promoting healthy child development and maintaining strong parent–child bonds. *Pediatrics, 119*(1), 182–191. http://pediatrics.aappublications.org/content/119/1/182.full.

Krashen, S. D., & Terrell, T. D. (1998). *The natural approach: Language acquisition in the classroom.* Prentice Hall Europe, Pearson Education, Upper Saddle River, NJ.

Morrow, L. (1990). Preparing the classroom environment to promote literacy during play. *Early Childhood Research Quarterly, 5*(4), 537–554.

Morrow, L. M., & Rand, M. K. (1991). Promoting literacy during play by designing early childhood classroom environments. *The Reading Teacher, 44*(6), 396–402.

Pyle, A., Prioletta, J., & Poliszczuk, D. (2018). The play-literacy interface in full-day kindergarten classrooms. *Early Childhood Education Journal, 46*(1), 117–127.

Roskos, K., & Neuman, S. B. (1993). Descriptive observations of adults' facilitation of literacy in young children's play. *Early Childhood Research Quarterly, 8*(1), 77–97.

Salinas-Gonzalez, I., Arreguín-Anderson, M. G., & Alanís, I. (2018). Supporting language: Culturally rich dramatic play. *Teaching Young Children, 11*(2), 1–7.

Smilansky, S. (1968). *The effects of sociodramatic play on disadvantaged preschool children.* John Wiley & Sons

Statman-Weil, K. (2015). Creating trauma sensitive classrooms. *Young Children, 70*(2), 72–79.

Streeck-Fischer, A., & van der Kolk, B. A. (2000). Down will come baby, cradle and all: Diagnostic and therapeutic implications of chronic trauma on child development. *Australian & New Zealand Journal of Psychiatry, 34*(6), 903–918. doi:10.1080/000486700265.

Stubenbort, K., Cohen, M. M., & Trybalski, V. (2010). The effectiveness of an attachment-focused treatment model in a therapeutic preschool for abused children. *Clinical Social Work Journal, 38*(1), 51–60. https://doi.org/10.1007/s10615-007-0107-3

Weisberg, D. S., Hirsh-Pasek, K., Golinkoff, R. M., Kittredge, A. K., & Klahr, D. (2016). Guided play: Principles and practices. *Current Directions in Psychological Science, 25*(3), 177–82. doi:10.1177/0963721416645512

11 Reading Aloud

Focus and Big Ideas

- Early read-aloud experiences
- Why is reading aloud so important?
- Shared book reading aloud
- Creating text sets

Early Read Aloud Experiences

After reading a **text set** that included several versions of *The 3 Little Pigs*, Miss Joy asked the children to consider which version was their favorite. This led to a substantive conversation with the children about the character of the wolf. Some children thought he was bad, and others thought he was nice, but had to eat the pigs to stay alive.

> Armisha was very clear. "I like the *virgin* where the wuff don't eat other pig characters. Like at our class. We don't bite."
>
> "Oh, you like the *version* of the story where the wolf doesn't eat the pigs. The characters are following the rules of our class!"
>
> (The teacher modeled the new vocabulary *version*)

Armisha's attempt to use Tier 2 (Academic vocabulary) words and to participate in the discussion in a familiar context indicates she is adding to her understanding about language and literacy. Miss Joy encouraged the other children to consider Armisha's point.

"Do you agree with Armisha? Do you agree that the best *version* is where no characters get eaten?" And the conversation continued…

The value of reading aloud to children is not only counted by the number of books a child hears in the early years, but also the quality of the interactions between the adult and the child "around" the book, before, during, and after the read-aloud. The interactions that occur between adults and child/children during the read-aloud are some of the most powerful learning opportunities teachers can create. There is little or no opportunity for literacy learning when read-aloud is used as a time-filler, background entertainment

DOI: 10.4324/9780429284021-11

for bathroom breaks, or as randomly chosen books that connect to nothing else in the day. Well-planned, well-implemented read-aloud, and Shared Readings impact the development of the Foundational Anchors of literacy. Children must learn how to interact with books and become cognitively active when being read to, especially children who have not been read to frequently at home or early care. Watching television, including children's television, is generally passive and can be tuned in and out as the child does other things, playing with cars, eating lunch, or falling asleep. There are few demands on executive function.

According to a New York State Early Childhood Data Report (2008), data show that 48.4% of parents of children under the age of six reported that their children were read to every day. Over 20% of parents of children under six reported that they read aloud to their child two or fewer days per week. Nearly 10% reported not reading to their child at all. This data is represented in Figure 11.1.

What does that mean in a group of pre-school children? Four-year-old children who have been read to daily arrive in kindergarten having had nearly 1500 **experiences** listening to books, talking about books, choosing books, finding favorite books, and enjoying social emotional interactions with an adult and a book (see Figure 11.1). These positive experiences foster *initial* understanding about the role of print and plant the seeds of curiosity about how print works.

Why Is Reading Aloud to Children So Important?

Research indicates that reading aloud to children is the single most important activity for building the knowledge and dispositions required for eventual reading success (Lonigan, Schatschneider, & Westberg, 2008). But why is that? Becoming familiar with how books and written language work may have been modeled for some children more than a thousand times by the time they are four. Each experience potentially includes rich conversation with the adult reader. Children with this wealth of experience arrive at the same time, in the same settings and classrooms as children who have rarely or never

Parent–Child Read-Aloud Experiences by Age 4		
Children read to daily (48.4%)	**Children read to occasionally** (20%)	**Children not read to** (10%)
1500 experiences with books Source: Created from data in the NYS Early Childhood Data Report	200–400 experiences with books	0 experiences with books

Figure 11.1 Parent-Child Read-Aloud Experiences by Age 4

heard a book read-aloud or perhaps have never even seen an adult read. The children with limited read-aloud experiences are thus **school-dependent**, meaning that school-like settings (preschool or childcare) and classroom teachers must provide the contextual experiences and explicit teaching they need to foster the same strong Foundational Anchors of literacy their peers developed at home or early care during many unplanned literacy events. School-dependent children need their read-aloud experiences to be as powerful as possible, making every book count, in order to develop understandings their peers had years to accumulate. For teachers, knowing how to get the most learning out of read-aloud events is important.

Shared Book Reading Aloud

"The term read aloud has been applied generally to a literacy event in which the teacher reads the text aloud while children listen and may interact to varying degrees. Other terms specify more or less child interaction and control over the experience" (Sanden, Mattoon, & Osorio, 2021)

The label **Shared Book Reading Aloud** applies to "an interactive method of reading books aloud to children during which the adult encourages the children's engagement in book related conversation" (Milburn, Girolametto, Weitzman, & Greenberg, 2014, pg. 109). This is not to be confused with **Shared Reading**, an event where teachers and children have eyes on large print in classroom charts, poems, Morning Messages, and Big Books. The procedures and instructional goals of these two literacy events are quite different. Shared Reading is explained in Chapter 15.

Shared book reading means that the teacher has planned an introduction to pull children into the story, pre taught unfamiliar vocabulary and idioms, and marked places in the text to stop and invite conversation about what the children are thinking. The goal is to interact with the children while helping children interact with the book and each other. Storybook reading in early childhood classrooms has historically been a one-way activity. The teacher reads the book, does most of the talking, and asks a few questions before and after the reading. Children are primarily a passive audience, quiet and listening (or not) to the adult read and comment on the book. Research, however, has long disputed this way of reading aloud to children, indicating that critical opportunities for literacy learning are lost (Whitehurst et al., 1994). When teachers engage young children as active participants in their own thinking, talking, listening, and learning from the book, they are supporting comprehension.

It is clear from seeing how Alize prepares for and organizes her *shared book reading aloud* time that the practice of grabbing a book and reading "if time allows" will not suffice (Figure 11.2). It never has. Unplanned, random practice may replicate what happens in some homes. The children we serve, however, must have well-planned and well-implemented practice for the purpose of developing strong Foundational Anchors.

Anchor Under Construction

In the fall, Alize begins her *shared book reading aloud* with her four-year-old class with short books that have brief text. She sits with her side to her students so they can see the pictures the entire time she is reading, or else she uses a document camera to share the pictures while she reads. Because listening to a book is new or unfamiliar to 20% or more of her students, she keeps the sessions brief and reads during several times in the day. As this community of learners progresses, she can offer longer, more complex texts. She provides small group support to her children who have limited language and vocabulary, multi-language learners, and children with learning challenges/struggles, prior to whole group reading to make the books understandable. She chooses books by authors and illustrators that represent diverse backgrounds and diverse cultural perspectives. She offers many genres, including poetry and informational texts to provide the greatest range of experience.

Figure 11.2 Planning for Shared Book Reading Aloud

Using Shared Book Reading Aloud to Support the Foundational Anchors of Literacy

Let's look at each of the anchors that can be constructed and extended during an effective *shared book read aloud*. In order to choose the most appropriate books and plan the most appropriate interactions, the teacher must be familiar with each child's background knowledge and current anchor status. In this way, the teacher can build on what children already know about literacy, genre, and informational topics. By choosing books that expand or enlighten the topic and theme of socio-dramatic play, the teacher helps the children create scenarios to play out.

Shared book read alouds have the potential to support the construction of all ten Foundational Anchors of literacy. Shared book readings include very effective strategies for developing active listening and reading comprehension strategies such as problem-solving, making connections, and drawing inferences. This pedagogy is best practice in early childhood education and supports children transitioning from active listeners to active readers. Stories read repeatedly with expression become stories that children emergently read in the voice of their caregiver or teacher and later influence their attempts at fluency.

1. **Oral language**

    Listening comprehension, the ability to listen to and construct the meaning of a text, is a part of enjoying a read-aloud. When children put their own responses into language, oral language increases. There is a positive impact on children's literacy development when adults encourage young children to think deeply and talk around and about the actual text during read-alouds (Wasik & Bond, 2001). Teachers should encourage children's spontaneous conversation and to pose and respond to each other's questions as they are engaged with the book. When children have to raise hands and wait for acknowledgement, the teacher remains in control of interactions. Talking about and practicing cognitive actions during read-aloud give children some understanding of their own thinking. This ability to think about your own thinking is called **metacognition**. Language play and flexibility with language are enhanced by the wide variety of texts the teacher carefully selects to share.

2. **Vocabulary and background knowledge**

   Vocabulary and background knowledge are infinitely expandable. Learners developing the tools of self-regulation/executive functions will notice and ask about words and ideas that are unfamiliar. Academic vocabulary is increased through repeated use during both reading and child talk. They will add these words to their receptive and expressive vocabulary. As the teacher provides planned vocabulary teaching before reading and interaction about the book during reading, children learn to use unfamiliar words from the book and from one another.

   Content and concept books such as number books, color books, shape books, and informational books are all excellent choices for read-aloud. They support children's development of vocabulary and background knowledge. Teachers should select books that will support specific instructional goals, whether the goal is the introduction of shapes or colors, initial information about the content, or more complex aspects of the content. If the theme of the socio-dramatic play area is a shoe store, finding books about getting new shoes, how shoes are made, or shoes around the world can add to play. Informational text is not just non-fiction. *The Very Busy Spider* by Eric Carle (1984) is a fictional story that illustrates the process of building an orb web. *The Mitten* by Jan Brett has a large number of animal names despite being fictional. Steve Jenkins, on the other hand, writes engaging non-fiction on many topics such as the *Beetle Book* (Jenkins, 2012) and *Biggest, Strongest, Fastest* (Jenkins 1995). The illustrations offer children a chance to study and understand many concepts within and outside of their own world.

3. **Book awareness**

   Repeated experiences showing how books work, front to back, left to right, constancy of print, relationship of print to pictures, and how to think about the content or story are cumulative in building a strong foundation. Intentionally sharing a wide variety of **genres** (e.g., poetry, fairy tales and fables from around the world, biographies and autobiographies of well-known figures, memoir, informational book, and story books) introduces and teaches children about the many ways authors can choose to write. Watching children discover how wide and deep the world of books can be is a thrill. When children begin to purposely pursue their own interests through books, teachers experience a satisfying result of reading aloud. When children become interested in megalodons in response to a popular movie, they seem amazed that a teacher could offer five books with pictures and information. They will make books of their own, just like they make towers with blocks. Making things is what they do to explore and understand their environment.

4. **Phonological awareness and phonemic awareness**

    By including books with rhyme and alliteration, the teacher can bring the children's attention to these literary features. The authors' use of rhyme and alliteration (words that begin with the same, e.g., Bando is a big, bold, brown bear.) are pleasurable to read and say. Calef Brown's book, *Polka Bats and Octopus Slacks* (Brown, 2005) is a favorite in many classrooms because it is a whimsical sing-songy book with poems children can soon recite. Reading books such as Llama, Llama, Red Pajamas (Dewdney, 2005) helps children develop an ear for the nuances of our language and encourages them to notice and manipulate onsets and rimes. Children will begin to notice and name these uses of the sounds of language when they listen to the teacher read. Being able to hear these parts of words (first sound, ending rhymes) is essential to reading and writing development.

5. **Alphabet knowledge and phonics**

    The use of quality alphabet books is an important part of reading aloud. Helping children see that the letters and sounds in the book are in the same order as the classroom alphabet chart helps them transfer learning from one circumstance to another. Letter names, sounds, upper and lower case forms, and the order of the alphabet are all available during shared book reading aloud (see Chapter 14).

6. **Print concepts**

    Shared book reading can easily be used to demonstrate book orientation (front to back of the book) and page orientation (the print is different than the pictures). Other print concepts are best taught in small groups and Shared Reading. Print concepts should not be emphasized when children are not interacting with print.

7. **Emerging reading**

    Emerging reading is heavily influenced by the fluent flow of the read-aloud. Children will imitate the reader's voice as they emergently read or retell a story. The teacher's reading fluency, with both expression and flow, increases listening comprehension and the child's future comprehension as a reader. Modeling is an effective strategy for developing reading fluency.

8. **Emerging writing**

As children learn and understand more about how texts work, they use that understanding to create their own books or Story Pictures during Assisted Writing time. Retelling a familiar story, innovating on a story (Goldilocks and the three Martians), using a text structure (All About My Dog or How to Get Dressed for Dance Class), or creating illustrations like Denise Fleming are all things emerging writers do as children learn to transfer knowledge from read-aloud to Assisted Writing.

Finding number and shape books that children enjoy can spawn another burst of excitement for Assisted Writing time as well. These books often transfer to children's writing. Making a number, letter, or color book is a text structure that children can follow as a model while sharing their own interests. Cedric made a fish number book because he had fish tanks at home (see Figure 11.3).

9. **Positive attitudes toward literacy and literacy learning**

Reading aloud to young children provides an opportunity for children to develop positive attitudes about literacy. As the parent or teacher reads and rereads interesting and engaging books, children come to recognize books as a source of joy and fun. They experience laughter, anticipation, and even suspense with an attentive adult. The big bad wolf can be frightening in a safe environment, and so exciting. Goose, Bear, and Fox (Alone Together, Bloom, 2014) can provide entertainment and companionship. Building this positive association with books and stories increases the child's desire to learn to read and to enjoy reading or looking at books independently. As their positive experiences accumulate, they become emerging readers, playing at, willing to attempt, and approximating being readers. They learn the power of books to inform them about everything from superheroes to the life of the pangolin.

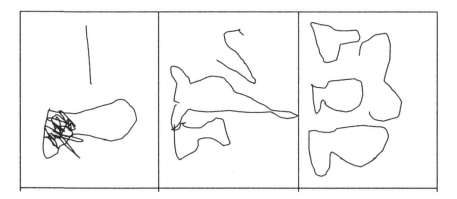

Figure 11.3 Cedric's Number Book about Fish

10. Executive function

Executive function skills include many aspects of behavior and thinking that can be developed and practiced during a shared book reading aloud. Like other Foundational Anchors, there is no limit to the depth and breadth of this anchor. Teachers support this development with explicit expectations for behavior and thought, and generous support for inexperienced children to meet the expectations. Every time a child practices and uses their executive function during classroom activities, the brain changes and strengthens their ability to manage their attention and responses.

Pitfalls to Avoid

Sometimes children bring books from home that do not meet the criteria for quality shared book read-alouds, do not fit with the current text set, or are inappropriate. These books can be shared during choice or center time with a small group, they can be displayed in the class library with the child's name on a sticky note, so others know who to ask about the book, or acknowledged in some other way. Including and celebrating books from home strengthens home-school connections which is an important goal, but these impromptu sharings must not be allowed to replace a planned, intentional read-aloud time for the class.

It is safe to say that during most story book reading, children are *exposed* to many of the Foundational Anchors of literacy. However, *exposure* is not the intended outcome and will not be sufficient to effectively add to children's funds of knowledge in a significant way, especially for the 50% of children without much prior read-aloud experience. Shared book reading aloud is a high-impact activity teachers must intentionally plan and explicitly teach to a desired outcome, thereby building and strengthening the Foundational Anchors of literacy. The practice of randomly pulling a book off the shelf or reading whatever children bring from home to the whole group during read-aloud provides only exposure and is not good practice.

As teachers collect and curate a shared book read-aloud library for themselves, they should organize a way to keep a summary of each text, notes on vocabulary, idioms and abstract ideas, an introduction, any realia needed, translations of the book or simple versions of the story, and additional information required for extra support. Large and small sticky notes are often used for this purpose. This will support the teacher in planning for the same read-aloud with different groups of children, year after year. Teachers will continually add new books that they discover and weed out books that do not engage the children.

Books presented in read-alouds should be available for children to peruse during independent emerging reading time. Many teachers prefer to have a bookshelf to which the children do not have access with their read-aloud book collection and that is understandable. Books are expensive and the teacher is developing a strong set of read–alouds to use long term. However, a second copy of a book the teacher has taught the children to love is another way to invite children to participate in literacy.

Creating Text Sets that Support Comprehension

A **text set** consists of several books that have a common thread or literary feature (e.g., setting, characters, events, problems, solutions, theme, genre, or organizing structure). Many teachers have created wonderful sets that include the same expansive vocabulary, or the same author or illustrator. Creating a text set is the intentional connecting of one text to another in order to support assimilation and accommodation of new information, to increase the level of language comprehension, and to scaffold understandings about books.

Sharing text sets with children builds an understanding that books on the same topic can explain things and be organized in very different ways. As teachers begin to create text sets, they will notice that children respond to each book in a set with anticipation. A set that lasts four days with the fifth day being a reread day of a class favorite has been an efficient pace for very young children. The number of days exploring a set may be extended over time. Text sets should also be created to align with class investigations and themes of socio-dramatic play.

Here are some examples of ways to group books together in text sets. Teaching children where to focus their attention within the set is essential if children are to fully benefit from these sets. Are you teaching them to compare characters, notice literary or informational structures, or accumulating knowledge on a topic? Share with children the basis of the set in order for them to focus attention on that feature. Some ideas for text sets are offered below.

Collect a text set:

- **in which all the stories have the same setting**. For example, when all the texts occur in winter, it gives children many opportunities to hear and discuss ideas like tracks in the snow, hibernation, shivering, and melting. Creating a chart of winter words during interactive writing helps focus attention on the vocabulary. Consider settings such as farms, in forests, or at sea and bring to the fore the literary feature of *setting*. Where and when the story happens affects the course of the story.
- **in which each book has the same main character or topic**. For example, when every book has a rabbit as a character or as the subject, including both fiction and informational texts, the set gives children opportunities to consider and talk about what is true and what is make-believe. Books about owls, rabbits, pirates, or ballerinas (or any interesting topic) with a mix of fiction and informational texts deepen children's knowledge and broaden their vocabulary.

- **in which the main characters share the same trait**. For example, the main character is brave, or jealous, or sly. This set helps children notice and name character traits. Brave Irene by William Steig (1986) and Flossie and the Fox by Patricia McKissack (1986) are books with brave girls as the main characters. Books with characters that share common features support children's prediction and comprehension (see Figure 11.4).
- **in which the character has to solve the same or similar problems.** For example, books in which the character has to have a babysitter, has a new sibling, or gets sick, all show solutions to problems children may encounter. Opportunities to see various solutions to a singular problem provide a means for children to learn to consider more than one response to a situation, a skill critical to executive function.
- **by one author/illustrator**. This gives children insight into how and why people create books. A collection of books by the same author or illustrated by the same artist can create a connected set of text with features that can be compared and explored in their own writing and artistic creations.
- **in a series**. Series with the same main character, such as Pete the Cat (Dean, 2006), support the predictability of the story and support children in using what they know about the character to predict and comprehend. Frog and Toad series by Arnold Lobel (2003), Commander Toad Series by Jane Yolan (1996), or the Mercy Watson series by Kate DiCamilla (2011) are books that each have their own story but that invite children to build and expand their background knowledge.
- **many versions of the same story.** As with all book selection, these stories must represent a variety of cultural backgrounds and a variety of authors. European folk and fairy tales do not represent the diversity of cultural backgrounds to which all children feel an affinity. Many cultures

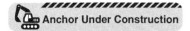
Anchor Under Construction

Ms. Kari had chosen a text set for the children featuring sneaky or sly characters. This character study involved noticing what the character did and said that showed they were sly or sneaky, a concept the children had, but for which they lacked words.

She had already read *The Enormous Crocodile* (Dahl, 1978) and the traditional tale, *How the Bear Lost his Tail*. Jason, a five year old, wrote her a note and read it to her, *Ms. Kari I hav a book of a sli karaktr*. The next day, he brought *Fantastic Mr. Fox* (Dahl, 2016) from his home library. He had seen a familiar book in a new way! And in this instance, Ms. Kari was able to plan and include Jason's book in the text set.

Figure 11.4 Jason Expands the Teacher's Text Set with a Book from Home

have similar cautionary tales which caution against being untruthful, unkind, or foolish. Examples include Folktales from Indigenous peoples across the globe. Asian, Arabic, and African stories can be the basis from which teachers expand.

- **with similar structures.** These are also fun for children to think about and talk about. *The Mitten*, (Brett, 2009), *The Old Lady Who Swallowed the Fly* (Taback and Chapin, 1997), and *The Big Enormous Turnip* (Tolstoy, 2012) are **cumulative** tales that use size as a feature of the story structure. The structure of *The Cat in the Hat* (Seuss, 1999) and *Jumanji* (Allsberg, 2017) are strikingly similar and end with the children deciding whether to tell the outlandish truth to their parents. Informational books also have a variety of structures, including question and answer, timeline or sequence, cause and effect, and lists of facts. When teachers show children these structures, they begin to notice them on their own and try them in their own writing.

Diverse characters, settings, and story structures all increase the child's vocabulary and background knowledge if they are attended to and talked about by the children during the reading and enjoyment of the book. A single book may appear in a number of text sets, for example, *The Very Hungry Caterpillar* (Carle, 1969) could be in a set of books authored by Eric Carle, and a set on insects or butterflies.

Connecting Shared Book Read Alouds with Writing

Children provided with many high-quality shared book read-aloud experiences know that every book has an author or writer who thought of the story and wrote it down. Telling the children about the author, showing them their picture, and wondering aloud about why Frann Preston-Gannon (2019) wanted to write about a sloth or why Donald Crews (1978) wanted to tell us about trains can be part of the read-aloud lesson. It supports concepts of reciprocity between reading and writing. With preschool and kindergarten children, teachers may choose to use only the authors' and illustrators' first names to bring them into the classroom as a peer or friend. Explaining to children that Frann or Donald had an idea and decided to make a book about their idea provides a model for children to create their own writing. By connecting reading and writing, children see writers and illustrators they come to know as mentors or models (Shanahan, 1988). The child's book knowledge and awareness of print are transferred to a new context when the teacher identifies the child as an author and illustrator when referring to the stories and pictures the child creates during Assisted Writing. Responding to children's attempts to record events as an approximation of being an author and illustrator scaffolds the transfer of learning from read-aloud to writing. When the child draws a picture, treat it as a book illustration. Respond with, "Tell me the story of your picture."

For example, some children may decide to write their own train book. Connecting their work to Donald Crew's book, teachers can notice and name the cognitive action of the child, "*Donald's book inspired you to write about trains! Writers are often inspired by other writers.*" "*Suz, you wrote a book about cats, just like Frann wrote a book about sloths! You made an informational book about things you know!*" Teachers must notice and name cognitive actions and make connections among shared book reading, emerging writing, emerging reading, background knowledge, and vocabulary (see Figure 11.5). Transfer makes learning more efficient and flexible.

Anchor Under Construction

Allison is reading to her preschool group of 15 children. They have read several books with bears in them in the last three days

Allison: We have another book that I know we will enjoy.

Nate: A bear!

Josias: Yeah a bear is on the front.

Other children: Another bear book.

Allison: We have been enjoying books with bears. Haven't we?

Several children reply excitedly. The titles of other books are in the conversation.

Allison: This one is called *Baby Bear's Not Hibernating* (Plourde, 2016). Lynn wrote this book. Hibernating is what it's called when an animal sleeps all winter, like the bear in *Time to Sleep* (Fleming, 2001). We read that yesterday. (She reads the first page.) "'I'm staying awake the who-o-o-o-o-ole winter,' said Baby Black Bear."

Allison <u>prompts</u>: What do you think his parents might say? Nicki, Bella, what do you think?

Nicki: No!

Allison <u>evaluates</u>. She considers what Nicki is trying to say and **elaborates.**

Allison: You think his parents will say no because bears have to hibernate?

Nicki: He has to.

Allison <u>repeats</u>: So what do you think his parents will say?

Nicki: You have to *hibrate!*

Allison: Let's read some more to see if he is going to hibernate.

She continues this procedure with each page, using the book as a medium to have exchanges with the children. On the following day, she will reread it fluently, stopping fewer times but always encouraging and accepting participation.

Figure 11.5 Teaching for Transfer between Books and Vocabulary

What are Children Expected to Know and Be Able to Do during a Read-Aloud?

The principal in an elementary school was called to a kindergarten classroom to intervene. Although it was only September, Theo had, for what seemed the zillionth time, disrupted the classroom read-aloud by walking around the room and talking to himself about the toys on the shelves. The principal took him out to the hallway to discuss the issue and began as she usually did, by asking, *"Theo, what were you supposed to be doing while the teacher was reading?"*

Theo: *"Not talking."*
Principal: *"And what else?"*
Theo: *"Not moving. Sitting still."*
Principal tried again: *"But what does the teacher want all the children to do?"*
Theo tried again: *"No touching?"*

The principal realized that Theo had begun kindergarten without knowing what this part of the day was about. For him, it was an exercise in self-control that he regularly failed. All those lost hours of learning for this boy were too many to consider. A significant portion of behavior management events focused on children who knew "what **not** to do" but had no idea of the cognitive activity involved in enjoying and benefiting from a read-aloud or for that matter, other learning activities. Without experience at home or explicit support and teaching of executive function and cognitive action at school, Theo had never had access to this learning. While some children in the class have learned these cognitive behaviors, teachers must not assume that all children have, regardless of age or grade. The teacher created a visual plan for the children to follow after realizing that stating expectations explicitly would support the development of the executive function necessary to learn (see Figure 11.6).

Focused attention and self-regulation, Executive Functions, are strongly supported when a teacher concisely states what the child **should be doing** and provides them a chart with pictures which they can refer to as a daily reminder during the shared book reading aloud. These cognitive, "inside the brain," actions (think about the story, remember the story) are some of the same cognitive actions required of the proficient reader and writer. They can

Figure 11.6 Creating a Visual Plan: Active Listening to a Read-Aloud

be learned and practiced during listening to a shared book reading aloud if the teacher has first identified them (named them) for the children, explicitly taught them to the children, and provided supportive feedback and coaching by reinforcing the child's actions. The teacher can say:

- Theo, you are looking at the <u>pictures</u>. That helps you remember the story.
- It looks like you are really <u>thinking</u> about what just happened in the story.
- I can tell that you are <u>listening</u> to the story when you tell us what you are <u>thinking</u>.
- Can you look at Our Read-Aloud Plan and give yourself a thumbs up? You are following the plan.

Noticing and naming the behaviors is far more reinforcing than praise. It allows children to identify the specific action they or another took to be successful. Remember, the child who is an active, engaged listener is more likely to become an active, engaged, proficient reader. When a child is actively listening, they are so cognitively involved that following the rules is easy. When you are spellbound, you don't move or talk or touch.

Complex Cognitive Activity

Teachers often find it helpful to consider what cognitive activities are involved in order for a child to perform a task. Although the tasks are mostly automatic for someone with experience, as a new learner the tasks are laborious and even exhausting. Think about learning to drive, using both hands, one foot, responding to all the activity in the car and all the activity in the environment. It is effortful and cognitively complex enough that 43% of first year drivers are involved in crashes. When children are participating in shared book read-alouds they are trying to

- be actively acting on the story in their own mind;
- hold events in their minds so they can access the arc of the story or remember information in informational texts;
- anticipate what will happen next based on the characters, settings, and plot line;
- recall the story;
- compare it to other stories;
- take an action if they don't understand a word or idea, such as speaking up, or raising their hand and holding their question until acknowledged;
- look at the pictures and make sense of what they are seeing and connect it to the story;
- ignore distractions and compensate for interruptions; and
- follow the rules on the chart.

With instructional support, feedback and practice they will be able to perform all these tasks at the same time, with an occasional fender bender.

Spotlight

Reading habits in the home differ widely, meaning children who begin preschool at the age of four have anywhere from 0 to 1500 experiences. Children entering preschool and kindergarten need daily shared book reading experiences that are well planned, interactive and use engaging, high-quality children's books. Text sets, books that are connected by a literary element have strong potential to support the development of the Foundational Anchors of literacy.

Children are expected to engage in complex cognitive actions during shared book read-alouds. Teachers can support these actions through explicit instruction and the use of a plan for shared book reading that includes Thinking about the Story. Children who struggle to attend to read aloud need more support and more experience in smaller groups and individually. Excluding these children who have not yet learned to actively participate only serves to further delay their learning.

References

Katrina, L. C. (2008). *NYS early childhood data report: The health and well-being of New York's youngest children.* Council on Children and Families.

Lonigan, C. J., Schatschneider, C., & Westberg, L. (2008). Identification of children's skills and abilities linked to later outcomes in reading, writing, and spelling. In *Developing early literacy: Report of the national early literacy panel* (pp. 55–106).

Milburn, T. F., Girolametto, L., Weitzman, E., & Greenberg, J. (2014). Enhancing preschool educators' ability to facilitate conversations during shared book reading. *Journal of Early Childhood Literacy, 14*(1), 105–140.

Sanden, S., Mattoon, C., & Osorio, S. L. (2021). *Book talk: Growing into early literacy through read-aloud conversations.* Teachers College Press.

Shanahan, T. (1988). The reading writing relationship: Seven instructional principles. *The Reading Teacher, 41*(7), 636–647.

Wasik, B. A., & Bond, M. A. (2001). Beyond the pages of a book: Interactive book reading and language development in preschool classrooms. *Journal of Educational Psychology, 93*(2), 243.

Whitehurst, G. J., Arnold, D. S., Epstein, J. N., Angell, A. L., Smith, M., & Fischel, J. E. (1994). A picture book reading intervention in day care and home for children from low-income families. *Developmental Psychology, 30*(5), 679.

References for Children's Literature

Bloom, S. (2014) *Alone together.* Astra Young Readers.

Brett, J. (2009). *The mitten.* Penguin.

Brown, C. (2005). *Polkabats and octopus slacks: 14 stories.* Simon and Schuster.

Carle, E. (1969). *The very hungry caterpillar.* World Publishing Company.

Carle, E. (1984). *The very busy spider*. Philomel Books.

Crews, D. (1978). *Freight train*. Greenwillow Books.

Dahl, R. (1973). *Fantastic Mr. Fox*. Puffin Books.

Dahl, R. (1984). *The enormous crocodile*. Bantam Books.

Dean, J. (2016). *Pete the cat storybook collection: 7 groovy stories!*. HarperCollins.

Dewdney, A. (2005). *Llama llama red pajama*. Penguin Young Readers Group.

DiCamillo, K. (2011). *Mercy Watson boxed set: Adventures of a porcine wonder*. Candlewick Press.

Fleming, D. (2001). *Time to sleep*. Macmillan.

Jenkins, S. (1995). *Biggest, strongest, fastest*. Houghton Mifflin Harcourt.

Jenkins, S. (2012). *The Beetle Book*. HMH Books.

McKissack, P. (1986). *Flossie and the fox*. Dial Books for Young Readers.

Lobel, A. (2003). *Frog and Toad are friends*. Harper Collins.

Plourde, L. (2016). *Baby Bear's not hibernating*. Down East Books.

Preston-Gannon, F. (2019). *Sloth slept on*. Cottage Door Press.

Steig, W. (1986). *Brave Irene*. Farrar, Straus and Giroux.

Seuss. (1999). *The cat in the hat*. Random House USA Children's Books.

Taback, S., & Chapin, T. (1997). *There was an old lady who swallowed a fly* (Vol. 333). Viking.

Tolstoy, A. (2012) *The great big enormous turnip*. Egmont UK Ltd.

Van Allsberg, C. (2017). *Jumanji*. Anderson Press.

Yolen, J. (1996). *Commander toad in space*. Putnam and Grosset Group.

12 Planning for Read-Aloud

Focus and Big Ideas

- Before reading
- Selecting quality children's literature
- Introducing the text
- During reading
- After reading
- Dispositions

Before Reading

It is interesting when university students are asked what they consider the most important thing about planning a wedding. They often suggest the venue, clothing, food, and cost. The most important thing, of course, is choosing the right person to marry. When planning a shared story read-aloud session for children, there are many things to consider, but the most important one is choosing the right book. Because reading aloud has so much potential for literacy learning, each book must be carefully selected and skillfully read aloud with purposeful interactions to further strengthen the targeted Foundational Anchors of literacy.

Selecting Quality Children's Literature

Teachers must identify quality children's literature that will serve as engaging read-alouds and generate new language, new understandings, and new connections. Quality children's literature should have many of the following characteristics:

- pictures that support the child's understandings;
- interesting language, literary language, or book language;
- information that is within the child's understanding, with adult support;
- genre diverse; for example, picture books, poems, informational text, and ABC and counting books;
- cultural diversity; representing multiple perspectives;

DOI: 10.4324/9780429284021-12

- ethnic diversity; characters in the books and authors who represent various ethnicities;
- gender diversity; characters in the text as well as the authors;
- compelling reads; interesting rereads;
- books that connect to other books and children's lives in and out of the classroom;
- books that can become familiar rereads for children;
- structures that will become recognizable, for example, beginning, middle, and end, cause and effect, timelines, field guides, concept books, etc.;
- books that support specific Foundational Anchors of literacy.

The teacher and the text must work together to further strengthen and extend the children's Foundational Anchors of literacy. Teachers must choose the best "partner" possible. There are many reasons the teacher might choose to read a **single book** rather than a text set. A single book might relate to a class issue, such as name-calling, friendship issues, cultural or community events, or other events. It may also provide a model or mentor for a Community Writing lesson (See chapter 16). The text structure, topic choice, or specific aspects of the illustrations that can be explicitly taught during the Community Writing What Writers Do lesson can be featured in the book the teacher chooses. During the What Writers Do lesson, the teacher can refer to the book without rereading the entire text.

Text sets, explained in detail in Chapter 10, are highly recommended as a means for children to accumulate oral language, vocabulary, and background knowledge across many texts. The goals the teacher determines for specific Tier 2 and 3 vocabularies can be supported by creating text sets in which the language is repeated and supported by pictures and story context. As children anticipate the content of each text, they are activating their background knowledge that now includes other books. Anticipation and prediction begin the cognitive action of comprehension.

Introducing a Text

After purposefully selecting a book, consider ways to introduce the book. The introduction should permit the teacher to connect children's current background knowledge, extend their background knowledge, and stimulate their interest and engagement in the book. The introduction is a jumpstart for comprehension and a means to awaken the child's enthusiasm for the text, like an engaging movie trailer. The introduction should provide the children with a short gist of the book so that their brains can call up appropriate schema requisite for engagement and deep comprehension.

In some cases, the children may have background knowledge that you can **activate**, while in other cases, you will be **constructing** new background knowledge, connecting to and **expanding** with what they already know. The teacher's awareness of the children's background knowledge informs which cognitive action they are supporting (activating, constructing, or expanding background knowledge). In other words, are you helping children think about things they already know that will help them understand the text (activating) or are you teaching the children new information that will help them understand the text (constructing)?

For example, in the Head Start classroom on the Eastern Navajo reservation, the children knew about sheep. They had experienced herding, sheering, slaughtering, cleaning, and eating sheep. They had extensive background about sheep that could be **activated** for listening to a book related to using wool to make clothing, such as *Charlie Needs a Cloak* (dePaola, 1973) or *Weaving a Rainbow* (Lyon, 2004), but the teacher would need to **construct** new information for the same children to understand *Deep in the Ocean* (Brunelliere, 2019).

Finding read-aloud texts that draw on, connect with, and add to children's background knowledge is an important consideration. The process of selecting books for a child from a wealthy suburb, or an urban housing project, for three-year-olds or six-year-olds, or to meet the needs of a specific subset of children in your classroom, is as important as selecting the right car to fit one's circumstances and budget. **The teacher's knowledge about their students matters** in all school experiences. If we are to lead children from what they know to new learning, it is essential that we have a firm, respectful grasp of the knowledge they bring.

Before reading the book to children, the teacher must read the entire book carefully, looking for ideas, concepts, words, idioms, or structures that will be unfamiliar to the children. When there is insufficient context or picture support, these (ideas, etc.) should be part of the introduction and part of the prereading lesson for language learners.

Introducing New Vocabulary

Part of a teacher's consideration of the text prior to reading are the word meanings, idioms, concepts, and abstract ideas that children may have trouble understanding without adult support. Teachers will need to decide which words or ideas to define quickly during reading **(implicit instruction)** and which to pre-teach prior to reading (**explicit instruction**). In the last chapter, the concept of sneaky or sly characters defined a text set. The children understood the concept because most had done something sneaky at one time or another. Still, they did not have words to label it. A concept like *bravery* may be unfamiliar in both understanding and vocabulary. Seeing the book through the children's eyes helps teachers identify what will be unfamiliar and require teaching.

Implicit vocabulary instruction supports children's comprehension of the book being read aloud. For example, the text says, "She felt hesitant about holding a snake," and the teacher says, "She felt hesitant about holding a snake. Hesitant means she didn't really want to hold it." Adding a **child-friendly** definition within the running text is implicit vocabulary instruction. Teachers plan what they are going to say in order to be clear, concise, and within the children's understanding. (Remember to write it on a sticky note.) Children's memory of the word and its meaning are increased by using the word in conversation after reading the text and connecting the word to other experiences, "*Do you feel excited or hesitant about going to recess?*"

Explicit vocabulary instruction involves directly teaching specifically selected words, or ideas, before, during, **and** after the reading in order for the word to be added to the child's receptive and expressive oral language.

> **Step 1. Before reading**: The teacher provides direct, accurate instruction. Asking children to guess what words mean prior to instruction adds confusion and slows learning. Teachers might say something like, "*In this book we are going to read, Carolina is hesitant to hold the snake. Hesitant means she held back because she wasn't sure she wanted to hold the snake. (Introduce a synonym or antonym that will add to the child's understanding.) Would you be hesitant or excited about holding a snake? How about holding some marshmallows? Would you be hesitant or excited? Turn and tell your talk-partner.*"
>
> **Step 2. During reading**: Repeat the sentence with the word in it and ask the children what it means. Give them time to explain in their own words.
>
> **Step 3. After reading:** Use the word in your discussion so that children once again hear the word used in context and have a chance to use it in their own conversation.

You cannot do this with every word or idea, so choose the most meaningful and useful words.

Examples of Introductions

The introduction of the book starts the comprehension, piques the interest, and promises an exciting, interesting experience. This comes after the vocabulary instruction. When the teacher develops a good introduction for a read-aloud, they write it out and keep it with the book. Introductions will get better over time and the teacher will discover which books work well for a specific purpose, considering the background knowledge their current group of children may have. The book introduction will not ruin the surprise of the text but instead increase the understanding of the text for the children. Here are some examples of introductions based on commonly retold stories.

Example 1: Purpose of introduction: To help children see the story arc and anticipate the magic that they will compare to the magic in other books of the text set.

Cinderella: We have been reading books (a text set) that have magic in them. Here is a new book with magic in it. This book is called Cinderella and it tells the story of a sad, lonely girl. Her family is very unkind to her. They are all going to a dance and they tell her she has to stay home. But then comes the magic! Are you ready for the story of Cinderella?

Example 2: Purpose of introduction: To help children focus on the theme of the text set, helping others.

The Lion and the Mouse: We have another book to read about helping each other. In this book, the mouse promises to help the lion. The lion thinks the mouse is so little he couldn't ever help a lion. Do you think you have to be big to help others? You are all good helpers and you are little. The lion had to learn a lot about who helpers are. Ready?

Example 3: Purpose of introduction: To reinforce the genre of informational and nonfiction books as compared to fiction; to activate and construct new vocabulary.

Vocabulary instruction prior to introduction: I have three important words that will help us understand the book we are going to read about wolves.

Predator: A predator is an animal that hunts for and eats other animals. In this book, the wolf is the predator.

Pack: A pack of wolves is a group of wolves that live together. We know some other words for groups of animals that live together; a hive of … bees (giving children time to answer) and birds that live in a flock. Wolves live together in a pack.

Den: That is what we call the hole that the mother wolf cares for her cubs in. It isn't a nest or a house, it's a den.

A book about wolves: Yesterday we read the Three Little Pigs. In that story, the wolf was scary and the pigs were afraid that they were going to get eaten. But the wolf and the pigs could talk to each other, so we decided it was a make-believe story. Today I have another book with a wolf in it. This one is not make-believe. It is true information about real wolves. Here they are on the cover. Are you ready to learn more about wolves?

Introducing the Book to Multi-Language Learners

It is important to consider the needs of multi-language learners (MLLs) and children with limited language in the language of instruction. Imagine trying to listen to an audiobook in a language you do not speak well. When the cognitive demand of making meaning from a read-aloud is overwhelming, or is incomprehensible, children can disengage. This means they do not have access to the learning their peers have. The teacher must plan ways to make the reading become **comprehensible input.** Comprehensible input is language input that the children can understand, although they cannot understand all the words. A bad phone connection may leave enough of the caller's words intact for their meaning to be comprehended even when the signal cuts in and out. This is what comprehensible input is like. The teacher has to consider what instruction can impact their ability to understand, learn from, and enjoy the larger group reading for the MLLs and low-language children. Because the read-aloud has been carefully planned, the extra time it takes to introduce the book to children who need extra support is well worth it. They, of course, have background knowledge that they might not be able to share with the teacher due to language barriers. Listen carefully to what the children are saying. Here are some strategies to employ individually or in small groups in the days **prior** to the read-aloud.

Strategies for Introducing Books to MLLs and Limited Language Children

1. Preview the text in a small group, using the pictures to explain and support the vocabulary and the structure of the text; fiction or informational.
2. Use realia whenever possible. **Realia** includes actual items named in the text which are unfamiliar to the children (a harmonica and a slide whistle that are mentioned) and representations of objects (plastic farm animals). Children need to examine, touch, manipulate, and talk about the realia provided.
3. Research available translations of the text that can be sent home with the child prior to reading the text in class. Encourage the family to read the book aloud to the child in their primary language.
4. Include a simpler version of the same story.
5. Using the book itself, show children the pictures page by page, and retell the story in a simple form.
6. Find simple books in English on the same topic of upcoming read-alouds to build or activate the child's background knowledge and vocabulary.
7. For informational books, find a simpler book on the same topic to share with the children. Support their use of the words in the text and create physical actions to support the concepts and ideas.
8. Using pictures from the book, ask the children what they think the character might be doing or saying so they can imagine the character's thoughts and actions.
9. Provide the children with a few photocopied pictures from the book to explore and discuss. Send these home for parents to see and talk about with their child.
10. Use photocopied pictures from the book to act out important parts of the story.
11. Use photocopied pictures of objects and settings from the book to support vocabulary development.
12. Read books more than once after providing language supports.
13. Teach for transfer. "We have read two books about animals in winter. What animals do you think might be in this book about animals that hibernate?"
14. Encourage children to ask questions as you introduce the text in a small group. As they begin to monitor their own understanding, reinforce their efforts with your response.

15. MLLs should only be invited (not pressured) to participate verbally in these supports. They may be in the silent period but will still benefit from comprehensible input.

The effectiveness of these strategies depends on the careful planning of the teacher for the shared book reading aloud that will occur throughout the year. Children who are learning language MUST have teacher support and scaffolding in order to access the read-aloud instruction. When we understand how important read-aloud learning opportunities can be, it follows that we want to include all of the children.

During Reading: Teacher Strategies and Interactions

Encouraging children to describe what they notice in the pictures, to share their ideas, and to ask questions about the story or topic during the reading, increases their oral language proficiency, both receptive and expressive. Don't assume that all preschool or kindergarten children know basic vocabulary such as the names of farm and forest animals like pigs and bears, or the names of their babies such as piglets and cubs. Spend time listening to and talking with children to identify their understandings about the content and the vocabulary they use to express their understandings. This permits the teacher to intentionally mediate during the shared book read aloud to further solidify and extend their concepts and vocabulary. Additionally, such conversations about the book give children time to take control of the ideas and the words. Children readily grow their receptive vocabulary as they learn the names of things and actions through read-alouds and try these names out in their own talk.

During reading, the teacher must read fluently, with expression, in a voice all the children can hear. This must sometimes be practiced with books that include words in another language or dialect other than that of the teacher. The teacher must check to see that all the children can see the pictures well enough to use them as a source of information to understand the story. Using technology, story readings available in video form, a document camera to enlarge pictures, or a listening center for repeated readings can help when the pictures are not large enough.

A focus on the learning opportunities during read-aloud will help the teacher make the most of shared book read-aloud time. By **repeating** a picturesque phrase, *hair the color of straw, fur as soft as a summer breeze,* teachers draw attention to the literary language of a book. Ask the children to listen again and notice how the writer used words to help readers use their imagination. **Inserting** a *child-friendly* definition of an uncommon or unfamiliar word provides input children can understand. Teachers must plan their exact words to avoid unhelpful definitions. Saying, "*Furious, that means the character was overwhelmed with fury,*" may be the first thing that pops out of the teacher's mouth if they hadn't planned to say, "*Furious, that means the character is so very mad. Jojo was furious. Jojo was so very mad.*"

Stopping to converse about what has happened or what could happen next gives children a chance to think about and process what is occurring in the story. This habit of stopping to intentionally think and process while listening to a story creates a model of the behaviors and thinking of a proficient reader. Proficient readers summarize the story as they read, adding new episodes or information to support ongoing comprehension. By saying their thoughts out loud, the teacher invites the child to share in the thinking or noticing. Noticing and naming one's own cognitive actions supports children's metacognition. These connections *appear* spontaneous but should be planned with a sticky note reminder. Say things like the following:

* This picture just woke up a story in my head.
* When I read that page, I thought it sounded scary.
* Were you as surprised (amused, confused, doubtful) as I was?
* I didn't really understand that part. I want to read it again.
* I wondered what that meant. Let's think about it.
* This seems similar to (another story) because they both …

As children become aware of words, they will ask what words mean, creating more opportunities to extend and use the vocabulary. If the group can manage without a formal hand raising routine, the conversation can flow much more naturally. The teacher can support vocabulary encountered during text sets by creating a chart that accompanies the set. For example, in the text set about wolves, the list might include den, pack, predator, prey, and any other words that children hear and wonder about or the teacher determines are appropriate given the books in the set.

After Reading: Teacher Strategies and Interactions

Considering what is the same, similar, and different about the stories gives children more to think about and talk about. Making maps based on stories that show where the character lived or traveled or creating scientific drawings or picture glossaries based on stories create many opportunities for children to talk about the book. Acting out the story as a large group or with stick puppets can be used for repeated retellings to increase comprehension. The key is for the children to talk (and talk some more) and for the teacher to listen. Conversation develops oral language and oral language helps ideas move into memory. Talk partners or activity groups that are creating products based on a book are about facilitating talk as much as about comprehension.

Questioning after reading can come in many forms and provide opportunities for conversation. An oral quiz, a quizversation becomes a high-risk context with right and wrong answers.

Appropriate questions can be **text based**, with the answers being either directly stated in the text or clearly shown in the pictures. Or they can be inferred by the text or pictures. Asking **inferential** questions helps children think beyond what is literally stated. **Opinion** questions do not have a correct answer but asking children to tell why they hold their opinion facilitates deeper thought. Armisha knew which version of the Three Little Pigs she preferred, and why. She could explain that she wanted the wolf to follow a "No biting" policy, just like she did in school. In all cases, listening with an **inquiry stance,** "Interesting, tell us more," to what the child is thinking or trying to say, as opposed to an evaluative stance "Good idea," decreases the risk of participation for the child.

Rereading familiar texts gives children another opportunity to think beyond the initial comprehension and notice new words, understand story structure, and integrate the story into their own background knowledge. For the least experienced children, reading the book aloud to a small group before presenting it to the entire group gives them a chance to begin to interact with and understand the text and it supports the development of Executive Function. The children get a chance to focus their attention on the extra scaffolding they need. Rereading a familiar text to a small group can also allow children to ask more questions and use new vocabulary.

Dispositions toward Literacy and Literacy Learning

Dispositions (attitudes, interest, inclinations toward literacy) are developed during shared book read-aloud time. Teachers must be aware, however, that this can work as both a blessing and a curse. The children with 1500 book experiences are already interested and anticipating enjoyment. The inexperienced children, the 10% who have not been read to, may behave as if your reading is like the noise of the TV in the background while they play. Taking time to choose engaging, initially participatory books, and teaching children what to do before, during, and after read-aloud time will give all children access to the benefits of this powerful experience along with success at doing "school." Excluding or being punitive with the child who has not learned to listen to stories, however, will teach the child that read-aloud time is painful and should be avoided. The **self-regulation** that the child learns while enjoying and comprehending a story can be taught and reinforced over time. The child may need many opportunities to attempt them with patient teaching, reminding, and positive reinforcement. They need encouragement and instruction to develop that relationship with books that will serve them well throughout school. They may need to practice while having read-aloud in a small group. Expecting a child to participate appropriately in any novel activity without teaching the behaviors and providing support that is gradually withdrawn as the behavior improves will lead to disappointment and failure for both the teacher and the child. Many teachers are tempted to exclude these children when they become too wiggly, disengaged, or disruptive. This sets up a negative relationship between books and stories. Young Cole said it best after preschool one day, "I hate when Miss Gwen wants to tell us books. I have to go to time out."

What Cole needed was time-in, not time-out; time to get connected to the books and the stories so that he could become part of the group. Using a clear set of expectations that include both behavioral and cognitive activities can make clear to Cole what his more experienced peers have already had many chances to learn.

Spotlight

Shared book reading aloud is full of opportunities for the children to learn and the teacher to provide instruction. Realizing the potential for learning makes the work of planning a worthwhile investment for the teacher. The first task is selecting quality children's literature. Teachers should seek support from both public librarians and children's book venders. The book and the teacher are partners in this endeavor. Teachers must make sure children see themselves on the pages of books and in authors' photographs.

Providing a strong lead-up to the reading includes vocabulary and concept exploration, specific support for MLLs and children with limited language, and planning a clear "movie trailer" introduction.

During the reading, clear, expressive, and fluent reading must be paired with children's ability to see every picture. Teachers should think aloud and engage children in talking about the events or content. Having planned child-friendly definitions will support vocabulary development and avoid confusing the child. What happens during reading, for better or worse, is the result of the teachers' planning.

After the reading is a time for more talk. Children can compare and contrast, make connections, offer reasoned opinions, and participate in making products like charts, drawings, or diagrams. Acting out stories and using stick puppets to retell stories can add to comprehension and enjoyment.

Finally, teachers must support the least experienced children, giving them full access to the learning available during shared book reading aloud.

References for Children's Literature

Brunelliere, L. (2019). *The ocean*. New York: Abrams Appleseed

DePaola, T. (1973). *Charlie needs a cloak*. Hamburg, Germany: Libri GmbH.

Lyon, G.E. (2004) *Weaving the rainbow*. New York: Atheneum/Richard Jackson Books

13 Phonological Awareness

Krista M. Griffin

DEPARTMENT OF ELEMENTARY EDUCATION
AND LITERACY, METROPOLITAN STATE
UNIVERSITY OF DENVER, DENVER, CO, USA

Focus and Big Ideas

- Phonological Awareness Skills
- The Two Dimensions: Unit and Manipulation
- The Progression of Phonological Awareness Skills
- Assessing and Teaching Phonological Awareness
- Daily Routines for Phonological Awareness

Fun with Language

Ms. Molina gathered her kindergarten class to the rug and told them they were going to sing Willoughby Wallaby Woo. The class cheered and joined in, gleefully singing their way through the first two lines: "Willoughby, Wallaby, Wee, an elephant sat on me. Willoughby, Wallaby, Woo, an elephant sat on you." They all began wildly raising their hands, and Ms. Molina picked Brandon and Daisha to stand up. "Willoughby, Wallaby, Wandon, an elephant sat on Brandon, Willoughby Wallaby Waisha, an elephant sat on Daisha!" they all sang/shouted. The enthusiasm was contagious, and the class continued on, happily rhyming the names of their classmates.

Even though the children may not have been aware of it, they were practicing one of the Foundational Anchors, **phonological awareness**, which is defined as *the ability to notice, think about, and work with the sounds of **oral language** at the word, onset and rime, syllable, and phoneme level (see Figure 13.1).* Young children develop and demonstrate aspects of phonological awareness by singing rhyming songs and poems, as in the example above, counting the number of words in a sentence, or clapping the syllables in their names. Ms. Molina called out the names of her students to line up for lunch by clapping out the syllables in each name. She clapped for each syllable and said "Jo-se". Then, Jose clapped out his name while he said each syllable and lined up. She continued with "A-dri-ann-a," who responded in turn. Even though these activities often just look like having fun with language, there is a huge body of evidence that links the awareness of speech sounds in words with later

DOI: 10.4324/9780429284021-13

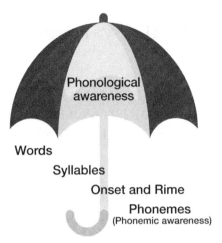

Figure 13.1 Phonological Awareness Umbrella

decoding ability (National Early Literacy Panel [NELP], 2008). Hooray for the research that supports children naturally having fun with language!

Phonological Awareness Skills

As we think about the Foundation Stage (Chall's Stage 0) and its focus on acclimation and early competence for emerging readers, we see how important it is for young children to use oral language to play with words and sounds. It makes sense that we need children to understand the sound system of their spoken language (speech) before we ask them to attend to the written system. As Yopp and Yopp (2009) put it, "Individuals who are unaware that speech is made of small sounds – those who don't notice and cannot mentally grab hold of and manipulate them—have difficulty learning to read a written system based on sounds."

There is much overlap in the development of the ability to hear sounds at the word, syllable, onset and rime, and phoneme level. There is a general linear development to phonological awareness but it is not strictly sequential. Children do not fully develop the ability to hear sounds in one way before beginning to hear sounds in a more complex way. Instruction and practice for younger preschool-aged children appropriately focus on the lower level **phonological awareness** activities such as rhyming words (first recognizing and then producing), counting out words in a sentence, and counting syllables in words. Building on their lower level phonological awareness, older children are prepared for a stronger focus on onset/rime and individual phonemes. Being able to identify and manipulate individual **phonemes** is the highest and most difficult level of phonological awareness. **Phonemic awareness** is the ability to notice, think about, and manipulate the *individual sounds* in spoken words.

Common Confusion of Terms

Educators often use the terms *phonological awareness* and *phonemic awareness* interchangeably, but as we have learned, this is incorrect. Phonological awareness is an umbrella term that includes the awareness of:

- the number of individual **words** in sentences;
- the number of **syllables** in words;
- the **onset and rimes** within syllables;
- and the awareness of **phonemes** (individual sounds) in words which is phonemic awareness.

All phonological awareness activities can be done in the dark, as there is no connection to **graphemes** (written letters), only to what can be heard. Children do not need to know the names of letters to successfully participate in phonological awareness games and activities. That brings us to another term that is often used interchangeably with these ideas, and that is **phonics,** the connection between letter and sound. Sometimes teachers will describe an activity where students circle the letter that a picture starts with and call that a phonemic awareness activity. You will know immediately that this is incorrect, because phonological awareness tasks are only concerned with the sounds in words, not letters.

That being said, combining phonics with phonological awareness tasks is appropriate when children have stronger lower level phonological awareness skills and are ready for that step, but it is important to know the difference between the terms. Studies suggest that kindergarten instruction that combines phonological awareness activities with sound-symbol relationships (phonics) has a positive effect on reading and writing success (Blachman, 1989). Therefore, teaching them in an interrelated manner acknowledges the important relationship between them. This assumes that they have developed phonological awareness in preschool. Teachers must have assessment data for all Foundational Anchors of literacy, rather than make assumptions.

The Two Dimensions of Phonological Awareness: Unit and Manipulation

Unit

Phonological awareness tasks can be thought of as having two dimensions—the size of the sound **unit** being considered and the type of **manipulation** (Yopp & Yopp, 2009). When we talk about the **size of the unit**, we describe them from biggest to smallest. The sequence is word, syllable, onset and rime, and phoneme.

A word is the largest phonological awareness unit, next, syllables, the onset/rime in a syllable, and then a phoneme. An **onset** is the first consonant sound you hear in a syllable, like the /p/ sound in pet (see Figure 13.2). The **rime** is

---

An Important Note for Our Readers: Backward slashes preceding and following a letter or group of letters indicate that it is a unit, **spoken** by itself. The smallest unit, a sound, is written /p/ and the slashes mean you should make the **sound** associated with the letter P. Another example shows onset and rime as units of sound. /ch/ and /in/ are the two sound units in *chin*. Finally, /city/ is a unit, a whole word, which is spoken as a whole word.

Figure 13.2 **An Important Note for Our Readers:** Explanation of Use of Brackets:/ sound unit/

the vowel and other letters that follow the vowel in that syllable, like the /et/ part of pet. A **phoneme** is the smallest unit of speech one can hear in a word. There are three phonemes in the word *pet*, for instance: /p/ /e/ /t/. But there are also three phonemes in the word *Pete*, even though there are four letters. The e at the end of the word *Pete* does not make a sound, it is silent. It's important to note once again that phonological and phonemic awareness are oral skills and provide a necessary foundation for instruction that connects sounds to letters.

Let's break down the word *planet* to see all of these units of sound displayed, building on what we did above with *pet* and *Pete*.

- **Word:** /planet/ (one unit)
- **Syllables:** /plan/ /et/ (two units)
- **Onset/rime:** /pl/ /an/ /et (three units including one onset, two rimes)
- **Phonemes:** /p/ /l/ /a/ /n/ /e/ /t/ (six phonemes)

Manipulation

The second dimension, **manipulation**, requires children to do something with (to move around, delete, add) phonological units (see above). It is generally easiest for students to *recognize* a phonological manipulation. For example, a child may be able to hear that /cat/ and /bat/ rhyme. Then, with experience, they can begin *performing* or *producing* phonological manipulations. When asked for a word that rhymes with /cat/, they may not be able to produce one. They may apply other manipulations saying, /Car/ or a non-word, /lat/. Therefore, recognition or identification of a manipulation is simpler than actually producing a manipulation.

The Progression of Phonological Awareness Skills

The following chart (see Figure 13.3) lists phonological awareness skills in order of the easiest to the most complex and gives examples of how children can be asked

Progression of Phonological Awareness Skills		
Unit levels	**Skill**	**Example**
Rhyme	<u>Recognize</u> when **words** rhyme	Which two words rhyme? /Dog/, /rug/, /log/
Word	<u>Recognize</u> the number of words in a sentence by clapping or counting	/Sherisa/ /likes/ /to/ eat/ /cake/.
Syllable	<u>Recognize</u> **syllables** by counting or clapping	/Pet/ clap one syllable /Carpet/ (clap two syllables) /Pretending/ (clap three syllables)
Onset and rime	<u>Blend</u> **onset and rime**	What is this word? /p/ /et/, /d/ /og/, /r/ /ug/
Rhyme	<u>Produce</u> a **rhyme**	What is a word that rhymes with /log/?
Phoneme	<u>Recognize</u> *matching* **initial sound**s in words	Which words start the same? /star/, /sun/, /lamb/.
Phoneme	<u>Produce</u> the **initial sound** of a word	What is the first sound in the word /car/ /bug/ /fin/?
Word	<u>Delete</u> part of a **compound word**	Say the word /sunshine/ without /sun/.
Phoneme	**Phoneme** <u>blending</u>	Blend these phonemes together: /g/o/, /b/ /i/ /g/, /p/ /a/ /n/
Phoneme	**Phoneme** <u>segmentation</u>	Hold up a finger (or move a chip) for each sound that you hear in /fish/ (f/i/sh), /no/ /n/ /o/, /send/ /s/ /e/ /n/ /d/
Phoneme	**Phoneme** <u>substitution</u>	Change the /n/ in name to /g/ (game) Change the /i/ in fin to /a/ (fan) Change the /m/ in dim to /g/ (dig)
Phoneme	**Phoneme** <u>deletion</u>	Say meat without the /m/ (eat) Say slink without the /l/ (sink) Say fork without the /k/ (for)

Figure 13.3 Progression of Phonological Awareness Skills

to demonstrate their understanding of each one. Notice how a more complex aspect of a lower skill may be developed further along in the progression.

Understanding the general order of phonological awareness complexity helps teachers identify and build on what children already know, rather than instructing them below or beyond their current understanding. A

3-year-old child who has learned to recognize rhyming words when they hear them said aloud is perhaps ready to count out syllables or produce rhyming words, as indicated in the progression above. An important element of working on these skills with young children is to make practicing of them as game-like and fun as possible. How much more engaged will children be when you ask them to help our friend, Blending Bat, blend sounds, so he can go home to his cave than if you just announce that it is time to practice phoneme blending? The Stellaluna bat puppet can represent Blending Bat. Children can be given the opportunity to move the bat's mouth as they blend the sounds together into a word. For example, the teacher says, "/c/ /a/ /t/" pausing briefly between sounds. The child moves the bat's mouth to say "cat."

Equally important, though, is showing children that what they learn by playing fun games can help them become readers and writers. Using what they have learned during game playing to solve problems they encounter in reading and writing is called **transfer**. Children cannot be expected to transfer information between contexts without teacher modeling.

Where Does Phonological Awareness Fit in Scarborough's Rope?

Referring back to Scarborough's Rope, we see that phonological awareness is a single strand in word recognition. It contributes to the development of word recognition through decoding and encoding. Decoding, making the sound represented by each letter or group of letters (e.g., ch, sh, th), is part of word solving in reading. Encoding, making the sounds in a word slowly and writing the representative letter, helps with word solving in writing. It isn't hard to see the connection between being aware that words can be both pulled apart and blended together, with the tasks of reading and writing.

A Caution

Because educators have become increasingly aware of the importance of a strong phonological awareness base for children, many now implement a phonological awareness curriculum in K-2 classrooms. Strong phonological awareness routines, instruction, and practice are necessary for children to learn and transfer. However, whole-class instruction alone cannot be relied on to meet the specific needs of every child. Children need different information and instruction at different times, based on what they already know and are ready to learn. A whole group, one size fits all, approach is never going to be effective for every child. This means that teachers will also need to work in small groups and one-to-one, depending on specific instructional needs. It is in the one-to-one or small group setting that the teacher can observe when children are struggling with phonological awareness and should consult the special educator for further insight.

Assessing and Teaching Phonological Awareness

Phonological awareness should be assessed both informally and formally. An informal assessment might look like a teacher asking children to do any of the tasks listed in Table 12.1 and recording their answers to determine the next instructional steps. Formal assessments such as the Phonological Awareness Literacy Screening (PALS) and the Phonological Awareness Screening Test (PAST) are prevalent at the district level. The PAST is designed to assess 14 different levels of phonological awareness and is individually administered orally to pre-K-2nd-grade students. The Acadience Phoneme Segmentation Fluency (PSF) test is a standardized, individually administered test of phonological awareness. The PSF assesses a child's ability to fluently segment three- and four-phoneme words into their individual phonemes. Progress monitoring using informal and formal measures allows the teacher to more precisely identify next steps for each child and analyze whether the current instruction is effective. This important use of data to inform instruction is called **formative assessment**.

The development of phonological awareness, like each of the other Foundational Anchors, is interwoven throughout the day. It is taught, practiced, and applied in both **direct** instructional contexts and **indirect** instructional contexts. The teacher's knowledge of these underlying tasks can add power and transfer to many lessons focused on other anchors. For example, Ms. Molina used a read–aloud selection to initiate the Willoughby, Wallaby game. Teachers must be intentionally aware of each child's level of phonological awareness to plan direct and indirect instructional contexts.

Direct Instructional Learning Contexts

A strong phonological awareness foundation in preschool is critical for children's receptiveness and success with phonemic awareness and phonics instruction in kindergarten and first grade. The following lessons reflect a sequence of teacher-directed phonological awareness instruction. They could be provided through whole group, small group, or one-to-one instruction. Whole group lessons (see Chapter 6) are appropriate for introduction of new skills, and practice of known skills to gain speed and flexibility. In the whole group, children may choose to participate or not, and the teacher is not able to hear individual responses. It is for that reason that information taught through small group instruction is more efficient and timelier.

Small group time should follow whole group introductions, allowing teachers to meet the individual skill needs of students, assess their understanding, and determine if the lesson is appropriate. Small group learning is as important for the most experienced learners as it is for the ones who are less advanced. It also allows for more modeling and specific feedback to students. Teachers can monitor responses in a small group much easier than with the whole class, and the pace can be adjusted for the needs of the group. The small group can be used to review previously introduced skills, provide teacher-directed practice with these skills, and introduce new skills when appropriate. Strategic, dynamic grouping supports effective instruction.

Lesson Examples

1. Recognizing when words rhyme

Very often, teachers use picture books to bring skills to life, especially rhyming. As shown in the table, recognizing rhyming words develops before producing rhymes. Luckily, there are many books that children love that feature rhyming words. Teachers can read a rhyming book such as *Rhyming Dust Bunnies* (Thomas, 2009), where dust bunnies who love to rhyme all have rhyming names (Ed, Ted, and Ned) except for Bob, whose name doesn't rhyme and who refuses to play their rhyming games. Just reading this book introduces children to the concept of rhymes in a fun way. The dust bunnies take turns introducing words for the other bunnies to rhyme, until Bob shows up on the pages and what he says decidedly does not rhyme. Ms. Molina decides to use the book for an explicit lesson on rhyming for her kindergarten class, as she has heard them begin to play with rhyming throughout the day.

"Class, please join me on the carpet for a fun read aloud that I love. I think you will love it too. The characters in the book are going to do something fun with words, and I want you to be on the lookout for what that is." The children join her and are excited to read a book their teacher loves. "When you think you know what the characters are doing with words, I want you to give me a secret thumbs up as you listen. The name of this book is 'Rhyming Dust Bunnies.' Does anyone know what a dust bunny is? No? It's not a real bunny. It's dirt and dust that clump together, like you might find under a bed. This author is making believe that these dust bunnies have arms and legs and mouths and can talk, and her pictures make me laugh. Let's read to find out what these dust bunnies are going to do."

Ms. Molina begins to read the book, thinking aloud on different pages, and noticing that many children are beginning to make the secret thumbs up. "I see lots of secret thumbs up. Who can tell me what fun thing most of the dust bunnies are doing with words? Yes, Thomas, they are rhyming! Rhyming is when the last part of the word sounds the same as the last part of another word, like Ted and Ned. The /ed/ part of the word sounds the same, or rhymes. It is fun to listen to rhyming words in books and poems, and the author of this book gives us lots of rhyming words to listen for."

Ms. Molina continued, "Let's practice some rhyming words from the book. I'm going to say three words, and you are going to tell me which two words rhyme. Ready? Ted, Bob, Ned. Which two words rhyme? Say them with me. Ted and Ned! Right! Which word doesn't rhyme? Ha, Bob. He doesn't want rhyme words in the story AND his name doesn't rhyme with the other dust bunnies. Let's try again. Stop, car, jar. Which two words rhyme? Right again! Car and jar do rhyme. You are all rhyming experts."

That afternoon before center's time, Ms. Molina demonstrated an indirect learning activity in which children could practice recognizing rhyming words. "I'm going to pull three objects out of this jar, and you are going to tell me which ones rhyme. What's the first one? Yes, that's a *star* I pulled out of this *jar*. Somebody stop me, I can't stop rhyming! Ok, what is this object? You are right, it is a cat. Here is my third object. It is a little car. So which objects rhyme, star, cat, and car? Exactly! This rhyming jar will be here for you to play with during center's time, and I can tell you will all be great at it."

2. **Counting words in a sentence**

In a small group of four children, Ms. Molina asked them to name one toy they had at home. She began with Callie. Callie named her bear. Ms. Molina said, "Shall we say *Callie has a bear*?" All the children nodded. "Let's count the words together," she said, and all the children held up their hands ready to count. She modeled along with the children. "Callie … has … a … bear." How many words is that? "Four! So we need 4 sticky notes." She put four sticky notes on the easel in a horizontal line, with an inch between them. She touched each one as she slowly said, "Callie has a bear," modeling word boundaries and setting the foundation for future understanding of voice-print match. Ms. Molina asked, "Who else wants to be the pointer?" Taking turns, children quickly touched each note and said the words. Then, the next child got to name a toy and they continued.

Why didn't Ms. Molina *write the words* on the sticky notes? You only need letters to represent sounds IF you can hear and isolate sounds already. She was helping the children HEAR word boundaries and use what they heard to match voice and "print" (the sticky note). At this unit level, and with this goal in mind, there is no benefit to writing letters.

3. **Counting/clapping syllables in words**

Remember the syllable game Ms. Molina played with her children as they lined up for lunch? This was a highly successful management transition (indirect learning context) and practice of phonological awareness because she previously directly taught each step. Let's examine the instruction that preceded this.

Ms. Molina gathered her students to the carpet. "Today we are going to learn a new game to help us break our names into syllables," she said, knowing that starting with children's names is supportive of positive learning outcomes. "Syllables are parts of words that contain a 'beat' and we can clap out our names to find that beat! Let's start with my son's name – Andrew. Say it with me – An–drew. Can you hear the two beats? Listen to me clap it." She clapped as she said "An" and then as she said "Drew." "Do you hear each beat? Let's try it with your names. Listen as I clap out a few, and then we can all try it together. A–lex. A–lyss–a. Doug. Now let's count the syllables we just heard. A–lex. How many times did I clap? Right, two! That means Alex has two syllables in his name. Let's listen to Alyssa's name. A–lyss–a. How many times did I clap? Yes, I clapped three times. That means Alyssa has three syllables in her name. Now let's try Doug. Ha! Yes, just one clap. Doug is a one syllable name. Let's clap and count the rest of the class." She repeated the sequence for the whole class. "Now I'd like you to turn to a neighbor and take turns saying and clapping your name and your partner's name." "How did that go? Noticing the syllables in words is an important step to becoming a reader and writer, and you all worked hard at being syllable clappers and counters!"

Ms. Molina modeled the process by demonstrating several examples: the names of Alex, Allyssa, Doug, and her son, Andrew. This was the "I do" part of the explicit lesson. She then gave many chances for whole-class practice with everyone's name. This was the "We do" part of explicit instruction. She then provided less support for additional "We do" practice when she asked students to try their syllable clapping in partners. She reminded students that, while this was a fun activity, it also has a purpose. This lesson was taught during the whole-class literacy block. This chapter, however, began with Ms. Molina encouraging children to practice the skill independently, the "You do" part of the lesson, by tying it to a classroom routine, lining up for lunch.

After progress monitoring her class on phonological awareness tasks such as syllable clapping, she will know if:

• syllable clapping needs to be explicitly taught again to whole class;
• a small percentage of students need more instruction delivered in a small group;
• a child or children were not understanding the concept and need 1:1 guidance;
• syllable clapping is a skill that all children can do successfully.

Children who have already successfully demonstrated "mastery" of the task may still enjoy practicing it in a fun, game-like way. Data on the progress of individual children will help her determine groupings and next steps for each child. Ms. Molina supports **transfer** of this skill during Assisted Writing, breaking words into syllables and stretching out the sounds in order to encode (see Chapter 15).

4. **Onset and rime recognition**

A logical next skill to work on in a whole group context would be onset and rime, so Ms. Molina plans a whole group lesson for the next week. Using the __**at** rime, she begins to model how the beginning sound (the onset) can be separated from the ending sound (rime).

"Today we are going to take the word /cat/. Let's clap the syllables. Yes, it has one syllable but we can still take it apart. We can break it into two parts, like these two unifix cubes that stick together." She demonstrates putting together and tearing apart two unifix cubes—one is green and one is red. She runs her finger across both of them and says, "cat." As she pulls them apart, she holds up the green cube, she says /k/ and then she holds up the red one and says /at/. She puts them back together and says, "/cat/. Who wants to help me? Watch me pull this green cube off. What's this part say? That's right, /k/. How about this red part? Yes! /at/. Let's put the word back together and say the word loudly and listen to our voices. Cat! Readers pay attention to the different sounds in words like cat! We can take the word apart and put it back together. Let's do that again."

You'll notice that Ms. Molina doesn't overwhelm children by going into a long explanation about onset and rimes—most of them do not understand the difference between consonants and vowels yet. She is giving them background and practice, taking apart one-syllable words, and using blocks so that they can visually attach the sounds to an object. The next day she may practice with the word /bat/ and begin setting the stage for listening for word families or rhymes.

Later on in the year, or in small groups if some children are ready, she can attach letters to the blocks and do the same thing. Since green often means "go," she uses that to designate the onset. Red is associated with "stop," so she uses a red cube to designate the rime. This can be a handy visual way of helping children understand where to start, but also reinforcing that we read text left to right.

5. **Rhyme production**

Ms. Molina knows that recognizing rhymes is easier than producing them, and that several of her children are ready for that next step. In a small group lesson with students whose assessments have indicated that they are ready to produce rhyming words, she rereads the Rhyming Dust Bunnies book. After she has finished, she asks the four students in her small group a question.

Ms. Molina: "Would you like to play the Rhyming Dust Bunny game? I thought you might." She points to the first three students and says "You three will be Ed, Ted, and Ned. Lucky you, Lindsey – you get to be Bob! Ok, Ed, you are going to start out by saying a word, and

Ted and Ned will each say a word that rhymes with the word you say. Bob will be last, and will call out a word that **does not** rhyme. You do not even have to choose a real word if you can't think of one, just one that rhymes. Are you ready?"

Ed: "Bird!"

Ted: (thinks for a minute and says) "word."

Ned: (triumphantly) "Kurd!".

Ms. Molina: "Those all rhyme, dust bunnies. Great job! Now Bob, what word will you say?"

Bob: "Green!"

Ms. Molina: "Ha, you are a good Bob, Lindsey. Ted and Ned both rhymed Ed's word, and Bob acted just like Bob in the book and came up with a word that didn't rhyme."

6. **Onset and rime: manipulation**

Before moving to individual phonemes, she decides that it is appropriate to work on onset and rimes further, but at a higher level. She knows that, while not all students in her class will master the skill of manipulating onset and rime that day, exposing them to it through a whole-class lesson is a good first step. She pulls the whole class together on the carpet.

"Good morning, class! Welcome to the carpet where we are going to be playing a fun game called Disappearing Sounds. I'm going to say a word and give you a hint on how to take away a sound to make a new sound. Let me give you an example. I'm going to say the word feet. Now I'm going to make the /f/ sound disappear and my new word is eat. Did you hear how I took off the /f/ sound from feet to make the word eat? Let's try another one, and you can say it with me. My new word is boat. I'm going to make the /b/ sound disappear and my new word is, say it with me, oat! Great job. Let's try another one as a class." Ms. Molina models the "I do and we do" parts of an explicit teaching lesson and then sets up the "you do." She tells them, "This is where you get to play Disappearing Sounds with a partner. I'm going to give you a word and I will tell you the sound that needs to disappear. You can then turn to your partner and whisper the new word together. Point to your shoulder partner so I know you know who to whisper too. Great! Here we go. Your word is coat. I'm going to make the /c/ sound disappear. Whisper the new word to your partner. Yay, I heard you all whispering oat! Way to make that /c/ sound disappear! Let's try another one."

7. **Initial sounds (phonemes): recognition and production**

Ms. Molina provided practice for children to hear the first sound in a word, phonemic awareness. Focusing on the /m/ sound, she said words that did and did not begin with /m/. Each time the children heard the

/m/ at the beginning of the word and they said, "Mooo." If the word did not begin with /m/, they covered their mouths.

As the game progressed, Ms. Molina asked the children to "come up with" (produce) words that start with /m/. Callie said, "My mom." "That is two words, Callie," said Ms. Molina. "*My* and *mom*. Like *My dad*." Callie said, "Oh that's ANOTHER WORD! Mydad."

Callie could hear the beginning sound but could not yet recognize boundaries between words. She thought the "word" *mydad* began with /m/. Ms. Molina instantly recognized that Callie needed further instruction and practice of boundaries between words, although she was beginning to isolate the beginning sound, a skill higher on the progression.

A lesson like the lesson above is all intentionally planned for the purpose of having young children listen for, hear, isolate, and produce sound units. Prior to the lesson, the teacher made a list of appropriate words to say to ensure that the children would not be confused. The /m/ sound is a **continuant sound** (also called a long and loud sound) that can be stretched a bit. Therefore, the words on the non-example list began with a **stop sound**, also called a "quick and quiet" sound. B, C, D, G, H, J, K, P, and T are stop sounds, so the words Top, Ball, Cat, Pink, and Goat were used rather than a word that also starts with a continuant sound such as l, r, n, or f. Planning for and scaffolding the children's success as they become aware of sound units is essential to developing positive dispositions toward literacy, another Foundational Anchor of literacy.

Initial Sounds Reteaching

Ms. Molina realizes that from her progress monitoring and from her own observations, there are several students who seem to be struggling with the initial sound isolation. This lesson is an example where children are working on two important and related skills—producing initial sounds and matching initial sounds. She will focus on the sounds /b/, /m/, and /s/ The children in this group are the ones that need this work.

Ms. Molina has created a three-column chart for herself with a monster, a ball, and a sun at the top. Later in the lesson, she will give a 9 × 12 envelope to each child with the same type of column and pictures on the back. The children practice saying the three key words with her and making their beginning sounds.

I **Do:** "Ok, friends, we are going to use some pictures to sort other words by their first sound. I'm going to show you how to play the game. I have some pictures for us to name and then listen to their first sound. Watch what I do." She picks up a picture of a mouse and says, "This is a mouse." It starts with /m/. "I'm going to put it in this column with the monster. Let's say those two words monster, mouse." She shows them pictures that start with m, b, or s and continues to model naming the picture, segmenting the sound, and matching it to the appropriate key word. She speaks slowly and clearly, giving time for students to process her words and watch her actions.

We Do: Ms. Molina can see that all the children are engaged and have been following along, so she says, "Let's try doing this together." She gives them each of their envelopes with a dozen pictures in it. She has drawn three columns with the monster, ball, and sun on the back. She asks them to empty the pictures and set up for the activity. "Can everyone find the picture of the bear? Great! All together, let's say the first sound in bear. /b/. Does it start like monster? How about ball?" The children place it under the ball. They make the two sounds together to check their work.

"Tashia, can you pick the next word? Pick up a picture, hold it up, say the word, and then we will all say the first sound together. Suitcase! Yes! Now let's say the first sound together -/s/. Good. Does that begin like bear does? No? So, what should we do with this picture? Yes, let's put it with the sun. Eduardo, can you pick the next picture, and say the word?" She continues to guide them to place pictures under the appropriate key word.

You Do: "Now I'd like you to choose a picture, say the word out loud. Say the first sound out loud and put the picture into the right column. I'm going to listen to you as you work." Ms. Molina uses the rest of the small group time to work individually with each child as they sort at least three words, providing scaffolding and feedback to each one.

8. **Phoneme deletion**

    A Sound Muncher puppet was used to help children learn to delete some sounds in words by eating the sounds so that the mystery of a new word could be solved. Ms. Molina says, "The word is window. Say the whole word with me before the Muncher arrives." Children say, "Window." The Muncher appears and munches, making the /w/ sound. The children listen and say, "indow." Phoneme deletion is never a chore for kindergarteners when they play games like this.

9. **Manipulating compound words**

    Ms. Cara introduced manipulating compound words to the whole group the month before and then worked with the students that had not mastered it in small groups. Her data revealed that one student, Brian, needed further work. She decided that one on one work would be the most appropriate.

    She asked Brian to join her at the back table and began the quick lesson. "Brian, I have some picture cards here that I want to show you. Can you tell me what this is a picture of?" "Oh, that's a baseball!" Brian said confidently. "Yes, and baseball is one of those special words we call a compound word," Ms. Cara answered "That means that it is made of two words we put together to make one new word. I can break it into two words, base and ball. Look at these two picture cards that I have – one is of a base, like you run to first base in a baseball game. One is a ball. If I keep each picture separate, I have two words. If I put them together, like this, I get one new word – baseball!" She puts the picture card for baseball in front of Brian, with the two individual picture cards, base and ball, underneath the baseball picture. "Brian, I can put these two words together, to make baseball, and then take them apart to make two words. Let's practice pushing these two word cards together and taking them apart."

"Let's try to do it with words instead of pictures. Say baseball." Brian says, "baseball!" "Now say baseball without the base," she prompts, because she knows this is the wording the PAST test uses. "Ball!" he says proudly. "Great job. Let's try it one more way. Say baseball without the ball." "BASE!" he says loudly. Ms. Cara could see that he seemed to understand the concept, so continued without using picture cards for the next words, bookcase and spaceship. Had he struggled with the oral example (just the words) on his own, she was ready to model with more picture cards, but they weren't needed in this case. She made a note to watch him when they played the deleting syllable game during transitions to make sure he was able to do it correctly.

Elkonin Boxes: Teaching Kindergarten Children How to Hear Individual Phonemes

Using Elkonin or sound boxes to help children hear the sounds in words as separate phonemes is effective and efficient when well-planned and correctly implemented. By the end of kindergarten, children need to be able to hear (isolate) each sound, or phoneme, in a word. The word *cat* has three sounds and three letters but the word *phone* has three sounds and five letters. Using boxes for the number of **phonemes**, and markers for sounds, begin with simple two or three sound words.

(All boxes should be of the same size and put next to one another with a space between them.)

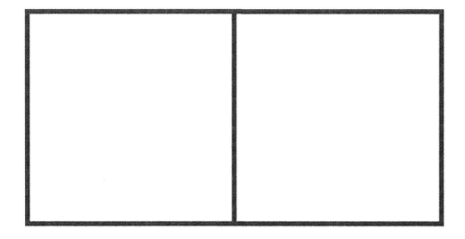

Goal: Teach children to segment words AND use boxes and markers to represent that understanding.

Materials:

- **Cards with two boxes and a card with three boxes**
- **Markers (pennies, cubes, poker chips)**
- **Words for the teacher to use with two or three sound (avoid vowel/r such as *ar* or *or*) combinations and consonant blends to start**
  - **Two sound words:** up, me, egg, she, odd, we, off, so, see, way, zoo, key
  - **Three sound words:** cat, mouse, head, lamb, feet, tub, bike, hid, (onset and rime words _at, _up, etc.)

1. **(I Do)** Model for the child how you **say the word**. Then, say it slowly to pronounce/hear each sound. Do not introduce the written word. Children are learning to **HEAR** sounds in words.
2. Say the word again, slowly this time, while pushing a marker into a box for each sound.
3. **(We do)** Take the markers out and stretch out the same word orally WITH the child.
4. Have the child push the markers while you both stretch the word.
5. Model this with several words making sure the sounds are coming out of the child's mouth. Modeling how to *stretch and listen* cannot move children to *independent stretch and listen* if the child is not making the sounds with you.
6. Stay with we do as long as the child needs assistance, pulling support back gradually.
7. **(You Do)** Teacher provides words for the child to stretch and use markers independently.

Reinforcing children's productive behaviors will help them master sound segmentation. Sentences that name the specific actions and thoughts are the most helpful. These include the following:

- You made the sounds all by yourself with your mouth.
- You listened to yourself making sounds.
- I could hear you taking that word apart.

- You found all three sounds.
- You moved the markers while the sound was coming out of your mouth.

The child MUST learn to make the sounds independently, listen to themselves making the sound, and pull the sounds apart independently in order to read and write. **Once the child is able to do this, do not make the sounds with or for the child.** Initially, make sounds for the child, then <u>with</u> the child, moving to having **only the child** say the word slowly and segment it.

When the teacher is modeling Assisted Writing routines, they can model how they are segmenting the words in order to write them. Asking children to make the sounds at the same time as the teacher reinforces for children how segmentation is used. Furthermore, segmenting words occasionally during Shared Reading or phonics games, and asking the children to blend them together, gives them practice in using sounds and blending them during reading. Teaching children to transfer learning between contexts, modeling "sounding out" during writing as well as reading, and supporting approximations of spelling using letter sound all contribute to the interconnected use of the Foundational Anchors of literacy.

Indirect Instructional Learning Contexts

When creating literacy learning events for independent practice, a natural place to start is with literacy centers. Literacy centers provide multiple opportunities for students to work on literacy skills that they are developing and often include the elements of differentiation and choice. There are some key things to remember when setting up independent practice situations, however.

The first thing to remember is that you need to have a strong purpose or objective for the activity. A fun activity without a strong objective is just filler. A fun activity with a strong objective is the sweet spot. The second thing to keep in mind is that students need to have both been taught the concept AND they need to know how to do the activity that practices the concept before they can do it independently. This is something that cannot be stressed enough. Teachers often get very excited about setting up fun literacy centers without thinking about the skills that need to be taught before students can be successful on their own. Or perhaps the skills have been taught, but when left alone at the center, students are unsure how to interact with the materials. Ensuring that students know what to do for each activity is imperative.

Examples of Phonological Awareness Centers

Teachers must provide lots of opportunities for active modeling and talking through the directions of a center. When they review center expectations each day, they make sure to remind children of steps they might be forgetting. At some centers, pictures can be included to help children remember the procedures or how to clean up.

1. **Rhyming jar**

    Ms. Molina had introduced the rhyming jar during whole group time. She modeled the "I do" portion, and the children practiced together for the "We do" portion over several days. When she decided the children were ready to play the game at a center, Ms. Molina knew that she needed to model the independent procedure for the game, the "you do" part. "We have been practicing together with the rhyming jar each day, and now it is time for you to get to play this game on your own," Ms. Molina began. "When you come to this center, you will sit down with one or two other friends. You will take turns pulling out bags of objects, like this. Do you see how there are three objects in each bag? It's just like what we did together, but this time you are pulling a bag out by yourself when it is your turn."

    Ms. Molina continued, "You will take the objects out of the bag and put them on the rhyming tray. You will say the names of the three objects out loud, and your friends will listen without saying anything. Friends will put up their thumbs if they agree and put them sideways if they don't agree. Then everyone will work together to make sure all the pictures are in the right spots. Let's try this out together." After several children modeled the procedures with teacher guidance, Ms. Molina explained the clean-up procedure. "When you are done with each bag you will put the items back in the bag, make sure the bag is fastened, and put it behind the jar. When everyone at the center has had chances to play the game, you will put all of the bags in the rhyming jar for the next group to play."

2. **Shopping center game**

    This center had been in the center rotation for a few days, and generally children were doing well with the directions. She decided to just do a quick recap. "Let's review the Shopping Center game directions. When you sit down, you will see the store shopping shelves, and 10 items on the shelves." (Ms. Molina made shopping shelves out of a shoe box and put five items on top of the box and five items on the bottom.) "You will each have your own small shopping cart. The first person to go will look at items on the shelves and ask for an item by giving a hint to their friend, telling them another word that starts the same as the one they are thinking of on the shelf."

    You can adapt this based on where students are skill level wise and what you want them to practice, as you could also include ending sound or medial sound. For this example, students will be focusing on the initial sound.

    "Got that, class?" Ms. Molina inquired. "YES!" they all replied. "Then," she continued, "without touching any of the items, you will say to your partner I'm going shopping and I want to buy something that starts the same as mouse." Your partner will look at the items on the shelf, and see that there is a magnet. They will pick it up and say "Magnet starts the same as mouse!" and put it in their shopping cart.

Then it is the other person's turn to secretly pick an item and think of another word that starts the same way, and the other person gets to guess and put it in their shopping cart. To clean up, you will unload your shopping carts and set up the shopping shelves again for the next group to come to the center.

Daily Routines for Phonological Awareness

When we began this chapter, Ms. Molina was inviting students to line up by clapping out the syllables in their name. Every day includes numerous transitions, i.e. lining up for lunch or recess. Including transitions as part of your instructional time allows you to double down on the skill and increases the effectiveness of your classroom management. Plan five minutes between the end of the lesson and the next place children have to be in order to work in routines. After enough practice, students can be invited to choose the activity. Described below are some class favorites.

1. **Moosey Moose (word play with initial sounds)**
   Moosey Moose, by Chris Raschka, is a book dearly loved by most kindergarten classes. It tells the story of a moose that is angry about wearing short pants. The author has several other books in his Thingy Thing series, including Crabby Crab, Doggy Dog, and Buggy Bug. One of the transition routines can be the game, Moosey Moose. Children are asked to think of a new title for a book the author could write. One by one, children raise their hands with an idea and are excused to the next activity or get their belongings and go home. Fishy Fish, Cowy Cow, and Dragony Dragon are all typical answers. Children love this silly game that celebrates and plays with phonological awareness and is connected to a book they adore.
2. **Broken word game (phoneme segmenting and blending)**
   Children spend a lot of time waiting quietly in the hallway during class bathroom breaks before lunch, etc. Effective teachers know better than to let that time be wasted, so another transition game is the Broken Word Game. The teacher says a broken word, a segmented word, very quietly. For example, /p/ /l/ /ay/. The children are asked to put the word back together, blend the sounds, and then whisper the whole word.
3. **Secret rule (flexibly applying phonemic awareness)**
   When there is less time and children need to be excused by groups, an effective teacher can say "Everyone whose name starts with a/d/sound can wash their hands for lunch." Sometimes teachers let children come up with a secret rule for who could be excused. They whisper it to the teacher who must make sure it works and announce the secret rule. This works for beginning sounds, middle sounds, ending sounds, blends …. The adaptations are endless and students enjoy the idea of a secret rule. They also enjoy the idea of going to lunch.

Spotlight

Phonological awareness, which is defined as *the ability to notice, think about, and work with the sounds of **oral language** at the word, onset and rime, syllable, and phoneme level*, is such an important foundational literacy skill. As students learn to understand the oral sounds in words, they are building the background to attach those sounds to letters to be able to decode and encode words. There are so many fun and productive ways to learn and practice rhyming, syllable, and beginning sound activities described in this chapter for teachers to try.

Phonological awareness can be attended to in many different ways throughout the day. Whole group, explicit, systematic phonological awareness instruction is a key part of early childhood classrooms. Also important are opportunities to work on these skills in small groups, one on one with the teacher, and independently. Teachers also capitalize on daily routines and transition opportunities for further practice. Understanding the progression of phonological awareness skills allows teachers to plan a classroom environment in which word play is both fun and strategic, building the Foundational Anchors new readers need.

References

Blachman, B. A. (1989). Phonological awareness and word recognition: Assessment and intervention. In A. Kamhi & H. Catts (Eds.), *Reading disabilities: A developmental language perspective* (pp. 138–158). Allyn & Bacon.

National Early Literacy Panel (NELP). (2008). *Developing early literacy: Report of the National Early Literacy Panel: A scientific synthesis of early literacy development and implications for intervention.* Washington, D.C. National Center for Family Literacy.

Kilpatrick, D. Ph.D. © (2003, 2010, 2019) PHONOLOGICAL AWARENESS SCREENING TEST (PAST) FORM A. Word Press by Kadence WP. thepasttest.com.

Yopp, H., & Yopp, R. (2009). *Phonological awareness is child's play. Beyond the journal, young children on the web.* National Association for the Education of Young Children.

14 Alphabet Knowledge and Phonics

Focus and Big Ideas

- Thinking about letters
- Examples of alphabet lessons
- Alphabet books and alphabet knowledge
- Phonics instruction

Thinking about Letters

A child's knowledge of the alphabet is the accumulation of a multitude of literacy events, many approximations during play and emerging reading and writing, direct teacher instruction, noticing print in the environment, small motor, and eye-hand development (see Figure 14.1) Reading and writing in an alphabetic system such as English means alphabet knowledge is essential. Emerging readers who are beginning to notice the print around them are accumulating alphabetic knowledge. Research has shown that the number of letters a child can name at the end of preschool is highly predictive of future reading success. Balancing across all diagnostic indices, optimal benchmarks of 18 uppercase and 15 lowercase letter names were identified (Piasta, Petscher, & Justice, 2012).

When we assess letter naming and related sounds for young children, we are quantifying the result of all of the experiences, instruction, conversations, read-alouds, writing, and drawing that have come before. Children from homes and care settings where these experiences are a regular occurrence often arrive at preschool naming many letters and attaching sounds to some. In other words, the number of letters a child can name is the tip of the iceberg. Teaching children 18 letters in isolation does not necessarily mean success will follow. It is important to realize that children learn about the alphabet during many literacy events in which the alphabet's purpose is modeled.

Some educators see what children need to know about the alphabet as hierarchical and would argue about what bit of information comes first. However, these pieces of the alphabet puzzle come together over time and do not follow a specific order. This is much the same as learning the name of the animal is *dog* and it says, "*Woof!*" It looks similar to a horse, but we expect children to notice and analyze the visual features to tell the difference and learn that the

DOI: 10.4324/9780429284021-14

What Children Need to Know About the Alphabet

Alphabetic knowledge is the basic information for young children and still it is multifaceted. They must know:

- letters are for reading and writing;
- the name of the letter;
- the forms of the letter (capital, lower case, variety of fonts);
- the sound(s) the letter(s) represents;
- the letter(s) used to represent a sound;
- how to write (or draw) the letter.

Figure 14.1 Components of Alphabetic Knowledge

horse says, "Neigh." No one would put off teaching their child animal names until they knew what 26 animals say!, or vice versa for that matter. A child from a literate home will know more about letters and sounds.

Children generally accumulate knowledge of letters and sounds between the ages of three and five. In any preschool or kindergarten class, there will be children who know a lot about all the letters and children who know no letter names at all. Ultimately, every child has to know all the pieces of information and learn to use the letters to create meaningful texts as well as comprehend texts. Through direct, systematic phonics instruction, guided practice, and independent approximations of reading and writing, children will learn to take words apart, put them back together, and manipulate the phonemes. They will learn how words work and how to transfer what they know to solve new problems in both reading and writing.

Research has shown that writing events, experience with writing, and opportunities to write are especially influential in children's acquisition of alphabet knowledge. "Children whose writing was more sophisticated knew the names of more letters, understood more about print concepts and were more sensitive to initial sounds of words." (Diamond, Gerde, & Powell, 2008). The most exciting part is that emerging writing accelerates the growth of alphabetic knowledge and alphabetic knowledge in turn accelerates the growth in writing competence. (Shannahan 2020). Direct and indirect **Assisted Writing** time, which includes many frameworks for writing in the classroom, is so often overlooked. This makes the teachers' job more difficult and the children's progress slower (see Chapter 16).

How Does the Alphabet Work?

There are 26 letters in the alphabet and two more to learn as children learn another form called book a (a) and book g (g). Letters represent units of sound called **phonemes.** The letters are divided into **vowels** and

consonants. The vowels are A, E, I, O, and U. Y acts as a vowel in words like try, myth, and ugly. Y acts as a consonant in words like yellow, yes, and beyond.

There are 44 phonemes in the English language because letters can make more than one sound (phoneme) like the hard and soft c and g, and long and short vowels. Phonemes made from more than one vowel are called **diphthongs**. Examples of two vowels that make one phoneme are *ee, oo, ae,* and *ou*. Two consonants that make one phoneme are called **digraphs.** The most common digraphs are *ch, th, sh,* and *wh*. Although there are nuances to these definitions, teachers must master the basic information in order to add to it.

Initially, the models of the alphabet provided to children and displayed in the classroom should be consistent and unambiguous because, really, the alphabet itself is rather inconsistent. The more teachers know about the alphabet, the easier it is for them to avoid confusing the children, recognize and analyze their confusions, and untangle confusions when they occur. Some examples are as follows:

- Some letter names begin with the sound of the letter e.g.; B, D, J, K, P, T, V, Z.
- Some letter names begin with the short e, e.g.; eff F, el L, em M, en N, es S, ecks X.
- The letter names of C (see) and G (gee) begin with soft C as in city and soft G as in gerbil, but children learn the sounds of hard G as in goat and hard C as in cat first.
- The vowels A, E, I, O, U, are taught as short vowels (ant, egg, impala, ox, umbrella) but are all named by the sound of the long vowel.
- The letters (aa<u>ch</u>) H, (kuoo) Q, (are) R, (double you) W, and (why) Y seem random.
- Some upper and lower case letters look the same or very similar, e.g.; Cc, Ff, Ii, Jj, Kk, Oo, Pp, Ss, Tt, Uu, Vv, Ww, Xx, Yy, Zz.
- The rest of the upper and lower case pairs look dissimilar, e.g., Aa, Bb, Dd, Ee, Gg, Hh, Ll, Mm, Nn, Qq, Rr.
- And finally lower case a and g have another form called book a (a) and book g (g).

The goal of offering this list is to help you think about how the alphabet works and the complexity of learning to use it. Alphabet knowledge must be taught explicitly, and its use modeled daily.

Teaching Materials

Teachers must provide many learning events that directly teach children the names and sounds of the letters. Materials (see Figure 14.2) in the classroom

---

Alphabet Teaching Materials

1. A consistent picture alphabet chart with one picture for each letter:
   a. A large one for the wall
   b. A large one that is loose for work on individual letters
   c. A small page copy of the entire picture alphabet for each child
   d. Copies of the picture alphabet to go in the centers
2. A set of name puzzle pieces for each child (see picture) or a set of magnetic letters that spell the child's name and an envelope to store each of them.

3. A classroom name chart with names of the children grouped by first letter. Leave room to add the names of new children.
4. Sets of magnetic letters with clear ball and stick letters (not letters like t and l with curls at the bottom)

Figure 14.2 Alphabet Teaching Materials

for direct teacher–led instruction for children beginning to learn about the alphabet and how to use it include the following:

The picture alphabet can be commercially purchased. Carefully consider the choice of pictures to serve as key words and mnemonic support. They can be problematic or confusing. For example, the name of the letter L is *el*. Using a picture of an el-ephant as a key confuses many children. Some pictures require teaching about the picture. For example, an igloo, a temporary ice dome made by Inuit people, is built out of snow blocks for temporary protection. Not all children know what an igloo is or the cultural information that surrounds it. If the picture reflects unfamiliar things for the children you are teaching, change the picture. A picture of George Washington for W might not be very helpful as a memory tool. Put a picture of a worm or a watermelon over top. Make the chart work for your class. It is best if teachers collaborate on the picture alphabet being used with children from three to six years old, so the model becomes solidly known and useful in a flexible way.

Word Walls

As children learn the letter names, sounds, and forms, a simple **word wall** becomes a useful tool for children aging four to six years old (see Figure 14.3). The word wall should have each letter and the associated picture in order to provide the most pathways for learning. It should be in alphabetical order to support future learning. A word wall allows children to connect sources

---

▰▰▰▰▰▰▰▰▰▰▰▰▰▰▰▰▰▰
Anchor Under Construction

- Child is trying to write *funny*. Makes the /f/ sound and the word fish pops out. They go find the picture of the fish to copy the F. (Child knows sound and picture.)
- Child is trying to write *egg*. Goes to the word wall and copies the name of the picture under E. (Child knows picture names are under each picture.)
- Child is trying to write *spider* but cannot yet easily segment blends (sp). Goes to the alphabet chart but doesn't find a spider picture. Asks a friend for help and together they stretch and write SITR.
- Children are reading a zoo book in a small group. Teacher points out the tiger on the alphabet chart, and children immediately notice the lion, iguana, and snake on the picture alphabet, connecting two sources of information in the classroom.
- While children watch, the teacher cuts apart the commercially produced color chart and adds color strips to the word wall. Children connect two more sources of information.

Figure 14.3 Examples of Children Using a Word Wall

of information about letters, sounds, and words that have previously been in separate categories. For example, a color chart, name chart, or classroom signage can become part of a word wall over time. Children use the word wall because the teacher models its use during Assisted Writing (see Chapter 16) and encourages its use by children. Teaching new words as they are added, noticing and reinforcing the word wall's use, and connecting it to reading and writing, makes the word wall meaningful. Otherwise, it is just wallpaper.

The word wall can become an indirect source of learning for children if its use is modeled by the teacher daily during Assisted Writing and if the teacher refers children to the wall when asked for information. (Child: *How do you spell candy?* Teacher: *It starts like cat. You can look at the word wall to see what letter you need.*) Adding words is direct instruction, as is removing words when children confidently produce them from memory.

A final note on word walls: Magnetic word walls have been found to be very accessible as well as instructional for children. Magnetic vent covers, cut into strips for words written in permanent marker, can be removed by the child and taken to their writing spot. Returning the word requires them to, again, look at letter features and the sequence of the alphabet. Cookie sheets, hot glued to the wall, make an excellent display.

Examples Alphabet Lessons

The Alphabet Name Game

Beginning to teach alphabetic knowledge in the classroom begins with children's names. The teacher can move from most support to least support. Teachers like to teach this procedure in small group for a week before they do it with a large group. It allows them to see which children can already perform the task, and may need a different task, and which children they will need to assist. The procedure follows:

1. Materials prep: Make a set of name puzzle pieces for each child (see Figure 14.2) or a set of magnetic letters that spell the child's name. (Use upper case or mixed-case letters depending on the current alphabet knowledge of specific children).
2. An envelope with the child's name written on it in clear manuscript (ball and stick) letters. Put the letters in the envelope.
3. Hand out each child a set of letters. Have children dump out their letters and turn them all face up, right side up.
4. Ask the children to build their name, starting with the first letter. It is **always** built left to right.
    a. Most support: Children can use the name on the envelope as a model. A red dot on the left side of the name supports left to right directionality.
    b. Medium Support: Children turn the envelope face down, build their name, and use the model on the envelope to check their work and fix it if needed.
    c. Independent: Child can consistently build correctly, left to right, in the correct order without support. They can check using visual memory.
5. Each child in the group gets a turn to point and read their name, then point and name each letter. The teacher helps each child do this successfully, generously giving as much assistance as needed. Pointing with the child, saying the names for the child if needed is fine. They will be able to do it in time.
6. **Then you play the put away game.** Using the large, loose alphabet cards, hold up one and say, *"If you have an uppercase R or a lowercase r in your name, turn it over."* Scan so you can check and assist as needed. *"Scarlet, I see a lowercase r in your name, can you find it?"* (Do not include the letter cards that show a letter no one has in their name.)
7. Move quickly until all the letters are put away. Collect the envelopes.
8. As the children get more automatic, you can add to the *put away game* by adding sound clues for consonants,
    a. *"If you have a letter in your name that says/mmm/, turn it over."*
    b. *"If you have the letter that is at the beginning of the word Sun,* (use the picture from the alphabet card) *turn it over."*

c.   *"If you have any vowels in your name, AEIOU, turn them over."* Adding complexity with **support for success**, varying commands, and moving quickly, keep the game lively and interesting. You will see children help each other and notice letters in the room.

9. This game can be played daily in large or small groups.

Learning the Picture Alphabet

Many classrooms have a picture alphabet on the wall but surprisingly this tool is not of any use to most young children unless they are taught the names of the picture and how they are associated with the letter. This game, played frequently, is one way to familiarize the children with the chart. It is also a good way to reinforce for children the **alphabetic principle**, the concept that letters represent specific sounds:

1. Give each child a picture alphabet sheet in a sheet protector. Have them put it on the table in front of them. Give each child one penny or other game piece.

2. Explain that you will name the pictures on the chart and you want them to cover it with their game piece as fast as they can by sliding it. When you give the thumbs up, they move their game piece back to the upper left corner and wait for the next clue. The clues name the pictures *"Find the impala."* and quickly scan and assist if needed. Then give the thumbs up. *"Find the dog."* After each clue, quickly scan and assist if needed but keep the pace brisk.

3. Play this version until the children know what each picture is and then move to the associated letter. *"Find I for impala." "Find the letter I… Impala."*

4. The next level is to switch between letter and picture, *"Find the letter D." "Find the picture for the letter Q." "Find the violet."* Do not add new clues until the children are quick and confident with the current set of clues. For children who are not ready to move forward, use small group settings to provide more time to practice.

5. Finally, you can add in, *"Find the picture that starts with/mmm/." "Find the letter that says,/t-t-t/."*

The children can now be prompted to use the small picture alphabet chart or the wall chart when they are working on reading, writing, or phonics.

Child: *How do you write mom?*
Teacher: *It starts like moon.*
Child: *How do you make an r?*
Teacher: *It is on your ABC chart./RRRR/What picture can help you?*
Child: *Rabbit*
Teacher: *Good thinking!*

The pictures on the picture ABC chart create a key word for the child to use as one pathway to the letter and sound. By first grade, multiple versions of picture alphabets can be used, but using a simple consistent one with preschool and kindergarten children is efficient and effective.

Who Needs Alphabet Lessons?

While children are having opportunities to play the letter name game and learn the alphabet chart, participate in read-aloud of alphabet books, and Assisted Writing; the teacher should provide specific lessons on individual letters for children who do not know them. This is another path to alphabet knowledge. First, use the initial letter identification screening. Goal number one is to help the child explore and solidify the letters they know or almost know. For example, Ellie can name all the letters in her name on the letter identification screening instrument. She does not connect the upper and lower case e and could not find them on the picture alphabet chart, but she has partial knowledge. She knows the names of the letters and how to form them. The teacher must plan for time and instruction for Ellie to become quick and flexible with the letters she knows or almost knows. Goal number two is learning new letters. After the child has solidified a few letters, letter learning is easier. They have learned how to learn letters. Planning alphabet lessons using the *I Do-We do-(We do-We do)-You do* structure assures learning will take place. The teacher lets go a little at a time during *We-do,* while observing the child's growing competence. It takes time to teach and support the child toward mastery.

Alphabet lessons in early childhood curricula generally include activities, *some* of which assist children in learning about letters. Look back at Figure 14.1. Does the suggested activity assist the child to learn any items on the list? Does forming letters in clay help children notice circles, curves, humps, and lines? Certainly, the learning that occurs as the teacher directs the child's attention to the distinguishing features of the letter is clear and unambiguous. However, a child doing this same activity without direct instruction will not have the same outcome as a child who has. Practicing at a center, indirect learning, will help solidify the learning after direct, explicit instruction.

Adding to what a child knows or almost knows is powerful teaching. Adding new letters requires other considerations. Is the new letter visually similar to the last letter the child learned? The letters, **b, h, p, d,** and **q,** are all very similar and should **not** be taught close together. Teaching correct letter formation is formally introduced in kindergarten and the **verbal path for the formation of letters** helps children avoid confusion. Children learn to tell their hands what to do to make a letter. For example, lowercase b and d are formed differently. Lowercase b is formed by *a straight line down, back up, and around.* A lowercase d is formed by *a magic c, all the way up and back down.* Teachers should also learn how to model correct manuscript letter formation.

Alphabet Books and Alphabet Knowledge

Adding to **alphabet knowledge** can be a goal during read-aloud when you are reading alphabet books. The text of well-written picture books, poetry books, and informational books should be enjoyed and comprehended for their content and language. Alphabet books are different. The alphabet is usually the organizing structure of alphabet books. They can be a *text set* by themselves and can be included in other text sets as well. For example, Alphabet Under Construction could be included in a text set of *ABC Books, Books by Denise Fleming*, and *Books with Mice in Them*. Young children should experience the alphabet in many ways during their early childhood years. Reading aloud from alphabet books is a very productive and efficient strategy for encouraging children's familiarity with alphabet knowledge while enjoying the read-aloud process.

Various alphabet books focus on sharing different information such as letter names, letter shapes, letter sound, introducing lower case letters, matching upper and lower case letters, alliteration, and phonological awareness. These are most useful in increasing alphabet knowledge. Books that connect letters and sounds and **teacher talk** about the letterforms during repeated readings can support children in transferring what they know about the letters in one context to an unfamiliar book, a new context. For example, the letters always come in the same order and every letter has a **big, uppercase, or capital** letter and a **little, lower case, or small** form. Books use different terminology (Tier 2 vocabulary) for the pairs of big and little letters.

Some stories use letters as characters or as part of the plot. Stories such as Audrey Woods' *Alphabet Rescue* and *Alphabet Mystery* have letters that take action and solve problems. These are fun and interesting because they are narratives, organized by story with use of the letters. As with all well-planned and presented read-alouds, these are fun and inviting but are less focused on the essential alphabet knowledge.

Many alphabet books can be read with or without the accompanying informational text, making the book available to children at different levels of experience. Jerry Pallotta's informational alphabet books such as The Icky Bug Alphabet Book and The Construction Alphabet Book engage children in content vocabulary while allowing the teacher to decide how much information they will offer on each page. Teachers can direct attention to the letter and sound and name the picture without reading aloud the entire informational paragraph. These serve the purpose of knowledge building and adding Tier 3 vocabulary. Dr. Seuss's(1963) ABCs, an amazing alphabet book, offers several words for each letter, including inventive rhymes on each page. This is a book that children can chant along with the teacher while feeling letter sounds in their mouths and hearing themselves produce sounds. *Alphabet Under Construction* by Denise Fleming (2002) and *The Z was Zapped* by Chris Van Allsburg (1987) have more complex letter connections that are supported by enthralling illustrations. Teachers carefully choose books that will support the concepts they are teaching and lead to substantive conversations. Choose the best books available and reread them multiple times. The children will develop alphabet knowledge along with enjoying being read to.

Not all alphabet books are high quality or appropriate for young children. For example, there are several alphabet books on endangered animals that would be more appropriate content for older children who can understand man's destruction of habitat and the resulting extinctions. Add the best, most appropriate books to your read-aloud library and include them in more than one text set.

Alphabet Books as a Structure for Emerging Reading and Writing

Alphabet books use the alphabet as an organizing structure and young writers love to experiment with this structure. Teachers often begin by producing content-specific books for their children and making class books. Creating an alphabet book with names and photos for the class members is a way to use the genre for specific goals. There won't be a picture for every letter, but instead a page for every child. "C is for Carlos. We like Carlos. E is for Essie. We like Essie." Class-specific books can support letter learning and help children transfer alphabetic knowledge from one context to another.

Producing multiple alphabet books encourages children to interact with and emergently reread the **class books**. Twenty-six pages in a loose-leaf notebook can become an ABC book about soccer, the class pet or the current topic of investigation. Using page protectors allows the teacher and children to add to the book. Not every page has to be filled at first but more information can be added over time as children learn more information and add to the class book.

During Assisted Writing times, children can create their own alphabet books using a simplified structure by creating pages with words that begin like their own name. Marty's M Book is manageable, whereas a 26-page book is overwhelming. A second way for children to use letters as their organizing structure in a simplified way is to connect to a topic. "My Dog Alphabet Book," can have pages with B is for bark, W is for walks, L is for love, etc. without, again, trying to create 26 pages. These books both in their creation and in their rereading provide practice in alphabet knowledge and segmenting the first sound in a word.

Phonics Instruction

The terms phonics, phonemic awareness, phonological awareness, phoneme, and cell phones are all connected to the same morphological (meaning) base **phon** that is the Greek root word for **sound**. There are 44 sounds or **phonemes** in the English language. Infants hear and imitate the phonemes of the primary language around them. Babbling is the infant imitating sounds they hear. They make easier sounds first like baba, dada, papa. It's no wonder that these are words for *father* in many languages.

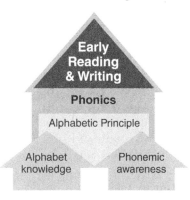

Figure 14.4 Phonics Instruction Is anchored by Phonemic Awareness and Alphabet Knowledge.

Children must be able to hear and manipulate individual sounds orally (phonemic awareness) before they can fully benefit from the inclusion of print (letters). Hearing and making beginning, ending, and middle sounds, hearing and clapping syllables, hearing and producing rhymes, and segmenting words into phonemes can all be done without having mastered all aspects of alphabet knowledge. Children need instruction and practice of phonics in direct learning contexts along with indirect learning. Center activities that support practice **after** the child has learned how to hear sounds can support the development of speed and flexibility to hear and use sounds. For example, picture card sets can be used, even by non-readers, to match beginning sounds after they have been demonstrated and modeled. These same activities, without the direct learning, cannot teach children new concepts.

Alphabet knowledge and phonemic awareness develop together and support the alphabetic principle, that is, sounds and letters work together. Speech sounds are represented by letters and combinations of letters and can be used to encode and decode written language. How that is actually done is phonics. Phonics instruction is supported by research and is required for children to learn to use the symbols of English (letters) to understand the written word and write meaningful text (U.S. Department of Health and Human Services, 2000).

If it seems like there are many moving pieces to teach and connect so that children can conceptualize the alphabetic principle, there truly are. Unfortunately, in avoiding the complexity and interconnectedness of the Foundational Anchors, many teachers skip the foundation and begin with phonics lessons before children have control of sounds. Others simply teach information in isolation; letter of the week, kindergarten sight words, and short vowel sounds. The least experienced children understand the least of what is being presented and most children are unable to transfer understandings from one context to the next. The teacher is still working hard but seeing fewer results.

Kindergarten Phonics

As children learn the pictures on the alphabet chart, the letter names, and sounds, they begin to learn words they care about (mom, dad, Rover) and make sense of how words work. They are ready to decode and encode words with a consonant-vowel-consonant (CVC) pattern, (e.g., cat, hot, pup) These words all have short vowels. Jumping to this instruction before children can hear and manipulate sounds, and use letters and sounds in their writing, can create confusion. Most children have control of letters and sounds during their kindergarten year (Pounds, 2013) Letter naming assessments can determine where children are in their alphabetic knowledge and what they are ready for next.

Manipulating onset-rime to make new words is a direct learning context. The making words professional books (Cunningham & Hall, 2009) include many examples of lesson formats for direct instruction. **Decodable texts**, texts that use the same word pattern repeatedly, allow children to practice what they are learning in the phonics lesson. As children are able to control these short vowel words, consonant blends and digraphs can be included in the consonant portion of the CVC pattern (e.g., chap, fish, spin, grin). By the end of first grade, these concepts and skills, along with the silent e, should be an automatic part of the child's phonics application.

Teaching Sight Words

The idea of teaching sight words in kindergarten and first grade is to create a bank of words the child can read and write with automaticity. Teachers are provided a wide variety of sight word lists, and the instruction tends to be primarily about visual memory. Boxes in the shapes of words, flash cards, and worksheets are about memorizing how words look, learning them by "sight." However, when teachers take time to analyze the list they are assigned, they can organize the word into word families (onset-rime) and word patterns. Using the Dolch list (Dolch, 1949), as an example, the words in Figure 14.5 have been organized for systematic instruction that can be generalized and transferred. From 52 sight words, there are more than 150 words children can control, using what they have learned to solve new words in both reading and writing. If you can read and spell *at*, you can read and spell ten more (_at) words using onset and rime. Using magnetic letters to manipulate sounds and make new words helps children uncover and practice using what they know (at) to solve a new problem (cat, fat, etc.). Teachers can analyze any sight word list in the same way.

A Phonics Curriculum

The selection of a phonics curriculum is most often done at the administration level. Teachers should have a curriculum that has a **systematic scope and sequence** of the teaching and learning to support their understanding of how knowledge builds from simple to complex. Children must learn to "sound out" words in reading while simultaneously participating in Assisted Writing routines. The *stretching and writing* and the *sounding and blending* of phonemes, now represented by letters, are reciprocal processes. Keeping these processes connected supports children using knowledge across contexts (Blevins, 2020).

The phonics curriculum must allow for differentiation. An experienced kindergarten teacher, implementing a new phonics curriculum was worried. The same lesson was supposed to be presented to the entire class. She was expected to deliver the daily lessons as written. However, the children who arrived at kindergarten reading text independently needed to learn to transfer what they knew to writing. The children who could not orally segment first letters needed phonemic awareness. No curriculum is appropriate to meet all the children's needs at the same time.

Decodable text along with Assisted Writing that supports the sounds and words being taught helps children connect what they are being directly taught in the phonics lesson to reading and writing. Teachers must use their professional judgment when using any text to support emerging readers. Decodable text can be nonsensical for children who struggle with language. Providing support for comprehension before the child reads builds language comprehension. The teacher says, "*On this page Sid and Min are playing hide and seek. Let's read the words.*" The child reads, "*Sid and Min hid. Sid hid in the big hat. Min hid in the bed.*" As the child practices sounding out and blending short vowel words, they are able to hold onto meaning. Making meaning from text is the goal of reading and children are easily confused about what reading is. Decodable text and Assisted Writing must build on what has been previously taught but must also include, review, and integrate prior learning. In the passage above, both *short a* and *short e* words are included, as is the sight word *the.* The text is creating opportunities for children to use what they learned from one lesson in the service of new learning.

The Phonics Developmental Continuum (PDC) (Pounds, 2013; http://yukonpssurrey.ss19.sharpschool.com) is an informational support if the teacher is not provided with a scope and sequence. Based on what children know about letters and sounds, the sequence in the PDC helps teachers determine the next set of concepts and information to be explicitly taught. This is also a guide to when and what information must be modeled and applied during Assisted Writing time. Learning the complexities of phonics is only a benefit to children when they have adequate opportunities to use and apply information in the service of reading and writing. Emerging reading and writing opportunities are essential for children to use and practice what they know (see Chapters 15 and 16).

Teaching phonics to three- and four-year-old children, instead of focusing on the other Foundational Anchors, will not help them advance. Alphabet knowledge and phonological awareness undergird the alphabetic principle (see Figure 14.5) Earlier is not better if children are unable to connect the pieces. It's like serving a T-bone steak to an infant. You may say you fed him, but he won't gain any weight.

Dolch Sight Words Kindergarten Words that work the same way in black							
All	**Am**	**At**	**Ran**	**Saw**	**Black**	**Get**	**Went**
Call	Ham	**That**	Ban	Draw	Hack	Bet	Bent
Fall	Jam	Bat	Can	Jaw	Jack	Jet	Cent
Mall	Pam	Cat	Dan	Law	Lack	Let	Dent
Hall	Ram	Fat	Fan	Paw	Mack	Met	Gent
Tall	Sam	Hat	Man	Raw	Pack	Net	Kent
Wall		Mat	Pan		Quack	Pet	Lent
		Pat	Ran		Rack	Set	Rent
		Rat	Tan		Sack	Vet	Sent
		Sat	Van		Tack	Wet	Tent
		Vat					Vent
Well	**Did**	**Will**	**Brown**	**But**	**Must**	**Eat**	**Came**
Bell	Bid	Bill	**Now**	Cut	Bust	Beat	Fame
Cell	Hid	Dill	Town	Gut	Dust	Heat	Game
Dell	Lid	Fill	Down	Hut	Gust	Meat	Lame
Fell	Rid	Hill	Clown	Mutt	Just	Neat	Name
Jello	Video	Jill	Cow	Nut	Rust	Seat	Same
Sell		Kill	How	Rut		Wheat	Tame
Tell		Mill	Now				Blame
		Pill	Plow				
Ate	**Say**	**He**	**White**	**Like**	**Ride**	**Too**	**No**
Date	Bay	**She**	Bite	Bike	Hide	**Soon**	**Go**
Fate	Day	**Be**	Kite	Dike	Side	**Who**	**So**
Gate	Hay	me	Lite	Hike	Tide	**Do**	
Hate	Jay	we	Quite	Mike	Wide	**into**	
Kate	Lay			Pike			
Late	May						
Mate	Pay						
Rate	Ray						
	Way						
Please	**New**	**Good**	**Under**		**There**	Words without pattern	
Ease	Dew	Hood	Thunder		The	**Pretty yes want**	
	Drew				This	**With four was**	
	Crew				They	**What are our On**	

Figure 14.5 Teaching Sight Word Patterns

Spotlight

When teachers look carefully at how the alphabet is put together and the relationship between letters and sounds, the amount of learning that has to take place seems unmanageable. Teachers and curriculum writers are tempted to teach each piece separately while disagreeing about the sequence. All the Foundational Anchors are linked and teachers must teach children to connect learning across tasks. Materials and lessons for direct learning contexts for alphabetic knowledge are provided to support teacher thinking and planning. Children's names are a great place to start.

Phonics curricula are not usually selected by teachers, vary in quality and usefulness, but may be adjusted to meet the needs of a particular group of children. Whole group phonics instruction provides the least learning for the children who need the most support.

Word walls can be a useful tool for children when teachers model and encourage their use. Word walls make clear what letters and sounds are used for and reinforce the alphabet sequence. Alphabet books can increase alphabetic knowledge, add to read–aloud time, and support content area learning. They also show ways in which the children and teacher can use the alphabet as a means to structure their own texts.

Teaching children to manipulate sounds and letters for encoding and decoding is phonics instruction. Teachers build the beginnings of phonics onto the strong foundation and continue the work in a direct and systematic manner. They check for understanding and monitor progress through alphabet screening, children's reading of decodable and predictable books, and their use of sounds in their emerging writing.

References

Blevins, W. (2020). *A fresh look at phonics; Make instruction active and engaging to turn students into skilled readers.* National Association of Elementary School Principals. NAESP.org

Cunningham, P. M., & Hall, D. P. (2009). *Making words first grade: 100 hands-on lessons for phonemic awareness, phonics and spelling.* Pearson Education.

Diamond, K. E., Gerde, H. K., & Powell, D. R. (2008). Development in early literacy skills during the pre-kindergarten year in Head Start: Relations between growth in children's writing and understanding of letters. *Early Childhood Research Quarterly, 23*(4), 467–478.

Dolch, E. W. (1949). *Problems in reading.* Garrard Press.

Piasta, S. B., Petscher, Y., & Justice, L. M. (2012). How many letters should preschoolers in public programs know? The diagnostic efficiency of various preschool letter-naming benchmarks for predicting first-grade literacy achievement. *Journal of Educational Psychology, 104*(4), 945–958. https://doi.org/10.1037/a0027757

Pounds, G. (2013). *Phonics developmental continuum.* Yukon Public Schools. Retrieved November 17, 2021, from http://yukonpssurrey.ss19.sharpschool.com/

Shannahan, T. (2020). *How can we take advantage of reading-writing relationships?* Reading-Writing Relationships | Shanahan on Literacy. Retrieved October 27, 2021, from https://www.shanahanonliteracy.com/blog

National Reading Panel (U.S.), & National Institute of Child Health and Human Development (U.S.). (2000). *Report of the national reading panel: Teaching children to read: An evidence-based assessment of the scientific research literature on reading and its implications for reading instruction: Reports of the subgroups.* National Institute of Child Health and Human Development, National Institutes of Health.

References for Children's literature

Fleming, D. (2002). *Alphabet under construction*, Henry Holt Publisher.

Seuss, Dr. (1963). *Dr. Seuss's ABC.* Beginner Books.

Van Allsberg, C. (1987). *The Z was zapped.* Houghton Miffin Co.

15 Emerging Reading

Focus and Big Ideas

- Emerging readers
- Daily reading contexts: reading to, with, and by children
- Shared Reading
- Planning time for emerging reading

Emerging Readers

Two-year-old Brennan sat by himself at the bottom of the stairs, rocking back and forth with joyous rhythm as held his book, Pete the Cat (Dean & Litwin, 2010), and chanted the words. He turned the pages back and forth, using the pictures of the prior page to remind himself of the colored mess that Pete would step in next. His voice was bold and confident as he used the expression he had heard his parents use during their many read-alouds of this favorite book. "But did Pete cwy?," he asked loudly with emotion. "Noodness no!"

How do we describe the exciting changes that occur when a young child begins to initiate interactions with books and print? We can see that they are on the cusp of beginning to read as they start to memorize books, recognize letters and their name in print, retell stories, make up silly rhymes, and give meaning to their own scribbles. Reading-like behaviors become visible; page turning, moving front to back through the pages of a book, moving their finger from left to right along the print, using the pictures to guide the reading, and recognizing a story by the cover.

At this point in their journey of learning to read, children are called **Emerging Readers.** They are in the Foundation Stage of Reading Development, the stage prior to their ability to rely exclusively on the print to read and write. Although not relying on the print, they are beginning to actively construct meaning with text, referencing their experiences with literacy, what they have been taught, and what they have learned about oral and written language, the Foundational Anchors of literacy. Emerging Reading can be described along a developmental continuum. The developmental

DOI: 10.4324/9780429284021-15

progress is led by both the quality and quantity of literacy interactions and instruction. Very young children who are just beginning to orally label pictures in a book are on the beginning side of the continuum. Children who use their memory of the story, knowledge of the genre, concepts of print, and some familiar words or letters to emergently read a familiar story are on the more advanced side. The Foundational Anchors comprise the information children reference to construct meaning from text. The extent to which each anchor is developed contributes to a child's overall level of Emerging Reading. It also influences the rate of a child's progression from Emerging Reader to Proficient Reader.

As indicated previously, the Foundational Anchors of literacy do not develop proficiency in a sequence, one before the other. For example, complete alphabet knowledge does not develop before concepts of print begin to develop. Executive function develops right alongside phonemic awareness. And although some educators are surprised by this, reading does not develop before writing but at the same time. While each of a child's Foundational Anchors of literacy may be at different levels of advancement, all develop concurrently, and each solidifies and expands the development of the others. This is called **reciprocity**.

Using Daily Reading Contexts to Support Emerging Reading

When children engage in emerging reading, they simultaneously apply their current understanding of each of the anchors in order to make sense of and bring meaning to print.

> The teacher had read aloud Make Way for Ducklings, by Robert McClosky, several times to the preschool class. Because the children enjoyed it so much, she put several paperback copies in the classroom library. One went into the tub about ducks, and two went into the Read Aloud tub. During Center's Time, Austin found the book and sat on the floor with his back against the comfy couch. He looked at the cover and opened the first page. After reading the title, he began the first sentence, sounding like he was actually reading the book. Continuing through the book, page by page, he paraphrased the action, using some exact wording and some informed improvisation. Because of the length of the text, Austin could not memorize the book word for word. He used his memory of the story, the pictures, the exact expression that the teacher used at various points, and some of the author's actual wording that had resonated with him. He included the word "molt" without missing a beat. The teacher had introduced and reinforced that word during the readings. He joyfully called out the rhyming names of the

ducklings, "Jack, Pack, Lack, Mack, Nack, Ouack, Pack and Quack. Duckling was a new word for him that he assimilated into his language comprehension with the teacher's support. Another child, Josie, sidled up to him to listen as he read, participating at times for clarification or to make a comment.

Quite a complex cognitive task for a preschool child and one that is not dissimilar to the thinking a proficient reader engages in while reading! **Emerging reading** is a legitimate stage of learning to read and a necessary opportunity for children to *practice* and *apply* the Foundational Anchors. Early childhood teachers plan for all children to engage in this cognitive work within **meaningful** instructional contexts multiple times throughout the day. Children who engage in emerging literacy through enjoyable, purposeful contexts are more likely to establish positive dispositions about literacy, develop background knowledge and vocabulary, and long-term memory for the concepts and conventions of print.

Daily Reading Contexts

Effective teachers plan for all children to engage in daily intentional opportunities for:

* **Reading to children**
* **Reading with children, and**
* **Reading by children** (Mooney, 1990)

Reading by children for those who are not yet reading conventionally is called Emerging Reading.

Reading to Children

The criteria for selecting books to read aloud to young children throughout the day was discussed in Chapters 11 and 12. Selecting texts for children to emergently read after they have heard the book read-aloud requires another set of criteria (see Figure 15.1).Any text that is read aloud to children to the extent they can anticipate what it says becomes what is called **familiar text**. All texts chosen or created for children to emergently read **must be** familiar texts. Familiar texts can represent a wide array of published or adult, class, or child created books; printed or handwritten.

When familiar text is provided, children have a high probability of successful, enjoyable emerging reading. They will orchestrate all of the information at their disposal to reconstruct the text, including their memory of hearing and seeing the familiar print read-aloud. The extent to which

---

Criteria for Selecting Future 'Familiar' Books

- Large, clear, well-spaced words
- Plain typeface
- Illustrations that support or extend the meaning of the words
- Genre structure that can be noticed and perhaps imitated (poetry versus a story or informational text)
- Story structure that can be noticed and perhaps imitated
- Length of sentences (mostly simple sentence structure)
- Number of sentences per page (1–2)
- Length of entire text
- Literary language that invites successful participation of students through features such as repetition, pattern, rhyme, rhythm, or song

---

Figure 15.1 Criteria for Selecting Future 'Familiar' Books

each of children's Foundational Anchors of literacy is developed will also have an impact on their ability to emergently read a familiar text. Because there is no expectation of precise reading, the child will actively attempt to make sense of text without fear of reprisal for their emerging but not quite accurate approximations. Their focus will be on the joy, meaning, and purpose of the print. With this comes the belief in themselves as competent readers. They will use semantic and syntactic knowledge of the language, and print or grapho-phonic information to the extent that they can as they self-monitor for accurate meaning, a critical strategy used by proficient readers.

Reading with Children

SHARED READING: A BRIDGE TO INDEPENDENT READING

The pedagogy of Shared Reading uses a memorizable, highly **predictable text** to read aloud to the children (see Figure 15.2). The predictability allows children to successfully anticipate the book's next word, next sentence, next character, or idea. After the teacher has read the book at least twice and it has become a familiar text, the teacher invites children to "read along" in places where it repeats and/or can be anticipated. After several Shared Readings of the text, many children can repeat the entire text with the teacher, with other children, or independently. Shared Reading books, therefore, become a source of familiar texts for children to emergently read.

Types of Predictable Books

- **Repetition of phrase**—the word order in a phrase or sentence is repeated.
- **Rhyme**—the book has rhyming words, refrains, or patterns that are repeated.
- **Chain or circular story**—the story ending leads back to the story beginning.
- **Cumulative story**—each time a new event occurs, all previous events are repeated.
- **Familiar sequence**—the book is organized around a recognizable theme or concept, such as days of the week, numbers, the alphabet, seasons, opposites.
- **Pattern stories**—scenes in the story are repeated with some variation.
- **Question and answer**—the same or similar questions are repeated throughout the story.

http://pabook2.libraries.psu.edu/familylit/LessonPlan/rover/Parent%20 Education/Types_of_Predictable_Books_Charts.pdf

---

Figure 15.2 Types of Predictable Books

To be effective, the practice of Shared Reading must focus, as all reading does, on the meaning of the text. What is happening, why is it happening, who is it happening to, all must be clearly developed. During Shared Reading, the focus can easily turn into just memorization, with children joyfully chanting along with the book. Children can easily chant along with a book refrain without any notion of the meaning in much the same way we recited prayers or hymns as children. We could repeat the words but may have had little access to their meaning. More than one child has named their teddy bear Gladly after singing Gladly, the Cross-Eyed Bear (Gladly, the Cross I'd Bear) in Sunday school. While memorization supports the child to independently interact with the book, it provides a very low level of cognitive activity.

Predictable Books and Shared Reading

There are many important purposes for Shared Reading. Preeminent is the continuous modeling of how fluent reading sounds and how the reading process works. **Predictable books** can be an indispensable part of this modeling. Effective Shared Reading of predictable books engages children's minds. It facilitates their understanding of the structure of a text and participation in the experience of fluent reading. After the second reading, it focuses children's eyes on the print. Shared Reading is a **Read With Children** routine in which children divide their attention between the meaning of the story and the print. It is a teacher-led group activity so children can participate (share the responsibility for the reading) to the extent they are able and they learn from other's attempts.

The term Shared Reading has lost favor in some schools due to its association with Whole Language, which was thought to rely on incidental versus explicit teaching. The routine of Shared Reading, however, presents a unique and valuable opportunity for children to engage in important reading behaviors in a highly supportive setting. It draws in reluctant children, risk-averse children, multi-language learners, and low language children, allowing them to participate successfully with their classmates in reading-like behaviors and enjoyment of the print. These children may be further supported to make meaning and gain vocabulary by working with the same text in small groups.

The predictable books used for Shared Reading are enlarged texts, Big Books, so that all children in the group can have eyes on the print. There are many books commercially produced for this use, however, these vary greatly in quality and appropriateness for Shared Reading.

Supporting Children's Background Knowledge and Vocabulary during Shared Reading

Consider the critical differences in children's development of their Foundational Anchors when (1) a teacher just reads the book, *The Old Lady who Swallowed a Fly* (Taback, 1997), for example, and then encourages the children to chime in for subsequent readings, versus (2) when a teacher includes discussion of the meaning of the text and the vocabulary with the children. Talking with the children about the old lady creates opportunities to consider each of the creatures she ate, the predator and prey relationship that she builds on, and then the graduated sizes. "What do you think she was thinking?"

Different teaching purposes and conversation to support the Foundational Anchors of literacy can happen before, during, and after subsequent Shared Readings (see Figure 15.3). The quality of the learning experience is what makes effective development of the Foundational Anchors possible. Preparing for and implementing effective Shared Reading must include a focus on comprehension. The advantage of understanding what the story is about, what the words mean, how to summarize the story, or share it with a peer is the access to literacy learning and language comprehension. As with shared book read-alouds, teachers should always conduct a Shared Reading by modeling fluent reading. They must make the reading sound like talk, and use expression, hand movements, and facial expressions to convey the meaning of the text. Having children act out the text while others read fluently also focuses on meaning.

Shared Reading can provide many opportunities to connect reading and writing, an important practice (Shanahan, 1988). The teacher can create an

Anchor Under Construction

Shared Reading

Alize begins a Shared Reading as she would a shared book read-aloud, with a planned introduction to the book. She then reads the book to the children with fluency, using a book stand to support the larger book. She stops to rephrase for meaning, and to check for understanding. The children and teacher enjoy the book together, discussing and responding to the content. She encourages and supports conversation about the book, what the pictures tell us, and what the children think.

After the second reading of the book, or when children become familiar enough with the meaning and cadence of the text, Alize brings the print to the children's attention. She uses a pointer to point **under** the words as she reads fluently, models left-to-right directionality with return sweep, and voices to print correspondence. Consider how this enjoyable Shared Reading routine can support the development of **several specific** Foundational Anchors.

For example:

- **Oral language, vocabulary and background knowledge** develop through a focus on meaning. When children understand and can talk about a text as a group, gains in oral language, vocabulary and background knowledge are often observed.
- **Book awareness and story structure** develop as teachers model and then guide children to read and reread predictable books together.
- **Phonological awareness and phonemic awareness** develop when teachers use predictable books that include rhyming and alliteration. Teacher guidance offers opportunities to model counting the number of words in a sentence and noticing the beginning sounds in alliterative passages (Big Bob the Bear went bang, bang, bump) and ending sounds in rhyming words.
- **Alphabet knowledge and phonics:** Some alphabet books are repetitive and easily memorizable. This makes them very appropriate for emerging reading. Teacher guided Shared Reading materials such as charts and morning messages can facilitate teachers pointing out letter names and sound/symbol relationships (phonics).
- **Print concepts:** Once children are familiar with the meaning and structure of the predictable text, Shared Reading provides an effective learning context to demonstrate and name concepts of print such as directionality and voice-print match. Teachers can help children notice and name print features and conventions such as capital letters and punctuation marks.
- **Emerging reading:** Encouraging children to access and reread the Shared Reading texts encourages children to engage in emerging reading with confidence and success.

Figure 15.3 Shared Reading *(Continued)*

- **Emerging writing:** Teacher guided small groups provide effective learning opportunities in which children draw, label, or write about aspects of the texts or use the text structure to make stories of their own.
- **Positive dispositions about literacy and literacy learning** are developed during Shared Reading as they are risk-free reading opportunities that support children's success and confidence as readers.
- **Executive function** is developed as teachers actively encourage children to think about the text, engage in synchronous reading with their classmates, and anticipate where and when to chime in, and to follow with their eyes during teacher modeling of directionality and concepts of print. Executive function is also practiced as children split their attention between the meaning of the story and the print.

Figure 15.3 (Continued)

Assisted Writing activity that uses the story structure of the Shared Reading text with a different twist. These are called **Innovations of a Text**. For example, "I Know a (Preschooler, Kindergartener, First Grader) Who Swallowed a Raisin." Then each food gets larger in size. This can be a teacher-guided activity on a single piece of chart paper or on a storyboard. During small groups, children can be reminded of the original story, or reread the story, after which they are provided a piece of construction paper with the new twist written clearly and in legible handwriting at the bottom. A blank line is included for the new word and can be written by the teacher or the child. Both activities can be made into class books. **Innovations** that use a repeated or definite story structure can bring the structure to the forefront while modeling how to be inspired to write by reading. Examples of predictable books to use for innovations can be found in professional books such as *Getting the Most From Predictable Books* (Opitz, 1999). Sharing these new individual or class books with friends and family, and making them accessible during an independent reading time, encourages emerging reading.

Beyond Predictable Books: Creating Texts for Shared Reading

Shared Reading texts are created when groups of children create charts, lists, letters, reminders, directions, and other meaningful messages. These should be read aloud **to** the children and then **with** the children as a Shared Reading. When children become familiar with the text, the text should be made accessible to the children for purposeful emerging reading. All teacher produced text must be written neatly in plain manuscript handwriting (e.g., Zaner-Bloser Manuscript writing chart) with adequate spacing. Black, brown, blue, and green ink are the most readable (https://www.printablee.com/post_zaner-bloser-handwriting-chart-printable_322618/).

Examples of texts created for Shared Reading include:

- an attendance chart,
- signs for a hospital being created in the block center,
- directions for using the listening center,
- a menu in the dramatic play restaurant,
- a morning message,
- a nursery rhyme written on an enlarged chart, or
- a class dictated story about a trip to the ice cream factory.

If the familiar text is teacher-made directions, signs, or charts, the teacher must bring them to the child's attention. A teacher who places this type of text in what they would consider full view cannot assume children will notice or use it. Teachers must also be mindful of demonstrating how the particular text is read. Examples throughout the day include using a finger to demonstrate reading environmental print, using a pointer or a finger to demonstrate the process of reading aloud each child's name on the lunch chart, or when reading the list of ingredients for making Stone Soup. Pointing should be fluid, not word by word. Pointing under each word can result in modeling disfluent word-by-word reading. Being aware that you are **always** modeling reading fluency when you read any text aloud will ensure you avoid that error. As discussed in Chapter 3, the National Reading Panel (U.S.) & National Institute of Child Health and Human Development (U.S.), 2000) found that fluency is critical to proficient reading.

Reading by Children

"Reading By Children," who are not relying on print or only beginning to notice print, is known as **Emerging Reading**. Emerging Reading is a critically important Foundational Anchor all too frequently missing from early literacy curriculum. Classroom teachers who would consider themselves remiss not to include daily shared book read-alouds and Shared Reading often neglect to provide routines for children to independently reread familiar texts in risk-free, pleasurable situations. This denies children the time to synthesize and apply their Foundational Anchors of literacy. It further denies them the opportunities to develop the habit and confidence of reading independently. This is especially true for the least experienced literacy learners. Research shows that they get more instruction and less practice (Allington, 1983). Daily piano lessons with no time to practice do not make one a better piano player. You have to practice by yourself, hitting the wrong note and finding your way. Your mom isn't listening, correcting each note, so there is no risk involved.

Emerging reading of a variety of familiar texts and the time allotted to read and enjoy them should be provided for all children on a daily basis. When the familiar text is a favorite book that has been read aloud, it is important to provide multiple copies of it in the classroom library. Teachers should point these books out to children and ensure they are easily locatable and accessible to the children.

What does Emerging Reading look like? This depends on the child's current foundation of literacy and their degree of familiarity with the book. When rereading a very familiar book, preschool children with a strong foundation of literacy will typically use their comprehension of the story, their memory of the book, their memory of the reading situation in which they heard the text, the pictures, and the genre of the story (for example, if it is a fairy tale, a cumulative or predictable book, or an informational book). They may point to print if it is a predictable book (and pointing has been modeled) or if the print in some way adds to the enjoyment of the story (as in *Good Night Gorilla* when the page is dark except for where the animals each say "goodnight" in speech bubbles to the zookeeper). Any child-reading that uses some print information but does not involve reading each word accurately based solely on the print is considered emergent. Very young children may emergently read books with one or two words per page, acknowledging the print but not using it, whereas kindergarteners may use some known words and improvise others.

Planning Time for Emerging Reading

Planning for Emerging Reading in Socio-Dramatic Play

When children play at a high level in socio-dramatic play, they use literacy props for functional purposes (see Chapters 9 and 10). In this type of play, emerging reading is done BY children to accomplish role-specific goals. As with all effective teaching, the emerging reading children will do during play must be carefully considered, crafted, introduced, and modeled for the children.

As teachers consider the theme for the dramatic play center, they determine three to four roles that children would take. If the theme is a restaurant, for example, the roles might be a cook, a waitperson, and customer(s). The children's prior experience with the theme (read-alouds, field trips, life experiences, videos, etc.) will impact the extent to which children understand the complexity of these roles. Teachers then consider the important ways in which each role would specifically use literacy and the literacy props to accomplish goals (cooking, explaining a menu, ordering). Creating literacy props can be accomplished by the teacher independently or with the children in small groups. The decision of who should participate in making the props depends on the accuracy and detail required to create a functional literacy prop and whether the prop needs to be constructed prior to children's play.

Ensuring children will use the literacy prop and use it purposefully is contingent on the teacher introducing the prop, explaining why it is necessary to a specific role, and how it is used. Using the I Do, We Do, You Do steps of explicit instruction for this purpose is more likely to result in the children using their emerging reading during play.

Planning for Emerging Reading during Center's Time

Center's Time is a valuable part of each young child's day in the classroom. It provides a significant amount of time, typically at least an hour, for children to engage in independent practice and application of many developmental domains, including the Foundational Anchors of literacy. If planned effectively, children's minds remain not only interested and engaged during the entire time but also important learning is solidified.

Centers' Time, also known as Choice Time, is most likely to support children's time on task and level of involvement when teachers allow children to determine the amount of time they spend in a center. Ringing the bell or turning off the lights to signal children to switch centers is not unlike being enthralled in a good mystery and being sharply signaled to shut the book, put it away, and find another book or task to engage in for the next 20 minutes. No one is inclined to commit to deep thinking and engagement when you know you only have a short time to enjoy it. Chapter 9 on Socio-dramatic play references the research and best practices for the appropriate amount of time children should be allowed to commit to socio-dramatic play, which is often a center activity. Some centers should be purposely designed to provide time for children's successful and enjoyable emerging reading. These include:

- a Big Book center or area;
- a listening center;
- a literacy area with charts of familiar nursery rhymes, finger-plays, songs, morning messages, and other authentic interesting print;
- the library area;
- and other literacy routines (attendance, the schedule, the job chart, and the read-aloud cover display) that children can revisit.

The **Big Book Center** is a designated center or area for children to emergently reread familiar books introduced through Shared Reading. It includes a collection of predictable Big Books well-organized and labeled so that children can find their favorites. The center should include pointers (teacher-created or purchased) for children to practice tracking print as they reread. Appropriate Big Books are collected over time, ordered with professional development funds, purchased on-line or at yard sales from retired teachers, and shared between classrooms. Like all effective centers, teachers should introduce and model the organization of the materials as well as the process for using them. A teacher created chart of directions may also be placed in the center to remind the children how to participate in the Big Book Center. Reading the directions chart must also be modeled so that it is effectively used and becomes a functional and authentic opportunity for emerging reading.

The Library Area should include a tub or tubs specifically designated for smaller versions of previously enjoyed Shared Reading books. It should also include a tub or tubs for multiple copies of the books teachers have read to the children during shared book read-alouds. These tubs should be explicitly labeled and pointed out to children so that they know how to locate their favorites. Some teachers have complained that children do not appropriately engage in sustained emergent reading of books during Center's Time. They may look casually at the pictures before tossing them off and getting out another one. To proactively prevent these behaviors, many teachers use explicit instruction (I do, We do, You do) during whole or small group time to teach children how to choose books of interest, where to find them in the tubs, and how to emergently read them for maximum pleasure and engagement. Once children demonstrate they can independently read books emergently during Center's Time, teachers sometimes teach children how to read with a partner. They will be taught and will practice how to take roles of both a reader and a listener.

The Listening Center should include well-organized and maintained equipment that children have been taught to use and care for appropriately. YouTube videos, apps, DVDs, or other technology that allow the children to hear the story AND see the print, using the actual corresponding books, encourages children to enjoy books. Materials should be neatly organized for access and clean-up. Listening books should span a variety of genres to develop the child's ear and familiarity with many types of books. This is a Reading To learning event that offers additional opportunities to hear (and see) books fluently read-aloud. These, in turn, become books for emerging reading and should be made available in the classroom library. Once again, effective learning will not be facilitated if the teacher does not carefully explain and demonstrate use of the materials at the center.

Useful and Authentic Assessment Strategies

A teacher's focused observation and thoughtful analysis is key to their understanding of individual children's control of the Foundational Anchors of literacy and their ability to synthesize them during emerging reading. The information gleaned provides teachers with knowledge to guide day-to-day planning and teaching. It illuminates concepts and understandings that children need to have reinforced, clarified, scaffolded, or introduced in direct contexts such as read-alouds, teacher-led group creation of texts and innovations, or small group instruction.

The following chart (Guided Observation of Emerging Reading, Figure 15.4) was developed by the authors. It was informed by the work of early literacy researchers such as Sulzby (1985) and Valencia and Sulzby (1991). It is intended to be used only with **familiar** books that have been read aloud to

Guided Observation of Emerging Reading	
Continuum of development	**Observation**
Picture labeling	Child emergently reads by commenting about each picture. The talk does not create events in a story.
Story-teller	Uses story memory and the pictures to tell a connected story. The story may or may not be the story in the book. The child sounds like they are talking or telling the story rather than reading.
Mixed reading and story-telling	Uses story memory and the pictures. Story isbased on the story in the text. Alternates use of actual wording with improvisation. Sometimes it sounds like actual reading. Sometimes like oral story-telling.
Sounding like a reader (the progression)	Uses the pictures. Partial memorization improvises parts. No more improvisation. Child says all the words. Tracks print with finger but does not use print to read words. Moves finger left to right, top to bottom. Notices when their emerging reading does not match the print and attempts to make it match. Recognizes some known words and begins to use some grapho-phonic information such as beginning sounds.
Beginning reader (no longer emerging reader)	Actual reading that relies on the print to read the story.

Figure 15.4 Guided Observation of Emerging Reading

children to the extent they can anticipate the meaning, structure, and content. This guide can also be used by the classroom teacher as they incidentally observe children emergently read environmental and teacher-created texts.

Using the Emerging Reading Guide

Teachers will notice that the book being read influences where the child performs on the continuum. Observing a child reading a predictable book may fall into the *sounding like a reader level-level 3* because it lends itself to memorization. A familiar read-aloud story book may fall into a lower level such as *mixed reading and story-telling* because the child is using more comprehension to recreate a longer, more complex story. Every reading instructional event is supporting the child in moving forward. The teacher must observe children emergently reading a variety of texts that are used for instruction and made available to the children. This observation guide informs the teacher of where to focus instruction. By the start of kindergarten, children should have enough experience to *sound like a reader* with familiar books.

Spotlight

Emerging Readers are in the Foundation Stage of Reading Development, the stage prior to their ability to rely exclusively on print to read. Although not relying on the print, they are beginning to actively construct meaning with text, referencing their experiences with literacy, what they have been taught, and what they have learned about oral and written language, the Foundational Anchors of literacy.

Teachers plan literacy learning to occur in many contexts throughout the day; Reading to the child. Reading with the child. And reading by the child. Reading to the child is detailed in Chapters 11 and 12. When reading to children, the focus is on comprehension, story structure, and vocabulary. This changes when the children can see the print on charts or in predictable Big Books. In this context, teachers read to and then with children. Reading environmental print in the classroom to the children so that they become familiar enough to read it with the teacher and then by themselves is another daily routine. Shared Reading provides an opportunity for children to begin to balance comprehension of familiar text with looking at the print. This dual attention will develop as children gain concepts about print, alphabet knowledge, and phonemic awareness.

This leads children to phonics instruction so that they can read the words in unfamiliar text and apply all they know to make print meaningful. Reading by the children is **emerging reading,** when children are not yet relying on print or only beginning to notice print. Planning time for children's emerging reading is time for them to synthesize and apply their Foundational Anchors of literacy. It provides them the opportunities to develop the habit and confidence of reading independently. By continually connecting meaning and joy to reading, supporting children during their approximations, and providing phonics instruction as part of kindergarten reading instruction, we see children become proficient and willing readers.

References

Allington, R. L. (1983). The reading instruction provided readers of differing reading abilities. *The Elementary School Journal, 83*(5). https://doi.org/10.1086/461333

Mooney, M. E. (1990). *Reading to, with, and by children*. Owen Publishers.

National Reading Panel (U.S.), & National Institute of Child Health and Human Development (U.S.). (2000). *Report of the national reading panel: Teaching children to read: An evidence-based assessment of the scientific research literature on reading and its implications for reading instruction: Reports of the subgroups*. National Institute of Child Health and Human Development, National Institutes of Health.

Opitz, M. F. (1999). *Getting the most from predictable books (Grades K-2)* New York, New York. Scholastic.

Shanahan, T. (1988). The reading writing relationship: Seven instructional principles. *The Reading Teacher, 41*(7), 636–647.

Sulzby, E. (1985). Children's emergent reading of favorite storybooks: A developmental study. *Reading Research Quarterly, 20*(4), 458–481. https://doi.org/10.1598/RRQ.20.4.4

Valencia, S. W., & Sulzby, E. (1991). Assessment: Assessment of emergent literacy: Storybook reading. *The Reading Teacher, 44*(7), 498–500.

References for Children's Literature

Brown, M. (1947). *Stone soup.* Scribner Press.

Dean, J., & Litwin, E. (2010). *Pete the cat: I love my white shoes.* New York, N.Y. Harper Collins.

McClosky, J. R. (1941). *Make way for ducklings.* New York, N.Y. The Viking Press.

Taback, S. (1997). *There was an old lady who swallowed a fly.* Viking Books for Young Readers New York, N.Y..

16 Emerging Writing

Why Teach Writing?

In Chapter 15, Emerging Reading, we explored why and how reading emerges, how the teacher encourages and enables this emergence, and how the teacher leads the child's reading development forward. Writing is also an emergent process and serves as an effective means for accelerating reading development. By connecting reading and writing for children, children's sources of literacy information become much more useful and more flexible. How children think about reading and writing is shaped, in large part, by their school experiences. The potential for learning is enormous (see Figure 16.1). In many classrooms, teachers omit writing or see it as optional or as an afterthought. **Assisted Writing contexts** are the learning events that teachers create to support writing and reciprocity in the classroom. These can contribute to building almost every thought and action needed by the successful reader. Timothy Shanahan (1988) composed these seven principles for teaching reading and writing as connected processes. He says of reading and writing, "The seven instructional principles include: (1) both reading and writing need to be taught; (2) they should be taught from the earliest grade level; (3) the reading-writing relationship should be emphasized in different ways at different levels; (4) knowledge and process relations need to be emphasized; (5) the connections between reading and writing should be made explicit for children; (6) the communications aspects of reading and writing should be emphasized; and (7) reading and writing should be taught in meaningful contexts." This list perfectly summarizes the teaching of reciprocity, or transfer, between reading and writing.

DOI: 10.4324/9780429284021-16

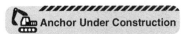

Anchor Under Construction

Teaching for Transfer

Jamie learned to write his J as soon as he arrived in the preschool class. He would soon be writing his whole name. His teacher connects this very beginning information to the Picture ABC Chart that the children use and later to the class name chart. "Jocelyn has a J to start her name, too."

Figure 16.1 Teaching for Transfer

Rethinking the importance of writing in the development of reading can change the trajectory of literacy learning for many children. It creates a reason to segment and sound out words that the child wants to write and reveals their control of letter/sound relationships. It models all aspects of alphabetic knowledge and adds meaningful use of sight words. Writing across different contexts supports the development of all the Foundational Anchors of literacy (see Figure 16.2).

Figure 16.2 A Kindergarten Child Rewrites a Familiar Story; The Three Billy Goats Gruff Saw a River across from a Field of Flowers

What Is Writing?

Writing is **composing** meaning into text (using print, visual, and/or computer applications) for a particular purpose and a particular audience. The essential elements of conveying meaning, holding onto ideas, organizing information, and communicating with self and others are the same for our youngest writers as they are for adults. For example, journaling has been used to benefit adults maintaining mental health (Purcell, 2006). This self-communication can help individuals gain insight and heal. There are many purposes, genres, and audiences for writing and these will become more apparent to children through the teaching that occurs in writing contexts.

Although one can find information on the steps in The Writing Process, this model is needlessly complex for our youngest writers. Their writing process is much more straightforward. They need support in:

1. **Composing** ideas
2. **Recording** ideas
3. **Rereading** the piece

In **composing**, pictures, oral storying, or big ideas are explored. The child chooses a small chunk (labels, sentences, etc.) to record.

Recording ideas occurs in levels of teacher responsibility (I do, We do, You do). Teacher transcribing supports the entire writing process and can move from modeled recording to shared recording. The child's approximations, their attempts at the recording task can range from purposeful scribbling to phonemic writing; encoding.

During **rereading,** the child looks at and reads what they recorded (at whatever level of recording) to make sure it communicates what they wanted it to. Sometimes during rereading, children add a letter, a word, or even a sentence. Our youngest writers are trying to **envision** their writing pieces rather than performing **revision**.

Assisted Writing

Assisting children to engage in the writing process occurs as teachers implement many instructional contexts. The procedures and benefits of several learning contexts will be explained. These procedures can be implemented in whole groups, small groups, and one-to-one. **Assisted Writing contexts** (see Figure 16.3) provide levels of instruction from direct learning contexts to indirect learning contexts with the teacher stepping in and out of the teaching and support role.

This chapter will explain four effective writing contexts: (1) Story Picture, (2) Modeled and Shared Writing, (3) Interactive Writing, and (4) Community Writing (CW). These contexts are a good starting point for teachers who are not familiar with writing with young children.

Preschool Assisted Writing contexts	Kindergarten and first grade Assisted Writing contexts
• **Story Picture;** Child composes aloud/ Teacher transcribes	• Writing center (Chapter 7)
• **Modeled and Shared Writing**	• Writing in play (Chapters 9 and 10)
• **Interactive Writing**	• **Modeled and Shared Writing**
• Writing center (Chapter7)	• **Interactive Writing**
• Writing in play (Chapters 9 and 10)	• **Community Writing (CW)**

Figure 16.3 Assisted Writing Contexts

When Do We Teach Writing?

There are many times during the day in which the teacher creates learning opportunities for children to learn about writing. Any learning context, (reading, writing, speaking, and listening) where children are talking about a topic, or noticing what an author did, contributes to writing. For example, Assisted Writing contexts, Read-Aloud, small group reading and writing instruction, extended conversation, Hands On/Words On experiences, exposing students to many different kinds of writing, demonstrating how to organize ideas in a way that readers can understand, modeling the use of conventions in writing, and showing students that there are different purposes for writing.

For very young learners and for multi-language learners (MLLs), sentence segmentation, a phonological awareness skill, will develop with focused attention and practice during Assisted Writing. Try listening to a language you cannot write and see if you can figure out where one word ends and the next one starts. (At night all the noise was intense. At night all the noise was in tents.) Sentence segmentation is made explicit by the teacher and is modeled and practiced in all Assisted Writing contexts.

The Developmental Stages of Writing

As children enter our classrooms we can assess their developmental stage of writing across contexts such as play, art, or small literacy groups. What they can produce independently will fit somewhere along the continuum (see Figure 16.4 and 16.5). Some children will arrive being able to use pencils and crayons, and some will not yet have had experiences with writing implements. With every writing demonstration and interaction, teachers are leading children to their next developmental level. Teachers are looking carefully at the writing children are producing in order to observe, teach, and accelerate their progress. In observing children's approximate recording of ideas and their use of pictures to hold and convey meaning, teachers can determine what to teach next.

Stage	Pictures	Approximate recording
Random scribbling	Pictures are unrecognizable but may be meaningful.	Children are reacting to and experimenting with the materials.
Purposeful scribbling	Some recognizable pictures begin to surface.	Children are trying to control the instrument and naming some of their work.
Letter-like scribbling	Pictures are developing.	Children have some actual letters and some invented letter-like shapes.
Letter inclusive	Pictures are very important to meaning.	Children include letters they know with intention and meaning.
Phonemic writing -initial sounds	Meaningful pictures precede writing.	Children include initial sounds and attempt some spaces between words.
Phonemic writing -ending sounds	Meaningful pictures precede writing.	Children include letters based on ending sounds and attempt accurate spacing.
Phonemic writing -middle sounds	Pictures may precede and/or follow writing.	Children include letters based on sounds they are able to segment and hear in the middle of words.
Using known words	Pictures may precede and/or follow writing.	Children include known words in writing (their name, mom, dad, love ...) and may include periods.
Transitional writing	Pictures may precede and/or follow writing.	Children problem-solve words in a flexible way (letter combinations, known words, and word families) as they move toward more conventional writing.

Figure 16.4 Stages of Writing; ECE to First Grade

Children do not always produce work at their highest level, but the teacher needs to be aware of where each child can perform and assist the child to inch to the next level. Pictures are not a distraction or an afterthought to children's meaning making, but often tell more of the message than a child can currently compose in words. The teacher must learn to see every picture as an event in a longer narrative and help the child compose the narrative.

Figure 16.5 Kindergarten Phonemic Writing with Middle Sounds: *I like Nicholas. He is my best friend because he is nice to me. He asks me if I want to play. I say yes*

Story Pictures; Assisted Writing Context

Beginning emerging writers record their ideas through both random and purposeful scribbling and both unrecognizable and recognizable drawings. More advanced emerging writers begin to use letters, words in their environment, letter/sound information, and known words to record their messages. We call these approximations of messages "Story Pictures" in order to imbue them with meaning and value, and to encourage oral language, vocabulary, and narrative formation (all aspects of reading).

The goal is to create a story with the child rather than label items in the picture. Recording the narrative can include any level of teacher support from writing down what the child would like written to working out what the child will write themself and coming back around to encourage or celebrate the work. The teacher begins by responding to a child's picture as if it were a moment in time in a longer story by saying, *"Tell me the story of your picture."* Such requests call for the child to respond with a **story**, whereas

---

Supporting Children's Composing of a Narrative

- *Tell me the story that goes with this picture.* Or *What is this story about?*
- *What will happen next?* Or *Where will they go next?* Or *What will they do next?*
- *What happened before this?* Or *What made them do that?*
- *What are they saying?* Or *Which one is talking?*

Figure 16.6 Composing a Story about a Picture

the questions, *"What's this?"* or *"Tell me about your picture,"* calls for minimal response from the child. We want children to see themselves as storytellers and to know that we value their stories (see Figure 16.6).

More about Story Pictures

1. **Composing:** The teacher says, **Tell me the story of your picture**. The teacher listens attentively to the entire story *without transcribing a word*. This allows complex oral language to be composed by the child as they tell their story. The teacher can prompt for events and dialog. They can ask for clarification to extend the language or understand the story.
2. After the oral storying is complete, the teacher asks, **What words do you want me to write?** The child offers a brief sentence or some labeling words. This is the step in composing where the writer goes from the big idea to the part they want to tell. Allow the child to compose this themselves. This is the cognitive work they will need to do independently as they move forward.
3. **Recording**
   - **Teacher Recording: Transcribing:** The teacher repeats the words or sentences the child offers. Teacher writes them neatly in manuscript print so the child can see what they are doing, leaving a space between words, and forming letters. Teacher and child reread the teacher's transcription together as the teacher points (see Figure 16.7).

An Example of One Child's Story Picture		
Process of composing	**Teacher language**	**Example**
Thinking of ideas	Tell me the story of this picture. What did you say when your dad put a swing in your big apple tree?	Child: I have a big apple tree in my yard and my dad put a swing in it. I like to swing and go really high.
Choosing one idea	What part will you tell?	Child: About my swing.
Deciding what to say or how to record it.	How will you say it?	Child: I'll write my swing is good.

Figure 16.7 A Composing Conversation

Figure 16.8 A Story Picture (Child Recording)

- **Child Recording: This includes levels of development from purposeful scribbling to transitional writing (see Figure 16.8.** The teacher imbues this work with meaning by asking the child to read what they wrote. If the child is hesitant, the teacher points to the writing and makes an action statement about the picture. (One may have to ask about the picture if it is unrecognizable.) For example, *"I think it says, My family is going to visit our friends. Is that right?"*

4. **Rereading:** The child then rereads the message on their own, attempting to match voice and print, going left to right. (Does this sound like emerging reading practice?) The teacher may send the child off to share their story with a friend. This brief interaction has supported the development of Composing, Recording, and Rereading.

The "Story Picture" above is about the apple tree swing. The writing says, "my swing." This process, or cognitive action of composing, is huge work for any writer and is the piece many children struggle with, and many teachers misunderstand. In the example above, the child had a longer story but only wrote the beginning sounds for My Swing. He still had to perform the many cognitive actions of encoding. After deciding what part to tell, he had to segment the phrase, hearing where one word ends and the next word begins. Then he had to connect a letter to the beginning sound, which he

Figure 16.9 A Kindergarten Child Begins a Scientific Drawing or Picture Glossary

did accurately. Finally, he had to remember the letter form and get it on the paper. M S may not seem like a big deal but when we consider the series of cognitive actions required, we can see how much there is to celebrate for this emerging writer.

A Closer Look at the Writing Process

Writing Begins with Composing

Composing is a process that moves from a whole big idea to the recording of the idea. A child's **oral storying** or talking about a picture they drew is more elaborate than what is recorded by the child or adult. Teachers encourage children to use their oral language in the most complex way they can, using questions to extend the talk. However, the recording of the idea in print is a smaller, more concise version of the conversation. A child may tell an elaborate story of their birthday party and choose to record, "I got a mask." Much

---

Composing

Think of ideas

Choose one idea

Decide what to say

Decide how to say it

Figure 16.10 Steps in Composing an Idea for Writing

of the composing process (from big idea to concise text) (see Figure 16.10) for adults is a quick, in the head, action. Whether you are composing a grocery list or thank you note, a Tweet or an email, you start broadly and narrow your communication to fit the purpose and audience, then record it. It is this same cognitive process we are supporting in children.

This process is unfamiliar to children and must be modeled over and over in many contexts. It must also be connected to texts the child is interacting with. After reading aloud, *Grumpy Monkey* by Suzanne Lang, the teacher might ask the children what they think made Suzanne choose that idea. Helping the children learn that books are ideas other people had and wrote down for us, demystifies the process of composing. For most writers, the cognitive process of composing is the most difficult and in our youngest writers, every story is a chance to practice that difficult task.

Recording

After the work of composing, the next set of actions for the emerging writer is creating the message in a symbolic form (see Figure 16.11). This may have already been created in a picture. The message a child records may appear as random scribbles, letter-like scribbles, actual letters, or letters that represent sounds of words. Their recording reflects the child's development in many Foundational Anchors. Phonological Awareness, Alphabet knowledge and Phonics, and Concepts of Print are interdependent in Emerging Writing. The Developmental Stages of Writing reveals the level of coordination between anchors.

Recording

Purposeful scribbling

Story Picture with transcription

Transitional writing

Figure 16.11 Continuum of Recording

In addition to remembering the message, and figuring out how to record it, the child has both the physical challenge of holding the writing implement and controlling their hand and eyes. This happens with time to write as well as other eye/hand activities and small motor activities such as play dough, stringing beads, melted bead designs, sorting with tweezers, guided drawing.

Pictures are an important way for children to record their thoughts and ideas. Teachers can become frustrated when children only draw and never write. This can lead to the requirement that children write first. This response is counterproductive, however, as pictures are the symbolic recordings of meaning. Letting children know that every picture has to have some writing on it (or a developmental approximation) is more appropriate and does not undermine the cognitive actions that occur when a child draws.

Recording can occur in a variety of ways depending on the group size, the child's confidence and capabilities, and the context. Moving the child toward independently recording at their own developmental level, while teaching to the next level, helps children's recording become more representative. Transcribing begins with the teacher modeling how they write the words but moves to having the child do some of the work that they are able to. For example, the teacher might say:

- *The next letter in dog is an O. You write that letter.*
- *That's the end of the word, put your finger here to hold a space.*
- *Help me make the first sound in pizza.*
- *The story is over. You make the period here.*
- *Let's make the S together. It is tricky for me,* and teacher and child work hand over hand.

When a child begins phonemic writing (also called phonemic spelling), the teacher assists the child to say the whole word slowly and listen for sounds they can hear. Assistance is NOT THE SAME as the teacher stretching the word and making the sounds for the child. Even if the child can call out a letter name, the teacher must stay focused on the goal; children practice segmenting words with their own mouths and voices. If the teacher does the segmenting and sounding, then children will not learn to do that work on their own. Stretching words out in writing is like sounding out words in reading. In reading, children blend the segmented sounds (that they make with their own mouths) back together. This is the reciprocity that is so important to accelerate learning.

Rereading: The Final Step

After the arduous work of composing and recording comes a rereading of the entire text. During the rereading, we want children to hear themselves reading their story out loud and make any changes that they want to make (see Figure 16.12). For preschool and kindergarten, adding is the main form of change or revision with either words or pictures.

```
┌─────────────────────────────────┐
│           Rereading             │
│                                 │
│          Fixing it up           │
│                                 │
└─────────────────────────────────┘
```

Figure 16.12 Rereading the Writing

This step will become revision and editing as the writers move into conventional writing but for most emerging writers, teachers provide as many rereading opportunities as possible without an expectation of revision or editing. In fact, the message may even change from one reading to the next. Reading and writing development go hand in hand, and the child may not yet know that text in a book says the same thing every time it is read.

Assisted Writing: Contexts for Supporting Writing Development

The contexts for Assisted Writing follow a progression from the highest level of teacher input to the lowest level of teacher input as children are able to do more with less support. The goal is to create a community of willing learners through differentiation and instruction, using all contexts depending on the level of assistance needed for the children to succeed and learn. The least experienced children will need small group writing with the teacher at all levels of the Assisted Writing context as well as joining the whole group events.

Modeled and Shared Writing

The teacher is responsible for planning all the **cognitive actions** in the context of modeled and shared writing, Composing, Recording, and Rereading. They invite the children to participate by thinking aloud about what they are doing.

Modeled or shared writing are intentionally planned learning contexts to provide a model of strategies, techniques, or genres that children are invited to try (see Figure 16.13). The topic must be a familiar topic or a shared experience. This models for children that ordinary life, written down, becomes a story. It also has a greater chance of reminding them of their own experiences. Reminding writers in the community of their own stories by sharing, reading aloud, or conversation causes a cognitive action that the authors have labeled, "Waking up a story in your head." Noticing and naming cognitive actions such as this helps children to incorporate them. We want children to begin to notice and name this thinking because (1) It is an ongoing source of writing ideas, (2) it is metacognition (thinking about your thinking), and (3) it is affirming to others in the writing community. For example, Josh begins sharing time by sharing a book he made about his new soccer shoes. Adolpho responds, "That woke up a story in my head! I watch soccer on TV with my dad."

Two Assisted Writing Contexts	
Modeled and Shared Writing	
Modeled Writing; *I DO* **Teacher takes full responsibility**	**Shared Writing;** *WE DO* **Teacher releases responsibility**
Think aloud (Big idea): *Today I wanted to tell you about my little dog Daisy. She is so funny. She sleeps on my bed and when I have waffles for breakfast, I always share them with her.*	Think aloud (Big idea): *Today I wanted to tell you about my little dog Daisy. She is so funny. She sleeps on my bed and when I have waffles for breakfast, I always share them with her.*
Think aloud (narrowing topic): *What part should I tell?* Children may have ideas here. *I want to talk about breakfast. I can say, "My dog Daisy loves waffles for breakfast."*	Think aloud (narrowing topic): *What part should I tell? What do you friends think?* Children share ideas and opinions. *That helped me think about the part we can tell. We will say, "My dog Daisy loves waffles for breakfast."*
Teacher counts words on her finger as she segments the sentence, pausing momentarily after each word: *My... dog... Daisy... loves... waffles... for... breakfast. Six words!*	*Help me count the words.* Teachers and children count words together. They say the sentence together, pausing momentarily after each word: *My... dog... Daisy... loves... waffles... for... breakfast. Six words!!*
Teacher begins to encode the first word and thinks aloud: *The first word is my. /M/* She invites children to make the SOUND with her. */M/ That's an M like Martha's name.* She adds a *y* to complete the word.	*I have the word my in my head.* Look in your head and spell it with me. Then says and writes M-Y.
Let's read the sentence to see what's next. My... dog. The next word is dog. The teacher will segment and sound out the word dog, letter by letter. She is modeling encoding with sounds although most of the children cannot segment sounds independently. This short word has a direct sound/letter correspondence.	*Let's read the sentence to see what's next. My... dog. The next word is dog. Stretch that out with me.* Although some children call out D, she insists they make the sound with their own mouth, then acknowledges, *That is the sound of D.* They sound out the rest together.
Let's read the sentence to see what's next. My dog ...Daisy...That's a word I know. I can look in my head for it. She looks "inside her head" to write words she knows.	*Let's read the sentence to see what's next. My dog ...Daisy...That's a word I know. I can look in my head for it.* She looks "inside her head" to write words she knows.

Figure 16.13 Comparing Modeled and Shared Writing *(Continued)*

Let's read the sentence to see what's next. *My dog Daisy … loves.* She will look on the word wall to spell the word love. *My dog Daisy loves…I need to add an s to make the word loves.*	*Let's read the sentence to see what's next.* *My dog Daisy … loves.* She will ask, *What tool can we use to spell the word love?* The children show her on the word wall and she writes L-O-V-E. *Let's read the sentence to see what's next.* They reread and most of the children say "love." The teacher asks the children if that sounded right. They tell her to Put an S on it. Teacher says, *we fixed it up.*
Let's read the sentence to see what's next. *My dog Daisy loves…waffles.* She will segment waffles, make the /w/ sound and the /f/ sound for each syllable. As she writes, she will connect the sounds to Wally's and Frida's name. She decided not to stretch and spell this longer word with silent letter e.	*Let's read the sentence to see what's next.* The teacher has the children clap the syllables in waffles. They hear the two parts and together write /wa/. Then she asks them to clap again and listen to the next part. She writes -ffles. She acknowledges that they heard many of the sounds in the second part.
Teacher segments each word into phonemes, encoding the sounds, pointing and rereading the sentence so far, and moving to the next word. She emphasizes ONE skill; initial sounds OR consonant sounds OR spaces between words OR segmenting words.	Teacher prompts children to stretch each word into phonemes, making the sounds WITH her. Together, they encode the sounds, pointing and rereading the sentence so far, and moving to the next word. She may be emphasizing one new skill or combining several known skills.

Figure 16.13 (Continued)

Figure 16.13 is a description of how modeled or shared writing might look in a classroom. The teacher begins with a blank sheet of chart paper and a black, blue, green, or brown marker. Paper is what the children will use so it is most appropriate for modeling. The teacher stands by the paper and begins to narrate their thinking process out loud so that children can see into the teacher's brain.

An emerging writer is only recording some sounds. However, as you model making sounds and recording letters, you add unvoiced letters so that the finished model is COMPLETELY CORRECT. The teacher's handwriting must be simple, consistent, and reflect correct manuscript letter formation. If this is not a skill the teacher possesses, it is important to learn how to form letters efficiently and legibly.

The final text created provides an unambiguous model of the recording of ideas. All words are correctly spelled and evenly spaced. When the sentence is complete, the teacher thinks aloud: *Now I'll read the whole thing and listen to my story.* Teacher points, reads sentences aloud, and tells herself that it is a good story. This same process of Modeled and Shared Writing can be used to model a list, a poem, a song, factual information, labeling, or other writing forms that children are invited to try.

Interactive Writing

Interactive writing is a context for writing in which the teacher AND the children create meaningful text together, sharing composing, recording, and rereading. **They also share the chart marker**. This work builds upon what children have learned from teacher transcription, and modeled, and shared writing. As the group works on stretching and encoding, the teacher invites a child to hold the space between words with their finger while another child writes a letter, a word, or adds a punctuation mark. The teacher includes the use of **tools children can use to help themselves write**. These include the picture alphabet, word wall, name chart, and environmental print. (See Appendix for complete list). She also calls on children to do what they can do successfully. If Ben can only write a B at this point, she will make sure there is a B in the composition and invite him to come write it.

Interactive Writing can occur in a whole group or a small group, depending on the goals. It can be used to create multiple genres as well as graphic organizers such as timelines, diagrams, and picture glossaries. For example, a thank you note to the custodial staff, labels for the job chart, or a timeline to show how an amaryllis grows from bulb to flower can all be created with interactive writing. The children and teacher work together to **compose** from the big ideas down to the words, together they decide what to write and how to say it. Then they work together to **record** by encoding the words, holding the spaces, rereading the writing after each completed word, and **rereading** at the end to fix up any missing parts.

Managing to let as many children as possible share their idea of what to say and how to say it, takes time but remember, composing is the hardest part of writing so practice time is important. The teacher makes the final decision about what to write, incorporating as many ideas as possible. Whenever there is a chance to model the use of a tool, use it! Teaching tool use and modeling it every time you write makes tools into so much more than wallpaper!

Community Writing Time

Why do we have **Community Writing (CW)** time in kindergarten and first grade? Community Writing time is a lively, playful opportunity for children to record ideas on paper. It is a time to have their efforts recognized and to have their actions imbued with intent.

Experience put into language becomes knowledge. Community Writing time is a time for children to put into language all their understandings of the world around them, to arrange that language in narrative form, the form that allows stories to travel through time, from one generation to the next, and to explain the world. It is a time to see and try forms for collecting information, sharing your interests, or creating a place in your mind for new information to be stored. The "All About" stories with facts like, "Cats have fur. Cats have kittens. Cats have claws. Cats are nice," shows how fact and opinion seem the same in the mind of a young child but more importantly, that as the child discovers more about cats, they will adjust their knowledge.

This 45 minute period during the day offers the kindergarten and first-grade teacher a time to learn about the children. They write about what they know and what they care about. What the teacher thinks matters is what the child thinks matters and the chance to get to know each child is a gift.

What Are the Important Components of CW?

1. **Setting the stage**

   Reading aloud and small group reading feed energy and inspiration into CW time. The teacher scaffolds reading like a writer, noticing and naming what writers do. This can happen at Read-Aloud or Shared Reading.

   When the time to gather is near, teachers use all kinds of ideas to signal the children. Providing children their own **writing toolkit** with their current work and tools such as the picture alphabet, names of class-mates, names of family members, etc. helps them feel ownership and agency. Have children place their writing toolkits in a work spot before gathering for the **What Writers Do lesson**. This allows them to leave the lesson and begin their projects without a long transition.

2. **What writers do lesson**

   The **What Writers Do** lesson is a chance for children to learn **one** thing about writing or writers. It takes 5–7 minutes only. This is presented in a short focused lesson and as an invitation for the community to try. *Here is something we can try…Here is something we can do that writers do…*It is an invitation, not an assignment. A list of possible What Writers Do lessons appears below.

3. **Worktime**

   Then there is work time. Teachers begin with 7 minutes of work time and build to 30 minutes over the first months of school. Here teachers are carefully establishing what writers in a community do and how they become independent. With the lessons clearly focused on independence, students should not feel that they need a teacher in order to get their ideas on paper any more than they need a teacher at the block center before they can build. The teacher is moving around the classroom to assist children to solve their own problems, thinking about where each child is developmentally and how future whole and small group Assisted Writing contexts can directly teach and model what children are moving toward. For example, only a few children have begun to leave spaces between words. Teaching children in small group to put a penny after each word helps them notice where words end. When they pick up their writing, they can count the pennies to see how many words they wrote AND there are no marks in the spaces. Teaching this one child at a time during work time is inefficient.

4. **Sharing time**

   Finally, there is sharing time. This is another chance to teach, prompt, and reinforce the actions that successful writers are taking. It is also where energy and enthusiasm is fed back into the CW time.

If the teacher reads the shared pieces with or for the child, then the group can hear the writing and respond. The teacher should lead the response with one smart thing the child-writer did in order to make their book or story picture. In this way, the teacher helps children notice and name the skills and strategies of successful writers and reinforces the behaviors and cognitive actions of the writer who is sharing. The teacher says, "*One smart thing I noticed that you did…*" And then adds the description of what the child did. Using the list of What Writers Do lessons (see Figure 16.14), naming one action reminds the writer and the rest of the children about what they need to remember to do.

What Writers Do

- Making stories and books
- Working on books over a number of days
- Finishing a book
- Telling parts of the story in pictures
- Trying something we learned in What Writer Do
- Making your pictures and words work together
- Making your Story have events
- Sharing the setting in words and pictures
- Adding details that you shared in words and pictures
- Spelling (or writing words) independently
- Using spelling tools
- Leaving spaces between your words
- Being inspired by others (writing a book like another writer)
- Inspiring others (writing a book that others will want to try)
- Retelling a story (A dozen writers have retold The 3 Billy Goats Gruff?)
- Putting words on each page
- Leaving spaces between words
- Writing the sounds you hear when you stretch the word
- Making the pictures and words match
- Not coloring over the words
- Working independently
- Writing about something you care about
- Adding the setting to the picture (a sun for daytime or a moon on a dark color for night)
- Putting a title on the cover (a promise to the reader about the book topic)
- Writing every page to match the topic (keeping the promise of the title)
- Using details in the picture to tell more of the story
- Trying a new genre. Your story about aliens is called Science Fiction
- Keep your toolkit organized so it helps you write more

Figure 16.14 What Writers Do Lesson Ideas

Sharing time is generally the last 10 minutes of CW time. In many classrooms, it is the part that teachers do not "get to" daily. Why is that? A common model looks like this. A few children sit in a special chair and slowly whisper or mumble their way through the text while the teacher gives audience members the hairy eyeball in order to keep them still and quiet. Then the other children get to ask questions or make "I like" statements. Although this procedure seems correct, the teacher wisely senses that the only possible benefit is to the one child who is sharing. So skipping this session seems like a very small loss.

In re-examining these procedures, teachers returned to the purpose of sharing the work that children have done. During sharing time we learn:

1. to write from one another. Our peers have understandings that could help us become better writers.
2. that peers at all levels of development model important aspects of making stories and books.
3. that listening to our peers makes us better authors and makes them authors. Authors want their work shared.
4. that sharing time is about feeding energy back into the CW.
5. that pace and volume matter. No one cannot listen to and respond to what they cannot hear. It is better to have the teacher read and the child show the pictures than to have inaudible reading.
6. that noticing and naming one smart thing a child does reminds and reinforces the learning for all children.
7. that children can notice and name their own smart actions and those of others.

How Does CW Change Over Time?

CW time begins with recording an idea and sharing it and moves to writing, talking, and drawing for 30 minutes with sharing time after the work time. Expectations and invitations change as well. In September, many children will do mostly drawing as a way to record their stories. Some will make the same story over and over with minimal writing attempts. As we move forward, the expectation that every page has pictures and words becomes explicit through What Writer Do lessons and teacher comments during sharing time, reinforcing the attempts at words.

By the end of the first half of the school year (just shy of 100 days) kindergarten teachers should be providing stronger small group assistance and support to children who are not recording words. These are most likely the same children who are finding learning letters, sounds, and alphabetic knowledge difficult.

Spotlight

It is not just what you teach, it is how you teach. Writing offers opportunities to support all the Foundational Anchors of literacy and to accelerate reading development. Sounding out a word and blending the sounds is the reciprocal process to stretching out a word and recording the sounds. When teachers make this connection for children, both processes work together. Who makes the sounds is of utmost importance. In both writing and reading, the **sounds must be made by the child**. Teacher models this out loud during Modeled Writing.

The writing process for young children is (1) composing, (2) recording, and (3) rereading. It is productive for young writers to practice this sequence on many pieces of writing and in many Assisted Writing contexts.

There are several different Assisted Writing contexts that can be used in whole, small, or individual groups. These include the Writing Center (Chapter 7), Writing in Play (Chapters 9 and 10), Story Pictures, Modeled Writing, Shared Writing, and Community Writing. Writers want to share their work with others, and this should be planned as a daily learning event so that all children benefit.

As children enter our classrooms, we can assess both their developmental stage of writing and their dispositions about writing. Both occur along continuums. What they can produce independently and how they feel about themselves as writers will fit somewhere along them. Demonstrating a personal joy of writing and presenting it so that every child can achieve and feel success, regardless of the level, is crucial to helping children develop strong foundations of literacy.

References

Purcell, M. (2006). The health benefits of journaling. Psych Central. Retrieved on February 5, 2014, from http://psychcentral.com/lib/the-health-benefits-of-journaling/000721

Shanahan, T. (1988). The reading writing relationship: Seven instructional principles. *The Reading Teacher, 41*(7), 636–647.

17 Delays in Literacy Development

Rebecca L. Dennis-Canges
DEPARTMENT OF SPECIAL EDUCATION
EARLY CHILDHOOD, AND CULTURALLY
AND LINGUISTIALLY DIVERSE EDUCATION,
METROPOLITAN STATE UNIVERSITY OF
DENVER, DENVER, CO, UNITED STATES

Focus and Big Ideas

*   Recognizing when children struggle
*   Why children struggle
*   Dyslexia: early warning signs
*   Eligibility for services
*   Providing interventions

Recognizing When Children Struggle

Children begin developing the skills they need to become proficient readers from a very young age. As it has been noted in previous chapters, the Foundational Anchors of literacy begin before a child even steps into a classroom. When a child begins to recognize print in their environment, they are given the opportunity to build their foundation for understanding oral and written language. For example, when a child recognizes the word STOP on a stop sign or flips through the pages of their favorite board book before nap time, they are taking their first steps into a literacy-rich world. While children learn to read at different ages and rates, there are common benchmarks that educators look at for typical literacy development. If a child's reading development falls behind their peers, they may experience difficulties not only in reading, but also in writing, math, and content area comprehension.

When a child is young, it may be challenging to determine if their delay is due to a limited literacy environment, they are simply experiencing a delay in literacy development, or if a child has an underlying disability that is causing the delay. The *why* of a delay in literacy development can be difficult to determine, especially at a young age. While educators may look at the foundational skills related to typical language growth and development when conducting observations of their children, they progress at varying rates based on their individual experiences and capabilities. Therefore, parents and educators should be cautious when making judgments about a child's literacy development. Nevertheless, what if a teacher or parent observes a child struggling with some of the early literacy milestones, such as letter recognition, issues with decoding, or shows disinterest in books, reading, and writing? By

DOI: 10.4324/9780429284021-17

observing the child's emerging literacy skills, a parent or teacher can identify the first signs of any learning difficulties that may be present. Through early identification of these delays, a child can receive the extra support they need to be successful as they begin formal instruction.

Why Children Struggle

A number of reasons can explain why a child may demonstrate confusions or delays when they begin to read and write. Struggles observed by a parent or teacher may indicate a learning disability; however, other elements should be considered before making the assumption that a disability is the underlying factor. Delays in the development of foundational literacy skills do not automatically mean that a child has a disability. Other risk factors should first be considered. If other factors are identified and supported with specific literacy interventions early in the child's educational experience, many reading difficulties can be prevented or resolved without intervention in a special education classroom setting. In this section, factors that should be considered when observing a child's progress in literacy development will be discussed.

Limited Experiences with a School Environment

When a teacher notices that a child is struggling to develop a strong foundation of literacy, one aspect to consider is the amount and quality of school-type experiences a child has had before entering kindergarten. While some children enter kindergarten with two to three years of quality early childhood classroom or care experiences, others may begin school without them. Research suggests that the quality of the classroom and the teacher play an important role in the academic success of children (Magnuson, Ruhm, & Waldfogel, 2007). In fact, it has been argued that a quality early education experience is linked to lifelong educational success. However, children with minimal exposure to language, reading, and other literacy-building activities may develop risk factors that hinder their success in the classroom (Burchinal, Vandergrift, Pianta, & Mashburn, 2010; Fuligni, Howes, Huang, Hong, & Lara-Cinisomo, 2012). Family members, caregivers, and early childhood teachers can play significant roles in developing children's Foundational Anchors of literacy. But, if a child enters kindergarten with a weak foundation of literacy, the gap created can follow them year after year as they progress in school. A teacher that uses an Anchored Literacy Curriculum can change the child's trajectory in a positive direction.

Limited Literacy Environments

Parental involvement in their child's education is seen to have the potential to positively impact a child's educational access, engagement, and success. Many view the parent as a child's first teacher (Echevarria, Short, & Peterson, 2012).

As was noted in Chapter 1, early home and care environments that provide supportive language experiences reduce the risk that children will experience delays in reading and writing. Furthermore, research has indicated that there is a positive relationship between parental involvement and a variety of school-related outcomes, including academic achievement (Ghanney, 2018). A child's cultural capital, that is what a child acquires from the home and what parents are able to transmit to their children, can play a vital role in determining their educational outcomes (Bourdieu, 1990). A parent with a low level of literacy may have limited involvement in their child's education (Donkor, 2010). While they may have the desire to support their child, they may be inhibited by their own limited education. Research also shows us that parental involvement, in general, is more important to a child's academic success than their family's socio-economic status, race, ethnicity, or educational background (Amatea & West, 2007).

Issues related to the home that may hinder a child's progress might include the following:

- The parents have a history of reading difficulty.
- The parents have limited or negative experiences with school.
- There is a focus on survival needs rather than education in the home.
- There is a lack of appropriate home literacy experiences or a lack of a role model for reading.
- There is limited vocabulary development in the home (for example, very little time is spent talking together as a family).
- There are very few or no books in the home.

Though parents play a huge role in making sure that their child's needs are being addressed by the school, these same needs must be addressed beyond the school environment. Both play an equally critical role in children's literacy development. Therefore, understanding key signs related to difficulties in literacy development is essential for teachers, care providers, and parents. Key signs they can look for are included in Figure 17.1.

- The child has difficulty thinking of rhyming words for simple C-V-C words like *cat* (such as *rat* or *bat*).
- The child does not show interest in language play or word games.
- The child shows no interest in reading or being read to.
- The child has problems with forming (articulating) words correctly.
- The child uses the wrong word in place of another.
- The child is confused by multistep directions.
- The child struggles with recalling a sequence of events (such as the events of a cartoon).

Figure 17.1 Key Signs Related to Difficulties in Literacy Development

Parental involvement is most effective when both parents and educators view it as a partnership. The teacher can establish the relationship by welcoming the parent and understanding that the parent may feel a power imbalance. Mutual respect and acceptance of the parental role of child advocate can help the partnership thrive. Due to this partnership, practices and expectations related to the literacy development of the child will be more consistent. The interactions children have with their parents (or other caregivers) during their early years can establish a basis for the child's learning and literacy development. As educators, it is vital to support, encourage, and partner with parents during this time in their child's life. The list provided in Figure 17.2 offers suggestions as to what and how parents can support their child's literacy development at home.

Supporting Children's Literacy Development in the Home

- Have an understanding or awareness of the school's reading program and what it focuses on.
- Ask if there is an option for small group instruction to support your child if needed.
- Discuss your concerns with your child's pediatrician and teacher.
- Do activities at home to help your child develop their sound skills (make sure they are short and fun; avoid allowing your child to get frustrated). For example:
  - Help your child think of a number of words that start with the /m/ or /ch/ sound, or other beginning sounds.
  - Create a basket of toys or items in the house that all have the same initial sound (for example a basket that has: box, ball, bow, bear) and talk with them about which sound all of the items share.
  - Make up silly sentences with words that begin with the same sound, such as "Nobody was nice to Nancy's neighbor."
  - Play simple rhyming games with your child, such as taking turns coming up with words that rhyme (*go—no*).
- Look at picture books with your child and create stories about what you see.
- Read books with rhymes.
- Teach your child rhymes, short poems, and songs.
- Practice the alphabet by pointing out letters wherever you see them in your environment (for example, on street signs or in a grocery store).
- Read alphabet books together.
- Involve your child with household tasks that will increase their verbalization. For example, make a grocery list, cook using a recipe, and talk about what they see on a cereal box.
- Allow your child to play computer games that focus on developing phonological and phonemic awareness skills.
- Discuss environmental print. For example, when walking or driving, point out words to your child on signs, billboards, or even the letters and numbers on a license plate.

Figure 17.2 Supporting Children's Literacy Development in the Home

Language Differences (Multi-Language Learners)

When a child enters school speaking a language(s) other than the school language, they may struggle to keep up the same pace of learning as their peers. Acquiring both their home language and English simultaneously may appear as a delay. However, when multi-language learners (MLLs) are supported in both home and school language, they not only catch up to their peers, but also they are multi-language speakers. MLLs need quality school experiences to ensure effective literacy skills in both languages, which become a strength.

While we know how important it is for teachers to create learning environments for the success of all their students, many teachers feel unprepared to support the needs of MLLs in their classrooms. In fact, studies have noted that more than 50% of teachers have stated that they never received training for working with MLLs (Echevarria et al., 2012). Currently, there are an estimated 5.1 million children in the United States public K-12 schools that are identified as MLLs (https://www.readingrockets.org). The cultural and linguistic diversity of the United States will continue to increase over the upcoming decades (Federal Interagency Forum on Child and Family Statistics, 2010). Therefore, school administration must provide teachers the support and extended education required to meet the needs of MLLs.

Figure 17.3 presents a list of essential understandings of teachers who work with children identified as MLLs.

Essential Understandings to Effectively Work with MLLs

Knowledge of:

- second language acquisition
- how to create a safe environment for the student to practice English
- the child's cultural norms and their potential effects on a teacher–child relationship
- strategies and techniques to develop the child's language skills. For example, the teacher should:
  - understand the ability to use cognates (words in multiple languages that share the same meaning and have similar spelling and/or pronunciation)
  - use a high level of visuals during lessons
  - introduce new vocabulary at the start of a lesson
  - use hands-on activities
  - develop background knowledge
  - provide native language support (Echevarria et al., 2012)

Figure 17.3 Essential Understandings to Effectively Work with MLLs

Medical Conditions

Medical conditions are a potential cause of delay of a child's language and literacy performance. A speech delay, for example, can be related to an underlying medical condition and this possibility should be investigated prior to attributing delays to disabilities.

A teacher can use developmental milestones to gauge a child's progress in speech and language development. For example, a child with a speech delay has typically not met their milestones for speech for a particular age. The following are presented as **guidelines** to consider as opposed to hard and fast rules. Behaviors that may indicate a speech and language delay may include:

- The child is not babbling (making speech-like sounds) by 18 months.
- The child does not use at least 25 words by age 2.
- The child does not use unique two-word phrases by 2½, such as "put on" or "play now."
- The child does not call things by name, by age 3, but instead will say things like "that" or simply point to items without any verbal language being used.
- The child is difficult to understand (even by those who live with them) at age 4.
- (https://devdis.com/sld.html)

Children diagnosed with *ankyloglossia* have a physical problem with their mouth, tongue, and/or palate. This can cause challenges with pronunciation of certain sounds. Discussing these concerns with a child's doctor or dentist is important. Another physical disorder that could produce delays in language development is *apraxia of speech*. This is a physical disorder that makes it difficult for children to form sounds in the correct sequence in order to form words. According to research, this rarely affects nonverbal communication or language comprehension (Pavey, Meehan, & Davis, 2013), however, can hinder reading development.

The child's hearing acuity, their ability to hear, should also be considered. A child who cannot hear well is likely to have difficulty forming words. Hearing distorted elements of language can delay the understanding of particular sounds and, as a result, play a role in a delay in developing literacy skills. Some signs of hearing loss are very subtle; in fact, if speech and language delay is the only visible sign, an issue with hearing may be overlooked.

When a speech delay is related to an underlying medical condition, or occurs with a coexisting disorder, it's essential to address it. Primary medical diagnoses often present with reading problems as a secondary symptom (Snow, Burns, & Griffin, 1998). That said, as a reminder, children develop at their own rate. If a child has a speech delay, parents and teachers should examine all related factors.

Learning Disabilities

Some children may be at risk for reading difficulties due to a specific learning disability (SLD). Learning disabilities are due to genetic and/or neurobiological factors which can affect multiple cognitive processes related to learning (Learning Disabilities Association of America, n.d.). The following section will discuss the learning disability called dyslexia, along with other reading disabilities that children may experience.

What Is Dyslexia?

Dyslexia is a learning disorder in which the fundamental problem involves the brain's ability to process language, decode and spell words, and identify speech sounds (Hudson, High, & Al Otaiba, 2007). As a result of these areas of weakness, a child will often struggle with comprehending written material. It must be noted, however, that this is not due to low intelligence or inadequate instruction (Hudson et al., 2007).

There can be confusion about the terminology surrounding dyslexia which may complicate the way schools define it. For example, while medical professionals refer to it as *dyslexia* or a *reading disorder*, schools may use the term *reading difficulty* or *SLD in reading* (Hudson et al., 2007). The language used in schools should be guided by the criteria established by the Individuals with Disabilities Education Act (IDEA) where dyslexia falls under the category SLD.

Under IDEA and its implementing regulations, SLD is defined, in part, as:

> A disorder in one or more of the basic psychological processes involved in understanding or in using language, spoken or written, that may manifest itself in the imperfect ability to listen, think, speak, read, write, spell, or to do mathematical calculations, including conditions such as perceptual disabilities, brain injury, minimal brain dysfunction, dyslexia, and developmental aphasia.
>
> (20 U.S.C. §1401[30]; 34 C.F.R. §300.8[c][10])

A total of 2.3 million students are diagnosed with SLDs and receive services under IDEA. This represents 35% of all students receiving special education services (National Center for Education Statistics, n.d.). While many of the students identified with an SLD struggle with reading (~75% to 80%; National Institute of Health, n.d.), additional reading disorders can be observed. Many identified with an SLD may have additional difficulties in writing (dysgraphia), mathematics (dyscalculia), motor coordination (dyspraxia), organization, focus, listening comprehension, or a child may have a combination of some or all of these.

Eligibility for Services

In order for a child to be found eligible to receive special education services in kindergarten and beyond under the category of SLD, educational data must be taken within an intervention process, whether it be Response to Intervention (RtI) or Multi-Tiered Systems of Support (MTSS). The data collected should demonstrate that the child's difficulties have a significant educational impact (Mather & Wendling, 2011). As a result, some students who have been identified with dyslexia may meet state-determined criteria for the special education category of SLD, and others may not. For example, it is estimated that 3%–10% of school-age children demonstrate adequate decoding abilities yet still struggle with comprehension (Cain & Oakhill, 2011; Leach, Scarborough, & Rescorla, 2003; Nation, 2001). These students may not be identified as having dyslexia, but, would demonstrate weaknesses in language abilities such as semantics and syntax (Cain & Oakhill, 2011; Cain & Towse, 2008; Cutting, Materek, Cole, Levine, & Mahone 2009; Locascio, Mahone, Eason, & Cutting, 2010).

Currently, 45 states have passed dyslexia-related legislation (https://www.dyslegia.com/state-dyslexia-laws/) in order to support the identification of students with dyslexia as well as provide children with the effective intervention tools. Many states have laws requiring public schools to screen children for dyslexia during kindergarten, first grade, or second grade (https://wapave.org). Adequate measures, however, for assessing and identifying children are not yet available. There continues to be widespread confusion throughout US schools about how to identify dyslexia (https://www.dyslegia.com/state-dyslexia-laws). The funding for testing and intervention programs is sparse. After a state passes the dyslexia-related legislation, it is up to the individual school districts to provide guidance to the schools and teachers for identification and intervention. It's important for teachers to be aware of early warning signs so that they can effectively support the children in their classroom.

Early Warning Signs of Dyslexia

As noted earlier, it can be difficult to detect if a child has a disability like dyslexia, early on in their life. Because learning disabilities like dyslexia cannot be seen, they often go undetected. Nonetheless, the earliest signs of dyslexia can emerge around one to two years of age when a child begins making their first sounds (Pavey et al., 2013). There have been links in the research to indicate that children who do not say their first phrases until two years old have a higher risk of being diagnosed with dyslexia at a later age (Fletcher, Francis, Foorman, & Schatschnieder, 2021). Signs of dyslexia can be a challenge to recognize before a child enters school. However, early clues may assist a parent or teacher in identifying the problem. Before a child enters school, a sign that they may be at risk of having dyslexia would include:

- Late talking
- Late choosing of a dominant hand
- Problems with learning and remembering the alphabet
- Not able to recognize the letters of their own name
- Problems in forming words correctly, or using baby talk
- Problems with remembering numbers and colors
- Difficulty in learning nursing rhymes
- Difficulty in remembering the rules of games

Even with these indicators, the teacher may be the first person to notice a problem once the child enters kindergarten. Some of the indicators that become more apparent as the child begins to learn to develop Foundational Anchors of literacy are:

- Difficulty in recognizing the individual sounds in spoken words (phonemes)
- Difficulty in sounding out written words (decoding) and recognizing familiar word parts
- Unable to recognize rhyming patterns or produce words that rhyme
- Issues with pronunciation
- Trouble concentrating
- Issues with proper interaction with peers
- Difficulty in following directions or learning routines
- Confuses left and right
- Difficulty in learning to tie shoes
- Difficulty with pencil grip or holding, scissors
- Difficulty with buttoning, zipping
- Problems with processing and understanding what he or she hears
- Problems with remembering the proper sequence of events
- Difficulty in seeing similarities and differences in letters and words
- Inability to sound out the pronunciation of words even when breaking the word into parts (phonological awareness)
- Anxiety when reading
- Difficulty in spelling
- Spending an unusually long time completing tasks that involve reading or writing
- Avoiding activities that involve reading and writing

The severity of a reading disorder is difficult to predict. Therefore, schools and teachers play a critical role in identifying children with potential reading difficulties, including dyslexia, once the child enters the classroom. It is a common understanding that when teachers deliver high-quality instruction, they can prevent some reading problems and lessen the impact of a more severe reading problem (Mather & Wendling, 2011). The task is to identify the learning challenges that may foreshadow a reading difficulty, use assessment data to make educational decisions, and link that data to literacy goals and instruction. Early identification of dyslexia is essential so that the child can find success with literacy and understand why reading and writing are a challenge for them. This will not only support children's literacy development but also combat social and emotional difficulties that may arise as they progress through school.

Providing Interventions

The disparity between a child's capacity to learn and their rates of reading failure can be linked to lack of early and effective interventions. While many interventions have focused broadly on emergent literacy skills, the NAEYC and the International Reading Association have issued a joint statement emphasizing that appropriate literacy assessment and individualized intervention strategies should include early, intensive, focused instruction to support the specific needs of a child who is struggling.

What Role Does RtI/MTSS Play in the Classroom?

RtI is a multi-tier approach to the early identification and support of children with learning and behavior needs (rtinetwork.org). Likewise, the MTSS is a framework in which data-based decisions are made in order to plan interventions for continuous improvement in learning and behavior. While MTSS is now seen across all ages and grade levels, RtI is typically seen in elementary schools but has been increasingly emerging in early childhood programs. It is within this framework that teachers can provide interventions that increase in intensity based on the child's instructional response. Different levels of instruction and intervention support are provided to children based on their need within three tiers (see Figure 17.4.).

Tiers of Instructional Need

Tier 1: Whole class instruction where the teacher provides all students with a research-based curriculum and instructional strategies.

Tier 2: Small-group interventions provided for students who are demonstrating specific learning needs.

Tier 3: More intensive intervention (in small groups or one on one) for those children who have not progressed adequately during Tier 2 Intervention or are demonstrating significant deficits in a specific area.

Figure 17.4 Tiers of Instructional Need

Response to Intervention: Ignoring the Process

Lance is a five-year-old child in Ms. Tacklind's kindergarten class. In December, all of the students were given an assessment before winter break to measure their current academic progress. It was observed from the data that Lance could not identify the letters of the alphabet outside of those in his name. Ms. Tacklind was concerned. She remembered that Lance's mother told her that he had not spoken until he was nearly three years old. Ms. Tacklind wondered if Lance's past issues with his speech and language were causing problems with his literacy development. Upon returning to school after winter break, she referred him to the Special Education team for an assessment.

Figure 17.5 Response to Intervention (RtI): When the Process Is Not Followed

It is important to note that movement between these three instructional tiers is fluid. In other words, a child's progress should be assessed and monitored throughout the intervention process. Based on their demonstrated learning and/or progress toward a clearly defined goal, the child can move in and out of support within these tiers at any time.

The problems exposed in the scenario (Figure 17.5) did not begin in December. Ms. Tacklind should have had four months' worth of data on the progress Lance was making in letter learning. A first screening in September would have caused her concern because it would have revealed how few letters he knew. The research indicates that he should have had 18 upper case and 15 lower case letters at the end of preschool (Piasta, Petscher, & Justice, 2012).Lance had the need for small group instruction from day 1. Ms. Tacklind would have seen that after several weeks of small group instruction, in addition to whole group, he had not added any letters to his repertoire. Lack of very simple data collection and observation to direct her instruction shows that Ms. Tacklind is making random instructional decisions for all of her children. A successful example is provided below (see Figure 17.6).

RtI is a promising model for meeting all children's needs. Children who do not respond adequately to the interventions within the three tiers may be referred for a comprehensive evaluation for special education services. However, when teachers provide direct and indirect instructional contexts, plan small group differentiated instruction based on assessment, and provide early and effective interventions with consistent progress monitoring for children who are not progressing with their peers, a child's chances for academic success are increased.

Response to Intervention: Implementing the Process

Debbie is a five year old in Mr. Katin's kindergarten class. During a parent-teacher confer-
ence early in the school year, Debbie's parents informed Mr. Katin that she had not attended
preschool and they were nervous about how she would perform academically now that she was
in kindergarten. Mr. Katin observed that Debbie struggled with learning her letter names and
was falling behind the progress that the rest of the students in class were making. To assist
Debbie, Mr. Katin sent home alphabet resources so that she could also learn the names of
her letters with her parents. In the classroom, he implemented small group instruction with
Debbie so that he could provide her more support. After a few weeks, Mr. Katin noticed
that Debbie was making very little progress. He decided to deliver one to one intervention
activities in order to focus on the letters she struggled with the most. After a few weeks of
intervention, Mr. Katin was pleased to see a dramatic growth in Debbie's letter naming on
progress monitoring assessments.

Figure 17.6 Effective Implementation of Response to Intervention (RtI)

Spotlight

Children enter the classroom bringing with them varying background experiences and knowledge. When children start school, teachers frequently observe each child's Foundational Anchors of literacy. They compare children's competencies with measures of typical language growth and development as they analyze their present levels and monitor their progress. However, it's important to note that children progress at varying rates based on their individual experiences and capabilities. There are many reasons for delays and these need to be explored. Having information about the child's background, previous school experience, and any potential cause of the student's difficulties will assist teachers in planning and providing instruction that is relevant and effective. Once teachers understand the underlying causes of reading delays and disabilities, they can use this information as they work with children and their families.

References

Amatea, E. S., & West, C. A. (2007). Joining the conversation about educating our poorest children: Emerging leadership roles for school counselors in high poverty schools. *Professional School Counseling, 11*(2), 81–89.

Bourdieu, P. (1990). *The logic of practice.* Polity Press.

Burchinal, M. R., Roberts, J. E., Hooper, S., & Zeisel, S. A. (2000). Cumulative risk and early cognitive development: A comparison of statistical risk models. *Developmental Psychology, 36*(6), 793–807. HYPERLINK "https://psycnet.apa.org/doi/10.1037/0012-1649.36.6.793"https://doi.org/10.1037/0012-1649.36.6.793

Cain, K. & Oakhill, J. (2011). Matthew Effects in Young Readers: Reading Comprehension and Reading Experience Aid Vocabulary Development, *Journal of Learning Disabilities, 44*(5), 431–443.

Cutting, L., Materek, A., Cole, C., Levine, T., & Mahone, M. (2009). Effects of fluency, oral language, and executive function on reading comprehension performance. *Ann. of Dyslexia, 59*(1), 34–54.

Donkor, A. (2010). Parental involvement in education in Ghana: The case of a private elementary school. *International Journal about Parents in Education, 4*(1), 23–28.

Echevarria, J., Short, D. J., & Peterson, C. (2012). *Using the SIOP model with pre-K and kindergarten English learners.* Pearson. Boston, MA. Allyn & Bacon

Federal Interagency Forum on Child and Family Statistics. (2010). *America's children in brief: Key national indicators of well-being.* Retrieved October 27, 2020, from http://www.childstats.gov/americaschildren/demo.asp

Fletcher, J., Francis, D., Foorman, B., & Schatschnieder, C. (2021). Early detection of dyslexia risk: Development of brief, teacher-administered screens. *Learning Disability Quarterly, 44*(3), 145–157. https://doi.org/10.1177/0731948720931870

Fuligni, A. S., Howes, C., Huang, Y., Hong, S. S., & Lara-Cinisomo, S. (2012). Activity settings and daily routines in preschool classrooms: Diverse experiences in early learning settings for low-income children. *Early Childhood Research Quarterly, 27*(2), 198–209.

Ghanney, R. A. (2018). How parental education and literacy skill levels affect the education of their wards: The case of two schools in the Effutu municipality of Ghana. *International Journal of Education and Practice, 6*(3), 107–119. doi:10.18488/journal.61.2018.63.107.119

Hudson, R. F., High, L., & Al Otaiba, S. (2007). Dyslexia and the brain: What does current research tell us? *The Reading Teacher, 60*(6), 506–515. Retrieved October 27, 2020, from http://www.ldonline.org/article/14907/

Leach, M.L., Scarborough, H.S., & Rescorla, L. (2003). Late-Emerging Reading Disabilities. *Journal of Educational Psychology, 95*(2), 211–224.

Learning Disabilities Association of America. (n.d.). *New to LD.* Retrieved from https://ldaamerica.org/support/new-to-ld/ on October 17, 2020.

Locascio, G., Mahone, M., Eason, S., & Cutting, L. (2010). Executive dysfunction among children with reading comprehension deficits. *Journal of Learning Disabilities, 43*(5), 441–454.

Magnuson, K. A., Ruhm, C., & Waldfogel, J. (2007). Does prekindergarten improve school preparation and performance? *Economics of Education Review, 26*, 33–51.

Mather, N., & Wendling, B. (2011). *Essentials of dyslexia assessment and intervention.* John Wiley & Sons, Inc., Hoboken, New Jersey.

Pavey, B., Meehan, M., & Davis, S. (2013). *The Dyslexia-Friendly Teacher's Toolkit* (1st ed.). SAGE Publications. Retrieved from https://www.perlego.com/book/3013487/the-dyslexiafriendly-teachers-toolkit-pdf (Original work published 2013).

Piasta, S. B., Petscher, Y., & Justice, L. M. (2012). How many letters should preschoolers in public programs know? The diagnostic efficiency of various preschool letter-naming benchmarks for predicting first-grade literacy achievement. *Journal of Educational Psychology, 104*(4), 945–958. https://doi.org/10.1037/a0027757

Snow, C. E., Burns, S. M., & Griffin, P. (1998). Chapter 4: Predictors of success and failure in reading. In *Preventing reading difficulties in young children.* National Research Council, National Academy of Sciences. Washington, D.C. pp. 100–134.

Appendix

1. The Ten Foundational Anchors of literacy

> **The Ten Foundational Anchors of literacy**
> 1. Oral language
> 2. Vocabulary and background knowledge
> 3. Book awareness
> 4. Phonological awareness and phonemic awareness
> 5. Alphabet knowledge and phonics
> 6. Print concepts
> 7. Emergent reading
> 8. Emergent writing
> 9. Positive dispositions about literacy and literacy learning
> 10. Executive function

2. Guided Observation of Emerging Reading

Guided Observation of Emerging Reading	
	Observation
Picture labeling	Child emergently reads by commenting about each picture The talk does not create events in a story
Story-teller	Uses story memory and the pictures to tell a connected story The story may or may not be the story in the book The child sounds like they are talking or telling the story rather than reading
Mixed reading and story-telling	Uses story memory and the pictures Story is based on the story in the text Alternates use of actual wording with improvisation Sometimes it sounds like actual reading Sometimes like oral story-telling
Sounding like a reader (the progression)	1. Uses the pictures. Partial memorization; improvises parts 2. No more improvisation. Child says all the words 3. Tracks print with finger but does not use print to read words. Moves finger left to right, top to bottom 4. Notices when their emerging reading does not match the print and attempts to make it match 5. Recognizes some known words and begins to use some graphophonic information such as beginning sounds
Beginning reader (no longer emerging reader)	Actual reading that relies on the print to read the story

3. Stages of Writing Development; ECE to First Grade

Stages of Writing Development; ECE to First Grade		
Purposeful scribbling	Some recognizable pictures begin to surface	Children are trying to control the instrument and naming some of their work
Letter-like scribbling	Pictures are developing	Children have some actual letters and some invented letter-like shapes
Letter inclusive	Pictures are very important for meaning	Children include letters they know with intention and meaning
Phonemic writing *initial sounds*	Meaningful pictures precede writing	Children include initial sounds and attempt some spaces between words
Phonemic writing *ending sounds*	Meaningful pictures precede writing	Children include letters based on ending sounds and attempt accurate spacing
Phonemic writing *middle sounds*	Pictures may precede and/or follow writing	Children include letters based on sounds they are able to segment and hear in the middle of words
Using known words	Pictures may precede and/or follow writing	Children include known words in writing (their name, mom, dad, love ...) and may include periods
Transitional writing	Pictures may precede and/or follow writing	Children problem-solve words in a flexible way (letter combinations, known words, and word families) as they move toward more conventional writing

4. Progression of Phonological Awareness Skills

Progression of Phonological Awareness Skills		
Unit levels	Skill	Example
Rhyme	<u>Recognize</u> when **words** rhyme	Which two words rhyme? /Dog/, /rug/, /log/
Word	<u>Recognize</u> the number of words in a sentence by clapping or counting	/Sherisa/ /likes/ /to/ /eat/ /cake/.
Syllable	<u>Recognize</u> **syllables** by counting or clapping	/Pet/ clap one syllable /Carpet/ (clap two syllables) /Pretending/ (clap three syllables)
Onset and rime	<u>Blend</u> **onset and rime**	What is this word? /p/ /et/, /d/ /og/, /r/ /ug/
Rhyme	<u>Produce</u> a **rhyme**	What is a word that rhymes with /log/?
Phoneme	<u>Recognize</u> *matching* **initial** sounds in words	Which words start the same? /star/, /sun/, /lamb/
Phoneme	<u>Produce</u> the **initial sound** of a word	What is the first sound in the word /car/ /bug/ /fin/?
Word	<u>Delete</u> part of a **compound word**	Say the word /sunshine/ without /sun/
Phoneme	**Phoneme** <u>blending</u>	Blend these phonemes together: /g/o/, /b/ /i/ /g/, /p/ /a/ /n/
Phoneme	**Phoneme** <u>segmentation</u>	Hold up a finger (or move a chip) for each sound that you hear in / fish/ (f/i/sh), /no/ /n/ /o/, /send/ /s/ /e/ /n//d/
Phoneme	**Phoneme** <u>substitution</u>	Change the /n/ in name to /g/ (game) Change the /i/ in fin to /a/ (fan) Change the /m/ in dim to /g/ (dig)
Phoneme	**Phoneme** <u>deletion</u>	Say meat without the /m/ (eat) Say slink without the /l/ (sink) Say fork without the /k/ (for)

5. Early Signs of Dyslexia

Early Signs of Dyslexia
Signs that preschool children may be at risk of dyslexia
• Late talking • Late choosing a dominant hand • Problems with learning and remembering the alphabet • Not able to recognize the letters of their own name • Problems forming words correctly, or using baby talk • Problems with remembering numbers and colors • Difficulty learning nursing rhymes • Difficulty remembering the rules of games
Signs that kindergarten and first-grade children may be at risk of dyslexia
• Difficulty recognizing the individual sounds in spoken words (phonemes) • Difficulty sounding out written words (decoding) and recognizing familiar word parts • Unable to recognize rhyming patterns or produce words that rhyme • Issues with pronunciation • Trouble concentrating • Issues with proper interaction with peers • Difficulty following directions or learning routines • Confuses left and right • Difficulty learning to tie shoes • Difficulty with pencil grip or holding, scissors • Difficulty with buttoning, zipping • Difficulty processing and understanding what he or she hears • Problems remembering the proper sequence of events • Difficulty seeing similarities and differences in letters and words • Inability to sound out the pronunciation of words even when breaking the word into parts (phonological awareness) • Anxiety when reading • Difficulty spelling • Spending an unusually long time completing tasks that involve reading or writing • Avoiding activities that involve reading and writing

6. Factors that Impact Children's Literacy Foundations

Factors that Impact Children's Literacy Foundations
Physical acuity: The extent to which a child can accurately hear, see, and access text and instruction, clearly articulate speech, and coordinate physical motor activity.
Cognitive factors: The extent to which a child can take in and comprehend information, develop schema, remain focused, regulate attention and emotions, and access information stored in long- and short-term memory.
Early language and literacy experiences: The extent to which a child has substantive conversations with adults and peers, and frequent positive interactions with more literate others who read aloud, converse, build background knowledge and vocabulary, draw attention to literacy in their environment, provide access to age-appropriate literacy materials, and offer positive affirmations to their emerging literacy behaviors and understandings.
Psychological factors: The extent to which a child can maintain a positive self-concept, motivation and confidence to learn, a feeling of trust in adults and others, positive dispositions toward learning and literacy, and resilience after experiencing trauma.
Language and literacy processing abilities: The extent to which a child can interpret information taken in by sight and sound, perceive and process visual and auditory information, and extend language comprehension and development.
Ecological factors: The extent to which a child's family or caregivers can access community resources and opportunities, maintain financial stability, meet the child's physical and safety needs, and support their language and culture.

7. Anchor Status Template

Anchor Status Template	
Name:	Date: Age of child: _____ years _____ months
Anchor	**Anchor status** *These skills are listed in order of complexity and development. Use tasks as appropriate for the age level being assessed*
1. Oral language	• Number of conversational exchanges _____ • Complexity of sentence structure: • Engages in conversation with peers _____ • Engages in conversation with adults _____ **Notes:**

2. **Vocabulary and background knowledge**	• Range of word choice: The degree to which the child uses three tiers of vocabulary. Provide examples. Tier 1 words: Tier 2 words: Tier 3 words: • Uses background knowledge in conversation (concepts and knowledge of their own world and the broader world) • Uses vocabulary and information learned through investigations _____ **Notes:**
3. **Book awareness**	• Interacts successfully with books: • Can identify: Title _____ Author or Writer _____ Illustrator or Picture Maker _____ • Can distinguish between real and make-believe books _____ • Knowledge of and familiarity with different genres _____ Provide examples: **Notes:**

4. **Phonological awareness and pho-nemic awareness** *See Appendix 4 for appropriate focus of assessment* *Children demonstrate understanding of phonological and phonemic awareness using what they can hear, not by using print. These are oral tasks* *Document all assessments in Notes: Include informal, formal, published and online assessment information*	• Can clap words in a sentence _____ • Can clap syllables in a word _____ • Identifies words that rhyme _____ • Creates rhymes _____ • Blends onset and rime _____ • Hears beginning sounds _____ • Recognizes words with matching initial sounds _____ • Hears ending sounds _____ • Can blend phonemes into a complete word (describe): • Can segment a word into phonemes (describe): **Notes:**
5. **Alphabet knowl-edge and phonics** *Document all assessments in Notes: Include informal, formal, published and online assessment information*	• Can identify the letters in their name _____ • Letter names: _____ out of 26 capital letters • Letter names: _____ out of 26 lower case letters • Letter sounds: _____ /21 consonants .... _____ /5 vowels • Engages in ABC book read-alouds _____ • Understands alphabetic principle (each letter has a corresponding sound) _____ • Identifies beginning letter/sounds _____ • Identifies ending letter/sounds _____ • Decodes CVC words _____ • Uses phonemic spelling _____ **Notes:**

6. Print concepts	• Acknowledges difference between writing and illustrations/pictures _____
Broad literacy concepts and specific conventions	**Concepts of print:**

Concepts of print:

Reading	Writing
Demonstrates knowledge of the reading process: • points to print: • top to bottom • left to right • uses return sweep	Demonstrates knowledge of the writing process: • top to bottom • left to right • uses return sweep
_____ Demonstrates voice-print match (one spoken word matches one written word).	_____ Uses spaces or other delineation between words

Notes:

_____ **Conventions of print:**

Reading	Writing
Understands and can identify the following: • a letter _____ (the concept of *letter*) • a *word* _____ (the concept of *word*)	_____ Writes left to right _____ Writes top to bottom _____Uses letters or letter-like symbols in writing
Can identify the following use of punctuation marks: • period _____ • question mark _____ • exclamation mark ___ • capital letters _____	**Uses punctuation:** *May be random approximations* • period _____ • question mark ___ • exclamation mark • capital letters _____

Notes:

7. Emerging reading
 	
Use guided observation of emerging reading
Appendix 2
	• Is confident and interested in reading:
	    • independently _____
	    • with a group _____
	    • with an adult _____
	
	• Rereads familiar text fluently _____
	• Participates in Shared Reading _____
	• Notices environmental print _____
	• Uses emergent reading in socio-dramatic play _____
	
	Stage of emerging reading
	
	• Picture labeling _____
	• Story-teller _____
	• Mixed reading and story-telling _____
	• Sounding like a reader _____
	• Beginning reader (no longer emerging reader) _____
	
	Notes:

8. Emerging writing
 	
Use stages of writing development
Appendix 3
	• Is confident and interested in writing _____
	
	Stage of emerging writing
	
	• Purposeful scribbling _____
	• Letter-like scribbling _____
	• Letter inclusive _____
	• Phonemic writing _____
	    • *initial sound* _____
	    • *ending sounds* _____
	    • *middle sounds* _____
	• Uses known words _____
	• Transitional writing _____
	
	Notes:

9. **Positive dispositions about literacy and literacy learning**	• Engaged during group reading opportunities _____ • Engaged during group writing opportunities _____ • Enjoys shared book read-alouds _____ • Uses functional literacy in socio-dramatic play _____ • Associates literacy with pleasure and purpose _____ • Integrates teacher scaffolding into independent attempts _____ • Demonstrates positive perceptions of self as a reader, writer, and thinker _____ **Notes:**
10. **Executive function**	• Can pay attention during group time _____ • Remembers shared information _____ • Can organize themselves _____ • Can plan steps of a task _____ • Can start and stay focused (unprompted) on tasks _____ • Can manage emotions to meet the demands of a situation _____ • Can control and adjust behaviors during challenging situations _____ **Notes:**

8. Tool Use for Assisted Writing

Tools help writers write		Writing instruments
Tools	**Teacher talk to explain tool use**	
Environmental text	Use the words you can see around the room to help you write	Pencils Thin markers
Picture alphabet	The picture alphabet can help you remember how to make letters AND the sounds letters make	Regular markers Colored pencils Stamps (letters, animals, construction vehicles, etc.)
Class name chart	You can write your friends' names	Stickers
Words by heart	These are words you can stick in your brain so that later you will be able to write them quickly You can spell the words that rhyme with these words	
Personal dictionaries	Your own word list helps you learn words that really matter to you	
Words from familiar books	Books can remind you how to spell a word	
Peer-made books and picture stories	Your friends' books can help you write words AND can wake up stories in your head	
Class-made books	You can get inspired by these ideas AND check on how to spell words	
Topic-related words	Our word charts help us remember the wonderful words that we find. They can wake up stories in your head	
Your brain	The strongest tool of all. Look in your brain for the word you want to write. Wake up the stories that are sleeping in your head	

9. Lesson Plan Template for Play

Planning the investigation and the theme of the dramatic play center Planning for high-quality socio-dramatic play in which literacy is used for functional purposes	Notes and reflection
1. Topic: _____ 2. Theme: (dramatic play center) _____	
3. List five to eight concepts you want the children to learn about this topic? (baseline content knowledge)	
4. Background knowledge • How will you determine what the children already know about the theme of the dramatic play center? (schema) • What type of knowledge about the theme of the dramatic play center will you help them build **before** they play? • What key vocabulary (Tier 3) do you want them to learn and use?	
5. List the roles of people who participate in the theme: (who works, visits, lives there?)	
6. Design the dramatic play center.	
7. List and describe the props.	
8. How does each person (role) use literacy?	
9. List and describe each literacy prop. Explain how each prop is used and why?	
10. Introduction/ demonstration/modeling use of literacy props: (whole group, small group)	
11. Identify and describe each of the Foundational Anchors of literacy that you plan for children to develop through engagement in high-level play on this topic and theme? • Oral language • Background knowledge and vocabulary • Book awareness • Alphabet knowledge and phonics • Phonological and phonemic awareness • Print concepts • Emerging reading • Emerging writing • Positive dispositions toward literacy • Executive function	

12. Resources: • Read-aloud books: (informational and fiction) • Resource books on the topic (for adults) • Resource and emerging reading books (informational and fiction for children) • Videos • Guest speakers • Field trip (s) • Additional resources	

Topic-related materials in other centers Ensure that these materials are introduced to children so that they understand how they can be used and are authentically connected to the theme	**Related resource materials in the writing center** (Theme related: e.g., extra prescription pads, clipboards, blank books, list of children's names, printed words that children can copy and might use in their play)	

Introduction of the dramatic play center theme	

To the children: (i.e., read aloud, video, special guest, guided small group rotations)	**To the parents:** (i.e., letter, bulletin board)	

Small groups: (e.g., creating literacy props, language experience stories, class and individual book making)	

Share the learning	

How will children personally respond to their learning about the theme and the play? (substantive conversation, revisit their work products created along the way, language experience charts, art, book-making, Assisted Writing, and drawing)	

Celebrate the learning	

How will children share their learning? (with each other, with families, with the larger community if appropriate?)	

Reflect on the children's literacy learning	

Analyze and reflect on the children's use and understanding of each
  Foundational Anchor of literacy as it relates to the goals and outcomes set.

- Oral language
- Background knowledge and vocabulary
- Book awareness
- Alphabet knowledge and phonics
- Phonological and phonemic awareness
- Print concepts
- Emerging reading
- Emerging writing
- Positive dispositions toward literacy
- Executive function

Analysis and self-reflection	

Consider:

1. What worked well?
2. What was challenging?
3. Describe the children's use of functional reading and writing.
4. What supported their use of functional reading and writing?
5. What outside and inside Interventions were effective?
6. What would you do differently next time to further support children's use of functional reading and writing?

10. Lesson Plan for Oral Language Development

The Talking Bag
An Oral Language Lesson

Goal of the lesson:

- To increase use and understanding of Tier 1 and 2 words;
- To name and describe a series of items in a category;
- To involve the children in a conversation to reinforce the words *same, similar, compare, contrast, part,* and *whole.*

Materials:

- Five to seven items in the same common *category (common in the homes of the children)*
     (For example, tools, shoes, spoons, flowers, seeds, leaves, kinds of cups, fruit, musical instruments, tools to write with, toy animals, types of candy, toy cars, toy animals, yellow things)
- A large basket or bag that the children cannot see through
- Chart paper, markers

Lesson sequence: (teacher talk is bolded)

1. **Today I have many items in my Talking Bag and the items in it all go together.**
     Let's see what the first thing is.
2. Remove the first item and ask, **What's this? What do you know about this?**
     (Encourage children to speak out instead of hand raising/turn taking if possible. You want children to put their ideas into their own words to create a reduced-risk setting. Keep the pace lively and playful.)
3. **Does it have parts? Can you name the parts? This has a lot of parts. Let's talk about the parts we see.**
4. **I wonder. Where do we find these? What do people do with these?**
5. **Let's write the name of this object.** (Write it on the chart.)
6. **What else could be in the bag that might go with this? How would that go with this?**
7. Remove the next item and ask, **"What's this?"**
8. **What are some ways it goes with (item 1)? Is it the same, similar, or different? Describe how they are (same, similar, different)?**
9. **Does it have parts? Name the parts.**
10. **I wonder … Where do we find these? What do people do with these?**
11. **Let's write the name of this object.**
12. **What else could go with (item 1 and item 2)**
13. Repeat with each item, extending and expanding the talk.
14. **Let's name the category these items all fit into. They are all ___.** Write the category name on the chart.
15. Finally, add to the written list other items that could have been in the bag (for example, other fruit that you didn't bring). Reread the list together.

This lesson can conclude with children using emergent writing about the topic or adding pictures to the chart or expanding the category of things. You can revisit charts if there is something new to add.

   This lesson can be done weekly and the children will use more language over time. It can also be done in small group with children who are less apt to talk.

Glossary

Academic school language: Academic school language is the language of instruction and the oral language used by the teacher throughout the school day; the language structures and vocabulary used to teach and learn literacy and the content areas such as math, science, and social studies. In the United States, English is most often the academic language.

Acclimation stage: The first stage of reading beginning at six months of age; the phase during which young children become familiar with and accustomed to literacy.

Accommodate: To adjust your thinking when new ideas are taken in.

Active play: Play in which children use physical movements such as running, jumping, and playing games like chase, hide-and-seek, tag, and rough-and-tumble play.

Alphabet knowledge: Understandings about the letters of the English language. This includes the shape and names of uppercase and lowercase letters, the speed of letter recognition, recognition of sounds represented by letters.

Alphabetic principle: Understanding that sounds and letters work together; that letters represent sounds.

Anchor status: The understanding and performance a child currently demonstrates for each of the ten Foundational Anchors of literacy.

Anchored Literacy Curriculum: An investigative curriculum that intentionally incorporates effective literacy learning of the ten Foundational Anchors.

Ankyloglossia: A physical problem with children's mouth, tongue and/or palate. This can cause challenges with pronunciation of certain sounds.

Apraxia of speech: A physical disorder that makes it difficult for children to form sounds in the correct sequence in order to form words.

Approximations: The literacy understandings and behaviors a child demonstrates before it becomes conventional.

Area: Designated classroom learning area. Spaces designated for specific use, easily determined by the design, choice, and arrangement of associated materials. Areas always include a whole group area and classroom library.

Assigned curriculum: Required use of specific curricula, materials, and resources.

Assimilate: To take in and fully understand information, concepts, and ideas.

Assisted Writing: Learning contexts that teachers create to support writing and reciprocity in the classroom. **Assisted Writing contexts** provide levels of instruction from direct learning contexts to indirect learning contexts with the teacher stepping in and out of the teaching and support role. Contexts include Writing Centers, Writing in Play, Story Pictures, Modeled Writing, Shared Writing, Interactive Writing, and Community Writing.

Background knowledge: Children's accumulated knowledge of the world, how it works, and the vocabulary to label, think, and talk about it.

Baseline: Teachers' minimum of information (background knowledge and vocabulary) they want all children to learn.

Bilingual: The ability to speak fluently in two languages.

Book awareness: The ability to notice, think about, and interact successfully with books.

Centers: Smaller than areas, centers offer specific activities that children engage in individually or with peers that support practice of the Foundational Anchors of literacy.

Cognitive factors: The ability to take in and comprehend information, develop schema, remain focused, regulate attention and emotions, and access information stored in long- and short-term memory.

Comprehensible input: The home and school language that a child can understand, despite them not being able to understand all of the words and grammatical structures.

Concepts of print: Print is what is read, where to start reading, books are read front to back, directionality of reading and writing print, concepts of word and letter, word boundaries, voice-print match, etc.

Consonants: The letters of the alphabet that are not vowels. Some vowels may act as consonants but are not considered consonants. Y acts as a consonant in words like yellow, yes, and beyond.

Continuant sound: Also called a long and loud sound that can be stretched; for example, /m/.

Conventions of print: Text features such as upper and lower case letters, basic punctuation, start and end of a word/sentence.

Creative expression play: Children use materials in unique or unusual ways, stimulating new ways of thinking and problem-solving. Activities include painting, drawing, sketching, coloring, writing, making music and noise, creating sculptures and pottery, constructing crafts, and other forms of artistic expression.

Curriculum: Everything that happens in the classroom, planned or unplanned. All the classroom materials, the environment, the opportunities, the activities, the instruction, and the interactions children engage in with other children and with their teacher comprise curriculum.

Daily reading contexts: Daily intentional opportunities for reading to children, reading with children, and reading by children

Decodable texts: Texts that use the same word pattern repeatedly.

Decoding: Using letters and sounds to identify a word.

Differentiation: Meeting the varied instructional needs of each child.

Digraphs: Two consonants that make one phoneme. The most common are *ch, th, sh,* and *wh.*

Diphthongs: Two (or more) vowels that make one phoneme (an individual sound). Examples are *ee, oo, ae,* and *ou.*

Direct learning context: A teacher-planned learning event used to directly teach children **new** information about literacy. These events are teacher-led and include Guided group learning, Explicit anchor building, and Literacy games and activities.

Dispositions: Children's predominant approaches, attitudes, feelings, inclinations, and beliefs about themselves as capable readers, writers, and thinkers.

Dual-language programs: Programs in which approximately half of the students are native Spanish speakers, and the rest are native English speakers. Students receive instruction in both languages, with the goal of all students becoming fully bilingual.

Dyslexia: A learning disorder in which the fundamental problem involves the brain's ability to process language, decode and spell words, and identify speech sounds.

Early competence stage: The second stage of reading within the Foundation Stage of Reading Development. Teachers build on the Acclimation Stage and bring children's attention to concepts of print and the patterns of oral language. They model the process of reading and writing within authentic contexts and guide children to use print in their play and in the classroom environment. Children begin reading and writing emergently.

Early home and care literacy environment: The interactions between parents, caregivers, and young children related to language and literacy development and the availability of literacy materials in the home.

Early language and literacy experiences: The extent to which a child has substantive conversations with adults and peers, and frequent positive interactions with more literate others who read aloud, converse, build background knowledge and vocabulary, draw attention to literacy in their environment, provide access to age-appropriate literacy materials, and offer positive affirmations to their emerging literacy behaviors and understandings.

Early production stage of second-language acquisition: The second stage of second-language acquisition. Children may try to engage in the play by using the vocabulary and short phrases that they have learned. They may use two-word sentences. They are collecting new words rapidly in this phase and benefit from explicit teaching of the vocabulary that will be used in the play.

Ecological factors: The extent to which a child's family or caregivers can access community resources and opportunities, maintain financial stability, meet the child's physical and safety needs, and support their language and culture.

Educational equity: Each child receives the instruction and resources they need to develop to their full academic and social potential. Each child's needs are met even though they are not the same needs of all children.

Elkonin boxes: Also called sound boxes. They are used to show children how to hear the sounds in words as separate phonemes.

Emerging readers: Children in the Foundation Stage of Reading Development, the stage prior to their ability to rely exclusively on the print to read and write. Although not relying on the print, they are beginning to actively construct meaning with text, referencing their experiences with literacy, what they have been taught, and what they have learned about oral and written language, the Foundational Anchors of literacy.

Emerging reading: The reading behaviors children demonstrate before they can read and write conventionally. These reflect their accumulated literacy experiences, both contextual and targeted, with more literate others.

Emerging writing: Marks, symbols, letter-like forms, or random letters that children imbue with meaning.

Environmental print: The print that is used in everyday life; signs, labels, directions, and logos.

Executive function: A set of mental skills that include working memory, flexible thinking, and self-control. We use these skills every day to learn, work, and manage daily life. Trouble with executive function can make it hard to focus, follow directions, and handle emotions, among other things.

Explicit anchor building: Sequenced instruction that results in children's unambiguous learning. The target learning goal and the steps for achieving that goal are clearly stated in detail and demonstrated by the teacher, leaving no room for children to be confused or in doubt. The steps of I Do, We Do, and You Do are used and represent a gradual release of responsibility for the learning.

Expressive language: Language produced to communicate.

Familiar texts: Any text that is read aloud to children to the extent they can anticipate what it says. All texts chosen or created for children to emergently read **must be** familiar texts.

Forms of print: As children purposefully use literacy, they begin to notice the forms of print and the way it is organized. This includes the genres, concepts, and conventions of print.

Foundational Anchors of literacy: Key literacy knowledge, skills, and dispositions that comprise a strong foundation of literacy and have been shown to support children's preparedness for formal reading instruction and later reading success organized into ten competencies.

Foundation stage of reading (Stage 0): Sometimes called school readiness or the reading readiness stage. From ages six months to six years, knowledge, skills, and dispositions of literacy should be developed during this stage in order to strongly support children's ease with learning to read and future proficient reading.

Function of print: The awareness that print has different purposes depending on the context in which it appears—for example, appointment books keep a doctor or hair dresser's schedule organized, menus list food choices, signs indicate the name and purpose of a store, and environmental print indicates how items are organized or used.

Genres of print: Print takes many forms: list, letter, sign, learning web, story, etc.

Graphemes: Written letters.

Guided literacy assessment: Literacy opportunities intentionally designed to observe children demonstrate what they currently understand and can do.

Guided play: Learning events that intermingle with the child-led nature of free play with a focus on learning outcomes and related teacher guidance. For meeting the outcomes of an effective literacy curriculum, guided play is used for the children to engage in **high-level socio-dramatic play in which children incorporate functional literacy**.

Hands-on/words-on activities: Teacher-planned activities that build vocabulary during hands-on activities.

Heritage language: The language spoken in the culture and community to which the child belongs. The child does not always have strong control of this language.

High-level socio-dramatic play: Children create an pretend situation, take on and act out roles, and follow a set of rules determined by those specific roles. Also called "mature" play.

Home language: The language spoken in the home by the parents or caretakers.

Immersion programs: Programs in which children who are native English speakers receive all of their instruction in Spanish (or another language) so that they can become fluent in the language.

Indirect learning context: Teachers plan learning events for children to apply, practice, integrate, approximate, problem-solve, reinforce, and extend their learning as they engage in child-led events. These events include socio-dramatic play, literacy learning centers and areas, and literacy learning games and activities.

Inside intervention: Used if outside intervention is not appropriate to the situation or successful. It requires the teacher to take a role or briefly step into the play as a co-player. It is the most supportive form of intervention and should be limited to a specific goal and then discontinued.

Instruction: The actions teachers take to reinforce and extend children's applications of the ten Foundational Anchors, e.g., model tasks, procedures, and activities; provide encouragement and reinforcement of productive learning behaviors; explain, clarify, and label concepts and information; and engage in substantive conversations that involve lots of sustained child-talk.

Interactive Writing: A context for writing in which the teacher AND the children **create** meaningful text together, sharing composing, recording, and rereading. They also share the chart marker.

Intermediate fluency stage of second-language acquisition: In the fourth stage of second-language acquisition, true conversations emerge. Children begin to think in a second language.

Invented spelling: See phonemic spelling.

Known: The known includes children's current understandings on which teachers help children build and connect with the "unknown" … new information and learning.

Language and literacy processing abilities: The ability to interpret information taken in by sight and sound, perceive and process visual and auditory information, and extend language comprehension and development.

Language play: Children manipulate the forms and functions of language as a source of fun for themselves and/or for the people they are with.

Literacy centers: Centers that provide activities the teacher creates for children to apply and practice the Foundational Anchors of literacy they know and/or have been taught.

Language comprehension: Children's oral language, vocabulary and background knowledge.

Learning disabilities: Difficulty learning due to genetic and/or neuro-biological factors that can affect multiple cognitive processes related to learning.

Limited early literacy environments: Early home and care environments that provide fewer opportunities for young children to develop and use language and literacy.

Literacy-enriched early environments: Early home and care environments that provide frequent positive and supportive language and literacy experiences.

Literary language: The language of authors that is different from the oral language children typically use in day-to-day conversations.

Literacy learning contexts: Intentionally planned teaching and learning literacy events that help children construct a strong foundation of literacy. They are designed to provide opportunities, activities, strategies, and instructions that support children's development of the Foundational Anchors of literacy.

Literacy props: Materials and resources used to support literacy development during socio-dramatic playLiteracy props should be authentic and natural to the play

Low-level play: Children take on imaginary roles in pretend short episodes driven by realistic props. It involves low-language use and little incorporation of peers. Typically found in dramatic play centers that do not have a theme.

Manipulation: The ability to do something with (to move around, delete, add) phonological units.

Modeled writing: An intentionally planned Assisted Writing context to provide a model of strategies, techniques, or genre that children are invited to try. The teacher has the responsibility for the writing.

Multi-language learners: All students who speak a language other than English at home.

Multi-tiered systems of support (MTTS): A framework in which data-based decisions are made in order to plan interventions for continuous improvement in learning and behavior.

Multilingual: The ability to speak fluently in more than two languages.

Native language: The home language the child learned in the home and maintained.

Observer, onlooker: A teacher intentionally observes children's play to analyze and evaluate children's proficiency in play, use of literacy, and possible need for adult guidance.

Onset: The first consonant sound you hear in a syllable, like the /p/ sound in pet.

Open-ended: Activities that give the child more opportunities to explore materials or processes in a differentiated way, without requiring a specific product.

Oral language: Ability to (1) comprehend language produced by others (**receptive language**) and (2) construct and produce language to communicate (**expressive language**) with others.

Oral storying: Talking with a child about a picture they drew.

Outside intervention: A teacher provides guidance by making comments or suggestions to children while they are playing but remains outside of the play.

Pedagogy: The method and practice of teaching.

Phoneme: The individual sounds in words; the smallest unit of speech one can hear in a word. There are three phonemes in the word *pet*: /p/ /e/ /t/.

Phonemic awareness: The highest level of phonological awareness. It is the ability to notice, think about, and manipulate the individual sounds in spoken words.

Phonemic spelling: Listening for the sounds in a word and representing them with their corresponding letters. It develops along a continuum of the initial consonant, final consonant, medial consonant, vowel place holder, and vowel.

Phonemic writing: See phonemic spelling.

Phonics (graphophonics): The consistent relationship between the letters or groups of letters (graphemes) of written language and the sounds of spoken language (phonemes).

Phonics curriculum: A curriculum that has a **systematic scope and sequence** teaching of letter-sound relationships. Knowledge builds from simple to complex.

Phonological awareness: The ability to notice, think about, and work with (manipulate) the sounds of oral language at the sentence, word, and phoneme (individual sound) levels.

Psychological factors: Thoughts and feelings within the child's mind that can impact motivation, learning, socialization, attitudes, and beliefs.

Physical acuity: The ability to accurately hear, see, and access text and instruction, clearly articulate speech, and coordinate physical motor activity.

Play leader: The teacher models, participates, or coaches children as they play, reinforcing their attempts to try out new language and new actions. This is also called **leading the play**.

Predictable text: The predictability (pattern, rhyme, repetition, story structure) allows children to successfully anticipate the book's next word, next sentence, next character, or idea.

Prefrontal cortex: The area of the brain that is responsible for executive function such as planning and organization, self-regulation, managing frustration, modulating emotions, and working memory.

Preproduction stage of second-language acquisition: First stage, also called the silent, or receptive stage. Children may not speak in the classroom language at all but focus on watching the actions of play-peers, trying to make sense of vocabulary.

Pretend or imaginative play: Children play "as if" something or someone is real or different than it actually is. They are symbolically creating something beyond what is literally there.

Primary language: The language a person uses in most situations. For many children, their primary language is their native language, but for others, their primary language is another language.

Print concepts: Understanding how to follow print and write left to right and top to bottom with return sweep, the concept of a word, spacing between words, voice-print match (one spoken word matches one written word), and page orientation.

Proficient readers: Skilled, competent readers that continue to enjoy and improve their reading at or above grade-level expectations.

Receptive language: Language produced by others that the child understands.

Reciprocity: The concept that all Foundational Anchors of literacy develop concurrently and each solidifies and expands the development of the others.

Response to intervention (RtI):   A multi-tier approach to the early identification and support of children with learning and behavior needs.

Rime: The vowel and other letters that follow the vowel in that syllable, like the /et/ part of pet.

Scaffolding: Instructional scaffolding is a process through which a teacher builds on what the child already knows and adds support/assistance in order to facilitate new learning and the mastery of tasks.

Schema: Background knowledge.

School dependent: School-like settings (preschool or child care) and classroom teachers must provide the contextual experiences and explicit teaching they need to foster the same strong Foundational Anchors of literacy their peers developed at home or early care during many unplanned literacy events.

Shared book reading: A *reading to children* pedagogy; An interactive method of reading books aloud to children during which the adult encourages the children's engagement in book-related conversation.

Shared Reading: A *reading with children* pedagogy that uses a memorizable, highly predictable text to read aloud to the children. After the teacher has read the book at least twice and it has become a familiar text, the teacher invites children to "read along" in places where it repeats and/or can be anticipated. After several Shared Readings of the text, many children can repeat the entire text. Shared Reading books become a source of familiar texts for children to emergently read.

Shared Writing: An intentionally planned Assisted Writing context to provide a model of strategies, techniques, or genre in which children are invited to try. The teacher shares the responsibility for the writing with the children.

Sight words: Words a child can read and write with automaticity; without stopping to sound out.

Social language: Social language reflects children's use of the language of school to informally converse with peers and teachers about their needs, preferences, thoughts, and in play. The child's focus is on communication and meaning. Teachers may falsely assume that children's proficiency of social language spoken in the language of school indicates that the child is equally proficient in academic language. This may not be the case.

Socio-dramatic play: Children's play that includes both pretending and social interaction. It is a type of cooperative imaginative play in which children work together to take complementary roles in an agreed-upon imaginary scenario.

Sound spelling: See phonemic spelling and invented spelling.

Specific learning disabilities (SLD):   A disorder in one or more of the basic psychological processes involved in understanding or in using language, spoken or written.

Speech delay: Indicated when a child has typically not met their milestones for speech for a particular age.

Speech emergence stage of second-language acquisition: The third stage of second-language acquisition. Children combine or connect words into phrases and produce simple sentences.

Story pictures: Emerging writers draw a picture and record their ideas as approximations. This Assisted Writing context is designed to encourage oral language, vocabulary and narrative formation (all aspects of reading).

Stop sound: Also called a "quick and quiet" sound. B, C, D, G, H, J, K, P, and T are stop sounds.

Substantive conversation: A form of talk between adults and children that informs, explains, and elaborates on ideas.

Syntax: Language structure or grammar.

Task-specific: Activities that provide materials and directions for children to follow in order to complete a specific task.

Teacher: All individuals who care for and educate children, including the parents. Any person in one of these positions plays a vital role in impacting the future and constructing the foundation for children's literacy success or failure.

Text set: Several books that have a common thread or literary feature (e.g., setting, characters, events, problems, solutions, theme, genre, or organizing structure).

Theme: The organizing topic of a socio-dramatic play center. The most effective themes represent **places** where children can pretend to take roles of the people who work or visit the theme. For example, a bakery, pizza restaurant, hair salon, grocery store, and doctors' office or clinic.

Theme-based curriculum: Curriculum that ties together early childhood disciplines, subject areas such as math, literacy, oral language, science, social-studies, music and art, to a specific topic.

Tiers of instructional need: Different levels of instruction and intervention support provided to children based on their need within three tiers.

Tier 1 of instructional need: Whole-class instruction where the teacher provides all students with a research-based curriculum and instructional strategies.

Tier 2 of instructional need: Small-group interventions provided for students who are demonstrating specific learning needs.

Tier 3 of instructional need: More intensive intervention (in small groups or one on one) for those children who have not progressed adequately during Tier 2 intervention or are demonstrating significant deficits in a specific area.

Tier 1 words: Basic words that children typically learn in their early years through conversation with adults and peers and during read-alouds.

Tier 2 words: The language of school and books; words and language teachers use to model, explain, coach, organize, and encourage effective thinking and appropriate classroom behaviors. It includes **academic language and literary language**.

Tier 3 words: Content-area-specific words and language, technical words.

Tiers of vocabulary: A common framework for thinking about vocabulary development.

Transfer: Using what they have learned in one literacy context to solve problems they encounter in other reading and writing contexts.

Transitional bilingual programs: Programs in which native speakers of Spanish, for example, are instructed entirely in Spanish for a period of time before transitioning into English instruction.

Trauma: Negative experiences impacting children and their ability to learn. They can include experiencing parents' divorce, mental or physical illness of a family member, food insecurity, job loss, witnessing or being a victim of violence, homelessness, a car accident, bullying, or moving and changing schools. Occurs across all races, ethnicities, cultures, and socio-economic households.

Unguided literacy assessment: Teacher-planned observational opportunities are intentionally planned and encourage children to engage with print independently as they go about their day.

Units of sounds: Described from biggest to smallest. The sequence is word, syllable, onset and rime, and phoneme.

Vocabulary: The number and range of words a child can either understand or use.

Vowels: The vowels are A, E, I, O, and U. Y acts as a vowel in words like try, myth, and ugly.

What writers do lesson: A short focused lesson for children to learn **one** thing about writing or writers. It takes 5–7 minutes only. This is presented as an invitation for the community to try.

Writing: Composing meaning into text (using print, visual, and/or computer applications) for a particular purpose and a particular audience.

Writing process: The writing process for young children is (1) composing, (2) recording, and (3) rereading.

Writing tools: Resources for children to use during writing and reading times. They include alphabet/sound charts, word walls, and class name lists. Teachers model their use.

Index

Note: Page references in *italics* denote figures.